故宫博物院藏

中国古代窑址标本　河北

THE SPECIMENS OF ANCIENT CHINESE KILNS IN THE COLLECTION OF THE PALACE MUSEUM

HEBEI VOLUME

故宫博物院编　冯小琦 / 主编

COMPILED BY THE PALACE MUSEUM
THE CHIEF COMPILER: FENG XIAOQI

故　宫　出　版　社
THE FORBIDDEN CITY PUBLISHING HOUSE

凡例

一、本书分卷以省为单位，窑多者，一省单独成册，窑少者，数省成书。

二、每个窑的标本以时代为序，同时兼顾品种、器型、装饰分类排列。

三、在某些重要窑名下，为清楚地表达瓷片的采集地，又分若干小地名。

四、标本的年代参考各地考古发掘资料，资料不充分或有意见分歧者，以故宫博物院传统观点为准。

五、有些标本因器型不完整，时代特征不突出，兼具宋、金或金、元特征者，取其一，或以宋（金）、金至元的形式标出。

六、窑具的年代、时代特征不突出者，或不标年代，或把范围定宽，如金至元，均放在每个窑的最后。

七、书中所选完整器物与窑址标本对比，以附图形式出现。

八、全国窑址分布图中的窑址为历年资料汇集，窑址所在县市地名绝大部分沿用学界习惯称谓。

九、故宫博物院专家窑址调查报告以省区划分，附于本省瓷窑后，有的涉及两省或多省的，附主要省份论文的最后。

Notes on the Use of the Book

1, The different volumes of this series were classified mainly by the provinces, with more kilns in one province done on single book and less one put it together.
2, The specimens of one kiln sorted by time, also considering the variety, type and decorative method.
3, In order to introduce the locality of specimens gathering precisely, the specific place names were also used for some important kilns.
4, The judgment on time of specimens was on the basis of archaeological materials from place to place, and the specimens in dispute or inadequate data were dated by traditional viewpoint of the Palace Museum.
5, Due to the incomplete type, the time character of some specimens was not glowing. The one that has features of Song and Jin dynasty or Jin and Yuan dynasty at the same time was dated in single period, or marked with "Song dynasty (Jin dynasty)" or the time of "from Jin dynasty to Yuan dynasty".
6, The kiln furniture in inconspicuous character of time could not indicate the specific date or broaden the period scale, then put it at last place of the kiln.
7, In contrast, the intact wares in the book appeared in attached figures.
8, Based on the materials over the years, we presented the distribution map of kilns in China, and most of the kiln names were followed by Scholar's idiom.
9, The investigation reports of experts of the Palace Museum were divided by different provinces and attached to the kilns of single province. The reports including two provinces or more attached behind the major province.

序

为加强故宫学术研究，在纪念故宫博物院成立 80 周年之际，建立故宫博物院古陶瓷研究中心，这是很有意义的一件事。

故宫博物院自成立以来，在中国古陶瓷研究方面，具有三个明显的优势：

其一是人才。故宫博物院是在明清皇宫的基础上建立的中国最大的古代艺术品宝库，凭借其得天独厚的条件，曾造就出一大批享誉海内外的文物研究专家。在古陶瓷研究领域，陈万里、孙瀛洲、冯先铭、耿宝昌先生等闻名遐迩，使故宫博物院在这一领域长期独领风骚。今天，在古陶瓷研究专业的人员构成方面，现有本研究专业在职人员 16 人，其中取得研究馆员任职资格的 5 人，副研究馆员任职资格的 4 人，馆员任职资格的 7 人，另有返聘研究馆员 2 人，退休研究馆员 3 人、副研究馆员 1 人、馆员 2 人。特别是拥有当今古陶瓷研究领域的泰斗、现已近 90 岁高龄的耿宝昌先生。因此，无论是在从业人员的数量还是人员的梯队结构方面，故宫博物院在这一研究领域都具有明显的优势。

其二是陶瓷类文物藏品。故宫博物院现收藏的古陶瓷可分为三大类：

1. 陶瓷类文物。总计约 35 万件，其中 32 万多件属原清宫旧藏品，1949 年以后通过拨交、收购、捐献等渠道又入藏 2 万多件。这些藏品，不但数量大，而且精品多，从新石器时代的陶器到明清各朝官民窑瓷器，无不包括，自成体系，这是国内外其他任何博物馆所无法比拟的。其中被初步定为国家一级文物的陶瓷器就有 1 110 件。宋代五大名窑（汝、官、哥、定、钧）瓷器、明清官窑瓷器是故宫陶瓷收藏中的强项，仅以宋代汝窑瓷器，明代永乐、宣德官窑瓷器，清代康熙瓷器为例：国内外收藏传世汝窑瓷器不足百件，故宫收藏 20 件，又收藏明代永乐、宣德官窑瓷器 700 多件，康熙瓷器 7 万多件。这些藏品无论从数量还是质量上看，在世界上都是名列前茅的。

2. 古窑址陶瓷标本。故宫博物院收藏有 20 世纪 50 ～ 60 年代以来从全国各地考察古窑址所采集的 300 余处重要窑址的约 6 万陶瓷标本，这在世界上也是独一无二的。标本的时代上起商周，下至清代，其中以唐到元代窑址的标本最为丰富。有的标本可与出土和传世器物相印证，有的标本则不见于出土与传世器物中。因此，对古窑址陶瓷标本的研究愈发显得重要，它能使我们更清楚地了解我国古代各地烧造陶瓷的情况，补充文献与传世器物的不足。目前有些窑址已遭破坏或深埋于地下，再前往采集标本，已几乎不可能有所收获，因此故宫所藏这批古窑址陶瓷标本就愈显重要。

3. 陶瓷类实物资料。 故宫博物院现收藏有原清宫因残淘汰下来的、古物南迁损伤的以及 1949 年以后收购来的数千件基本完整而被划归为非文物的资料，以及清宫淘汰下来的大量明清官窑瓷片标本。这些实物资料数量之大、包含的花色品种之全，在世界上是首屈一指的。其中有大量明、清、民国时期的陶瓷仿品，至今尚未全面向社会公开过，它们是学习古陶瓷鉴定的珍贵资料。特别是资料中还有一些品种弥补了现存古陶瓷文物中的空白。

其三是古陶瓷研究成果。在深入研究的基础上，故宫博物院已先后编写出版的陶瓷类图书有《故宫博物院藏瓷选集》（文物出版社，1962 年）、《故宫珍藏康雍乾瓷器图录》（两木出版社、紫禁城出版社，1989 年）、《故宫博物院藏清盛世瓷选粹》（紫禁城出版社，1994 年）、《故宫藏传世瓷器真赝对比及重要窑址标本图录》（紫禁城出版社，1998 年）、《故宫博物院藏明初青花瓷器》（紫禁城出版社，2002 年）、《故宫博物院藏文物珍品全集》（其中陶瓷类文物九卷：晋唐名瓷一卷、两宋瓷器二卷、五彩斗彩一卷、珐琅彩粉彩一卷、颜色釉一卷、青花釉里红三卷，香港商务印书馆有限公司）、《孙瀛洲的陶瓷世界》（紫禁城出版社，2003 年）、《陈万里陶瓷考古文集》（紫禁城出版社、两木出版社，1990 年）、《冯先铭古陶瓷论文集》（紫禁城出版社、两木出版社，1987 年）等。个人专著有陈万里《中国青瓷史略》和《瓷器与浙江》、耿宝昌《明清瓷器鉴定》、李辉柄《中国瓷器鉴定基础》和《宋代官窑瓷器》、叶佩兰《元代瓷器》、王莉英《陶瓷器鉴赏与收藏》、吕成龙《中国古代颜色釉瓷器》和《中国古陶瓷款识》、王健华《古瓷辨赏》等。另外，故宫的陶瓷专业人员还撰写了大量科研论文。这些已出版或发表的故宫专家和学者的研究成果，受到国内外古陶瓷爱好者的广泛关注。特别是 1982 年由冯先铭先生主编的《中国陶瓷史》，堪称我国第一部权威的陶瓷史，赢得国内外陶瓷界的极高赞誉，曾全文译成日文在日本出版。

正因为具备上述丰厚的藏品基础和研究优势，在加强故宫学的学术规划中，成立故宫博物院古陶瓷研究中心被提上了议事日程，在社会同行的支持下，并予以实施。故宫博物院古陶瓷研究中心设在延禧宫区，主要由三部分构成：一是设在延禧宫西司库的观摩室兼作小型会议室；二是设在延禧宫西库房的陶瓷专题陈列室，室内设触摸屏和等离子显示屏；三是设在延禧宫的古陶瓷检测研究中心，内设古陶瓷成分分析实验室，工艺研究实验室，结构分析实验室和物理、化学性质检测实验室，承担古陶瓷的分析检测研究工作。观摩室和小型会议室供来陶瓷中心访问的专家、学者观摩古陶瓷资料、标本以及进行小规模的学术研讨活动等使用。古陶瓷专题陈列室将定期举办院藏陶瓷专题展览，展示故宫古陶瓷专家、学者的研究成果，适当引进一些外展。

故宫博物院古陶瓷研究中心是一个高层次的国际性学术研究机构。该中心将在故宫博物院的领导下，在院学术委员会的指导下，由院古器物部和文保科技部具体负责其日常业务工作，积极开展国内外有关古陶瓷方面的学术研究和学术交流活动。

古陶瓷研究中心的研究对象主要是故宫博物院的古陶瓷收藏、古窑址陶瓷标本收藏和世界各地收藏的中国古代陶瓷。古陶瓷研究中心的研究内容包括对不同时期、不同产地、不同类型古陶瓷制作原料、工艺、结构及相关性质的科学研究；对古陶瓷年代、窑口、真伪的科学研究；对古陶瓷的科学保管、修复和复制等技术的科学研究，以及更多深层次、多视角的科学研究。

古陶瓷研究中心将利用故宫博物院在人才和收藏古陶瓷文物、资料、标本以及引进各种先进检测仪器设备等方面的条件和优势，为国内外专家、学者搭建一个开展综合性合作研究的学术平台，旨在使故宫博物院陶瓷藏品的诸多内涵为世人所知，以弘扬博大精深的中国陶瓷文化。同时，积极借鉴国内外同行的研究方法和学术成果，为故宫培养和造就一批古陶瓷专业的中青年专家，力求使故宫的古陶瓷科学研究水平位于世界的最前列。

为配合古陶瓷研究中心的成立，故宫博物院组织院内专家、学者在深入研究的基础上，将陆续编辑出版《故宫博物院藏清代御窑瓷器》、《故宫博物院藏中国古代窑址标本》、《故宫博物院藏古陶瓷资料选萃》等三套图书。清代御窑瓷器是故宫收藏中的强项，《故宫博物院藏清代御窑瓷器》一书将收录故宫收藏从顺治至宣统御窑瓷器 1 000 余件，配以大量辅助资料，这是故宫首次出版全面反映清代御窑厂生产工艺及产品的图录，其中绝大多数瓷器属首次公开发表。《故宫博物院藏中国古代窑址标本》一书，收录故宫自 1949 年以来赴全国各地考察古窑址所采集的 200 多个窑口的陶瓷标本，这是故宫首次向社会全面公布这批标本资料。《故宫博物院藏古陶瓷资料选萃》一书将收录 500 余件故宫藏器型基本完整的古陶瓷实物资料，其中有一部分属于珍稀品种，属于首次发表。我深信，这些古陶瓷图书的出版，必将对中国古陶瓷工艺学、鉴定学的研究起到积极的推动作用。

郑欣淼

2005 年春

Preface

Due to the goal to enhance the academic research level of the Palace Museum, the foundation of Ancient Ceramic Research Center of the Palace Museum was a very significant event during the 80th anniversary of the establishment of the Palace Museum.

The Palace Museum has following three advantages in research on ancient Chinese ceramic since its inception.

The first is talents. Based on the imperial palace of Ming and Qing dynasties, the Palace Museum was the largest treasure-house for ancient artworks in China. On account of these exceptional advantages, the Palace Museum brings up a large number of overseas renowned experts on cultural relic research. The well-known experts such as Chen Wanli, Sun Yingzhou, Feng Xianming and Geng Baochang took the Palace Museum lead in the research on ancient ceramic for a long term. Due to enough personned number and reasonable team structure, we still keep the obvious dominant position in the field of ancient ceramic at present.

The second is ceramic collections. The ceramic collections of the Palace Museum could be divided into three classes. One is the cultural relic of ceramic. There were nearly 350 thousand collections, among which over 320 thousand belonged to the Qing Court and the others were collected after 1949 through different approaches. The collections were not only large in number, but also high in quality, and have established a self-contained system from Neolithic Age to Qing dynasty. Then is the specimen of ancient kilns. The Palace Museum collected nearly 60 thousand specimens from over 300 ancient kilns throughout the country in 1950s and 1960s. It was really an unmatched accomplishment in the world. The last is the material of ceramic. The materials contained the following parts: incomplete wares of Qing Court, damaged wares due to removal for antiques, purchased wares as materials after 1949 and large number specimens eliminated by the Qing Court. It is also the second to none in the world.

The third is the research achievement of ancient ceramic. Based on deeply study, the Palace Museum compiled a great deal of ceramic books, such as *The Selected Works of Ceramic in the Collection of Palace Museum* (The Cultural Relic Press, 1962), *The Blue and White Porcelain of Early Ming Dynasty in the Collection of Palace Museum* (The Forbidden City Publishing House, 2002), *The Complete Works of Treasures in the Collection of Palace Museum* (The Hong Kong Commercial Press Ltd., 1996-2000) , *The Ceramic World of Sun Yingzhou* (The Forbidden City Publishing House, 2003), etc. There were also numbers of personal monograph as well, for example, *The History of Chinese Celadon* (By Chen Wanli, The People's Publishing House, 1965), *The Porcelain and Zhejing Province* (By Chen Wanli, The Zhonghua Book Company, 1964), *The Porcelain*

Appreciation of Ming and Qing Dynasties (The Forbidden City Publishing House, 1993), *The Inscriptions of Ancient Chinese Ceramic* (By Lü Chenglong, The Forbidden City Publishing House, 2003), etc. Besides, large numbers of papers were written by our experts on ceramic and attracted widespread attention.

Based on the abundant collections and research advantages, the establishment of the Ancient Ceramic Research Center of the Palace Museum was put on the agenda and carried out at last. The research center is located at Palace of Prolonged Happiness area, and could be further divided into three parts: small meeting room, ceramic showroom and laboratory for ceramic detection.

The Ancient Ceramic Research Center of the Palace Museum is an international academic research institution at high level. Under the leadership of the Palace Museum and the guidance of Academic Board of the Palace Museum, the Department of Ancient Cultural Relic and Technology for Ancient Cultural Relic Protection will be in charge of daily affairs of the center, and carry out academic research and communication on ancient ceramic in domestic and abroad.

The object of the Ancient Ceramic Research Center of the Palace Museum is the ancient ceramic collections and specimens in the Palace Museum and ancient ceramic collections all over the world. By these condition and advantages, the center will provide experts and scholars with a synthetic platform for academic exchange, and propagate the great and profound culture of Chinese ceramic.

To coincide with the launch of the Ancient Ceramic Research Center of the Palace Museum and on account of further study by experts and scholars in the Palace Museum, some related books will be published such as *The Imperial Porcelain of Qing Dynasty in the Collection of the Palace Museum*, *The Ancient Chinese Kilnsite Specimens* in *the Collection of the Palace Museum* and *The Selected Works of Ancient Ceramic Materials in the Collection of the Palace Museum*. It is convinced that the print of these books will contribute greatly to the development on handicraft and appreciation of ancient Chinese ceramic.

Zheng Xinmiao

目录

Contents

前言

冯小琦

中国陶瓷有8000年的历史，在世界工艺美术史上占有重要位置。半个世纪以来，我国文物考古工作者在20多个省、市、自治区的176个以上县市发现数以千计的历代瓷窑遗址，各地清理发掘的古墓葬也出土了数以万计的历代陶瓷器。新资料与文物的大量出土，为系统研究中国陶瓷的发展历史创造了有利条件。

本套书选用的标本源自20世纪50年代以来，故宫博物院的陶瓷研究专家和学者深入考古第一线，历尽艰辛，陆续在全国调查古窑址所得。特别是老一辈陶瓷专家陈万里、冯先铭、耿宝昌、李辉柄、叶喆民、李知宴、王莉英、叶佩兰等先生，他们在这方面做出了巨大贡献，在这里我们表示特别感谢。

陶瓷考古是一项非常艰巨的工作，瓷窑多依山傍水而建，20世纪50～60年代调查条件非常艰苦，没有汽车，专家们就搭乘拖拉机、马车、驴车，或租自行车，实在没有交通工具就徒步前进，去一处窑址往往要走上一天，他们冒严寒，战酷暑，肩背手提，把获得的第一手珍贵资料带回故宫；在这期间他们有的被蛇咬过，被蝎子蜇过，划破手脚更是经常的事，但是他们凭着对事业的执着，始终坚持深入考古第一线，克服了重重困难，收集了非常宝贵的资料，为故宫博物院的陶瓷研究工作作出了重大贡献。

这些窑址标本资料的时代上起商周，下至明清，系统地反映了中国陶瓷的发展概况以及各地瓷窑产品的特点及相互影响。其中有我国青瓷的发源地——浙江地区商周时期的青瓷、黑瓷和六朝青瓷标本；隋唐时期南、北方地区著名瓷窑邢窑、定窑、巩县窑、耀州窑、越窑、长沙窑等窑的标本；宋代著名瓷窑汝窑、官窑、定窑、钧窑、耀州窑、磁州窑、景德镇窑、龙泉窑、越窑的标本以及福建、广东等沿海地区生产的外销瓷器标本。

这批窑址资料涉及全国20个省区的180余个窑口、300余处窑址，约6万多片标本。其中以唐至元代的标本最为丰富。品种有青釉、白釉、白釉绿彩、黑釉、黄釉、三彩、绞胎、酱釉、黑花、绿釉、红绿彩、釉下褐彩、青白釉、青花等；造型凡生活所用盘、高足盘、碟、碗、高足碗、杯、盆、罐、坛、炉、瓶、壶、枕、灯、盒等应有尽有；装饰所见有划花、刻花、剔花、印花、彩绘、点彩、堆塑、浮雕、镂空等。其中有的标本可与出土和传世器物相印证，有的标本则不见于出土与传世器物。因此，对窑址标本的研究就愈显得重要。作为资料它能使我们更清楚地了解每个瓷窑生产的内涵，补充文献与传世器物的不足。尤其是目前有些窑址已遭破坏或深埋于地下，再前往采集标本，已难有收获，因此，这批标本就愈显珍贵。

故宫博物院收集的陶瓷标本，不论数量上还是质量上在全国都是名列前茅的。其中有些标本曾在英国、日本、香港等国家和地区展出，引起很大轰动，在世界范围内对中国陶瓷的研究起到了积极的推动作用。多年以来，全国各地的陶瓷工作者来故宫博物院参观学习，都曾希望故宫博物院能把这批窑址标本公开展示，并且出版，不少陶瓷爱好者和观众也希望能一睹故宫博物院这批收藏。为满足专业研究人员及广大观众的愿望，并为故宫博物院古陶瓷研究中心建立一个展示平台，我们将数十年调查的窑址标本全面地加以展示，期待它对于我国陶瓷的深入研究能够起到一定推动作用。本套书拟从 6 万多片陶瓷器标本中遴选 180 余个窑口、300 余处窑址的约一万余片古窑址标本进行展示，力求反映我国陶瓷的发展历史，同时也反映故宫博物院几十年来在陶瓷考古方面所取得的成就，弘扬我国的陶瓷文化，并藉以推动古陶瓷研究的深入。

Foreword

Feng Xiaoqi

The Chinese ceramic with a history over 8000 years was one of the most important inventions in China and occupied an outstanding position in the history of arts and crafts in the world. Our workers of cultural relic and archaeology excavated thousands of ancient kilns and tombs and discovered tens of thousands of ceramic specimens during half a century. The new materials provide us with useful advantage for study of ceramic systematically.

The selected specimens of the books were achieved by succession investigation of ancient kilns after 1950s, and our ancestors of ceramic made great contributions on the cause, such as Chen Wanli, Feng Xianming, Geng Baochang, Li Huibing, Ye Zhemin, Li Zhiyan, Wang Liying, Ye Peilan, etc. Here we should highly appreciate their hardworking and great contribution.

The ceramic archaeology was a kind of arduous task. Due to the poor conditions in 1950s and no cars available, the experts reached the destination often by tractor, carriage, donkey cart or hiring a bicycle. Sometimes they even went to the kiln site on foot. The experts took the firsthand materials back to the Palace Museum with the condition of severe cold or heat, and sometimes even bite by snake or scorpion, and cut feet and hands were in common. With the persistent pursuit of the objective, our experts overcame every kind of difficulties and collected valuable materials, and made great contribution to the development of our research on ceramic in the Palace Museum.

The period of specimens was from Shang to Qing dynasty, and it reflected the development of Chinese ceramic. The specimens included celadon and black glaze ceramic of Eastern Han, and celadon of Southern and Northern Dynasties; samples of Xing kiln, Ding kiln, Gongxian kiln, Yaozhou kiln, Yue kiln and Changsha kiln in Sui and Tang dynasty; samples of Song dynasty contained Ru kiln, Official kiln, Ding kiln, Jun kiln, Yaozhou kiln, Cizhou kiln, Jingdezhen kiln, Longquan kiln, Yue kiln, and ceramic specimens for export in Fujian and Guangdong, etc.

The specimens contained over 60 thousand pieces involving over 300 kiln sites from 20 different provinces. By variety, there was celadon, white glaze, black glaze, yellow glaze, tricolor, twisted-color glaze, dark reddish brown glaze, green glaze, red and green color, unglazed brown color, blue and white, etc. By type, there was plate, plate with high foot, saucer, bowl, bowl with high foot, cup, basin, jar, vat, censer, vase, pot, pillow, light and box, etc. By decoration, there was incised pattern, cut pattern, engraved pattern, stamped pattern and embossed pattern, etc. Some specimens have been confirmed by wares in excavation and collection, and the others were not common. The specimen materials could make a more clearly understanding about the production of kilns and make up the insufficient of ancient archives and material wares. So the specimens are precious to ceramic study.

The specimens in the collection of the Palace Museum ranked highest in quantity and quality nationwide. Some samples have been exhibited in Britain, Japan and Hongkong, and caused much of a stir worldwide and put forward to the development of study on ceramic. Over the years, the ceramic researchers throughout the country wanted publicity for these specimens in the collection of the Palace Museum, and the public audiences also hoped having a chance to watch the ceramic specimens. In order to satisfied the wishes of special experts and public audiences and construct a platform for the Ancient Ceramic Research Center of the Palace Museum, we will exhibit the specimens comprehensively. At the same time, the series of books will be published, including over 180 kilns and 10,000 specimens. We hope it will reflect the achievement on ceramic research of the Palace Museum and push the forward of the intense research on ancient Chinese ceramics.

故宫博物院陶瓷研究五十五年

李辉柄

瓷器是中国古代的重要发明之一，是对人类文明史做出的杰出贡献。因此，把它作为一门学科进行研究，向来受到国内外学者们的重视。

近代瓷学研究史可划分为两个阶段，一为文献考据阶段，一为考古调查发掘阶段。20 世纪 50 年代以前，学者们主要依据史部与集部有关陶瓷的文献进行考证，诸如《唐六典》、《旧唐书》、《新唐书》、《茶经》、《全唐诗》等典籍，尤其是宋、元以后的陶瓷著录、笔记及方志，如蒋祈的《陶记》、曹昭的《格古要论》、宋应星的《天工开物》、《大清一统志》以及相继出现的《陶说》等专著。因以上研究主要是以文献为基础进行的，即所谓"书斋考古"，所以学者们把它划归为文献考证阶段，该阶段的代表作品是吴仁敬、辛安潮的《中国陶瓷史》。虽然该书在学术上并无独到之处，不能代表当时的最高学术水平，但它毕竟是一部完整的中国陶瓷史。

故宫博物院著名陶瓷学家陈万里先生曾对这本《中国陶瓷史》作过这样的评价："这本书的最大毛病就是采取几个陈旧瓷书里的内容，因袭着以往的传统，作为正确史料，几乎成了一部变相的类书，不是一部陶瓷史。"

陈万里先生是我国第一位走出书斋，运用考古学的方法，对浙江龙泉窑青瓷进行实地古窑废址考察的学者。他认为过去只靠点滴文献史料进行研究的老路是无法取得显著成效的。他自 1928 年夏，八去龙泉，七访绍兴，搜集了大量瓷片标本，并对它们进行排比研究，开辟了一条瓷器研究的新途径，从而把我国的瓷学研究推进到了一个新的阶段，即考古调查发掘阶段，为现代陶瓷学研究奠定了基础。他撰写的《瓷器与浙江》就是这一阶段的重要代表作。该书可看作是从传统的书斋考古走向古窑遗址考古的一个里程碑性质的著作。

研究瓷器发展的历史，文献史料与实物史料是不可缺少的两个方面。陈万里先生在注重文献史料的同时，对于实物资料也给予充分重视，创造了文献与实物相结合的研究方法。实物资料来源于古瓷窑址与古墓葬发掘两个方面：窑址调查与发掘，目的是为了弄清各窑烧造器物的特征，以便区别窑口（瓷器的烧造地点），正确判断它的窑名；墓葬发掘特别是具有确切纪年的墓葬出土瓷器，可以用来印证古代瓷窑址的时代。陈万里先生从考古学的角度出发，以纪年墓出土物件或是文字记载作为科学依据，与窑址实地考察相印证，从而解决了不少瓷器的窑口与断代问题。

瓷器年代的鉴定与窑口的划分是研究瓷器发展史的基础。故宫博物院的陶瓷研究一直是院内学术研究工作的重点，为了解决陶瓷研究领域中存在的问题，提高陶瓷研究的水平与鉴定能力，从 20 世纪 50 年代开始，就确定了故宫博物院陶瓷研究的基本方针，并制定了长远的研究规划：陶瓷研究的工作分宋代以前与明清两大阶段，既分工又合作，同时进行。宋代以前的瓷器研究以陈万里先生为首组成调查组，对全国南北各地的古代瓷窑遗址进行调查，以解决宋代以前瓷器的窑口即产地问题。明清瓷器的研究则以著名瓷器鉴定专家孙瀛洲先生为带头人组成鉴定组，对故宫博物院藏 32 万多件瓷器，特别是清宫旧藏的明清瓷器进行断代研究，以解决明清瓷器的科学鉴定问题。

魏晋南北朝时期由于社会长期处于分裂割据局面，造成南方与北方青瓷生产与发展的不平衡，故有"南方青瓷"与"北方青瓷"之分。经过调查，南方青瓷的生产主要集中在浙江地区，窑址在浙江的上虞、绍兴、宁波、鄞县、萧山、德清、余杭、永嘉等县市均有发现，其中以上虞最为集中，大部分分布在曹娥江中游两岸，时代均为三国两晋至南朝。

在江浙一带墓葬中出土的南方青瓷极为丰富，以六朝古都南京出土青瓷最多，其中纪年墓葬出土青瓷为数不少，它们反映了不同时期青瓷的发展面貌与特征。绍兴曾发现有"黄龙"、"赤乌"、"永安"、"甘露"、"宝鼎"、"凤凰"、"天册"、"天纪"等年号的三国孙吴时代的墓葬，出土了一些青瓷，其中以刻吴永安三年 (260 年) 铭的青釉谷仓罐最为有名，器物上的纪年为这件器物的断代提供了科学依据。

然而，北方青瓷在中原地区魏晋时期的墓葬里几乎没有发现，北魏迁都洛阳以后的墓葬中，青瓷出土的数量渐多，至北齐时期骤增。最著名的是 1948 年河北省景县发现的北齐封氏墓所出青釉仰覆莲花尊，其造型雄伟、装饰富丽，器身堆贴飞天、兽面、蟠龙、宝相花等纹饰，并浮雕仰覆莲花瓣纹，莲花尊胎厚质坚，青釉润泽，是北方青瓷的代表。

邢窑是见于著录的唐代著名瓷窑之一，但由于长期以来未能发现它的窑址，因而也就始终没有弄清其真实面目。1980 年，首先在河北内丘与临城县交界之地发现了邢窑遗址，但根据唐代李肇《国史补》中"内丘白瓷瓯，端溪紫石砚，天下无贵贱通用之"的记载，邢窑遗址应在内丘，而不是临城。据此，文物工作者又在 1984 年于内丘境内进行调查，果然在 5 个乡方圆 120 公里区域内发现窑址十余处，并采集了大量标本。通过发掘证明了内丘城关一带的唐代瓷窑为当时邢窑瓷器烧制中心，所出白瓷也具备邢窑特征，与《茶经》中“邢磁类银，类雪”的记载相符。内丘城关白瓷窑烧制的器物，往往还在器底部刻划一个“盈”字。西安唐大明宫、唐长安西明寺遗址也曾出土过“盈”字款的碗底残片，与内丘城关邢窑遗址所出相同，应为当时邢窑的贡品。内丘邢窑遗址的发现，证明《国史补》中“内丘白瓷瓯”的记载是准确的，从而解决了中国陶瓷史上一大难题。

文献史料对研究陶瓷发展史也具有重要意义，然而有些文献记载的内容还要运用考古学的方法来加以证实和补充。如文献关于“秘色瓷”的记载，宋人赵德麟的“今之秘色瓷器，世言钱氏有国，越州烧造，为供奉之物，不得臣庶用之，故谓之秘色”。而从唐代陆龟蒙的《秘色越器》诗以及徐寅的《贡余秘色茶盏》诗的记载来看，秘色瓷并非始于五代，在唐代就有秘色之名。由于法门寺塔基出土了一批精致的越窑青瓷，物账单里又把这些青瓷称之为“秘色瓷”，这就有力地证明了越窑青瓷就是当时所谓的“秘色瓷”，从而使长期存在于学术界的这一悬而未决的问题得到了解决。

唐人陆羽《茶经》中记载的越州窑、鼎州窑、婺州窑、岳州窑、寿州窑与洪州窑等唐代六大青瓷窑，除鼎州窑外，其他五个瓷窑的遗址均已发现并进行了重点发掘。这些瓷窑烧瓷的历史以及烧制器物的特征，均与《茶经》记载相符。在全国各个地方志中所记载的瓷窑，有些已经发现，有些还有待考古工作来加以证实。但事实已经证明，通过考古学的方法，既可印证历史文献的内容是否属实，又可弥补有些文献的疏漏之处。

宋代瓷器发展的重要标志就是官窑的建立与民窑的大发展，窑址星罗棋布，遍布于全国各地。构成了宋代瓷器发展的主要特征。

1965 年，经调查首先在河南禹县城北门内的八卦洞发现了烧制宫中用钧窑瓷器的窑址，出土器物的造型、釉色与宫中收藏的钧窑瓷器相同，从而证实了北宋后期曾在禹县建立了官窑。钧窑瓷器完全是根据当时皇室设计式样与宫廷内陈设需要而生产的，器型多为花盆、盆奁、鼓丁洗、出戟尊等，釉色有玫瑰紫、海棠红、月白等，器底刻有一至十的数目字样。

汝窑也属于北宋官窑之一。根据宋代叶寘《坦斋笔衡》中“本朝以定州白瓷器有芒，不堪用，遂命汝州造青瓷器”的记载，汝窑是继定窑之后，为了满足宫廷需要建立起来的官窑。在河南宝丰清凉寺村发现了汝窑遗址，其中所出青瓷工艺之考究，造型之精美，与清宫收藏品完全相同，由此可以确认，河南宝丰清凉寺村即是宋代汝窑的所在地。

杭州乌龟山郊坛下官窑窑址早在 1930 年就已发现，1956 年浙江省文管会对其进行过一次发掘。1985 年冬至 1988 年春，考古工作者又相继对乌龟山窑遗址进行了两次发掘，不仅获得了大量实物标本，而且还揭露出龙窑与作坊等遗迹。

20 世纪 60 年代以来，沿着陈万里先生所开拓的道路前进的著名瓷器研究家冯先铭先生，集录了广博的古代文献和地方志中的陶瓷史料，在陈万里先生考察的基础上，调查了全国各地的古代瓷窑遗址，尤其是对北方的河南、河北、山西、陕西古窑址集中的地区，进行了较深入的考古调查，取得了巨大的成果，基本上弄清了中国古瓷窑的分布及南北重要瓷窑的发展历史与相互关系，为解决各大博物馆藏品的窑口（产地）问题提供了科学依据。冯先铭先生主编的《中国陶瓷史》是继《瓷器与浙江》之后的又一部重要著作。它总结了历代陶瓷的研究成果，代表了这一阶段研究的最高水平，为今后陶瓷史研究的深入发展创造了条件。

宋及宋以前我国瓷窑分布遍及南北各地，瓷器的窑口归属问题是根据古窑址调查发掘来判定的，瓷器的年代是根据墓葬特别是纪年墓葬出土瓷器作为标准器排比出来的。两者相互印证，是解决窑口与判断时代的科学方法。明、清时期，江西景德镇已成为全国的制瓷中心，绝大多数产品均出自景德镇窑。所以，明、清瓷器的鉴定与宋以前的情况不同，它不存在产地即窑口的划分，而只是一个时代的断定。由于已发掘的明、清时期有明确纪年的墓葬很少，出土的瓷器更少，很难作为我们断代的依据，而明、清瓷器也不像唐、宋瓷器那样有较固定的标准，再加上明、清各个具体时代的年限都不长，瓷器的品种又相当繁杂，后代和前代又存在着一定的连续性，因此，要想做到很精确地断代是困难的。鉴定明、清瓷器的年代，就成为一个主要课题。

20世纪50年代以来，故宫博物院除了以陈万里先生为代表的研究人员在全国开展古窑遗址调查外，还组织院内外专家对清宫旧藏的明、清瓷器进行了一次全面的鉴定。我国著名瓷器鉴定家孙瀛洲先生是采用类型学的方法对明、清带年款的瓷器进行排比研究的第一人。他以明、清带年款的官窑瓷器作为标准器，把不同朝代的瓷器所具有的不同时代特征排比出来，经过研究归纳，得出一些有关鉴定明、清瓷器的科学标准，并把它提到理论化的高度，用以指导实践。在他的指导和参与下，按照上述的科学方法，边排比，边研究，边进行鉴定，把原先对一些瓷器错定了的年代纠正过来，使故宫博物院这项“鉴定工程”得以顺利完成。

随着考古事业的发展与瓷器研究的客观需要，当前我国瓷器研究领域已在前两个阶段的基础上，进入到综合性研究的新阶段。故宫博物院陶瓷研究中心的成立，是这一新阶段的一个重要标志。陶瓷鉴定研究是一门艰辛的学问，尤其是进入现代社会，一些利欲熏心者不惜引进现代科技，仿制和伪造古陶瓷牟取暴利，给陶瓷鉴定带来了新的课题。对此，我们除了要对传统鉴定方法进行科学总结外，还要引进新的科学技术检测手段。在前人研究成果的基础上共同深入研究，不断解决摆在我们面前的疑难问题，把中国的陶瓷研究推向一个更高的水平。

The 55 Years of Research on Ceramic in the Palace Museum

Li Huibing

The ceramic was one of the most important inventions in ancient China, and an outstanding contribution for human culture as well. As an academic discipline, it is widely known by experts in domestic and abroad.

The history of ceramic study in modern times can be generally divided into two stages: one was the method of textual criticism, and another was archaeological investigation and excavation. Before 1950s, the scholars mainly carried out the study by textual research of ancient documents on ceramic. Chen Wanli was the first one to investigate the ancient celadon kilns of Longquan kiln in Zhejiang Province using the method of archaeology. Consequently, our study was put forward to a new level meaning stage of archaeological investigation and excavation. The book of *The Porcelain and Zhejiang Province* was an important representative in the period, and could be regarded as the landmark from scholar’ s room to field visit.

The ceramic appreciation on dating and kilns distinction was the basement of ceramic research. In order to solve the problem existed in our study and enhance the level of ceramic research and appreciation. In 1950s, the Palace Museum determined the basic roles on ceramic study and formulated the long-term research program. The work of ceramic research could be divided into two stages: one was before Song dynasty, and another was Ming and Qing dynasty. Under the leadership by Chen Wanli, the work team investigated the ancient kilns all over the country, and tried to judge the specific kiln site of ceramic before Song dynasty. The study of Ming and Qing dynasty was guided by Sun Yingzhou, the famous experts on ceramic. The appreciation team launched the study on over 300 thousand porcelains especially those collected by the Qing Court, and solved the difficult problem of appreciation on Ming and Qing porcelain.

Based on the investigation by Chen Wanli, the famous ceramic expert Feng Xianming successively investigated the ancient kilns all over the country after 1960s, especially in Northern China, such as kilns in Henan, Hebei, Shanxi and Shaanxi Province. The book of *The History of Chinese Ceramic*, which compiled by Feng Xianming, was another famous work after the book of *The Porcelain and Zhejiang Province*. This book reflected the highest level in the period and provided useful materials with study on ceramic history.

The ceramic appreciation on dating and kilns distinction, which belonged before Song dynasty, was mainly judged by kiln investigation and excavation. This is compared to the ceramic appreciation of Ming and Qing dynasty. In this period, Jingdezhen has become the center of ceramic making throughout the country. Due to lack of materials of tombs, the accurate judgment on Ming and Qing ceramic was difficult and became a main study in our work.

For this reason, beside the investigation, the Palace Museum also organized the experts of ceramic to carry out a comprehensive appreciation on Ming and Qing porcelain collected by the Qing Court. According to the method of typology, the famous expert Sun Yingzhou firstly put the porcelain with inscriptions in Ming and Qing dynasty as the standard and analyzed the feature of different period, and then made the conclusion on appreciation criterion. By appreciation criterion, the work went ahead smoothly.

Under the need of development on archaeology and porcelain study, the research has been step into a new stage of comprehensive study. The founding of the Ancient Ceramic Research Center of the Palace Museum became an important landmark in the period. Based on the scholars’ achievements, we still need studying deeply to solve the puzzling question and put the research into a new high level.

全国窑址分布图

The Distribution Map of Kilns in China

注：▲窑址

▲故宫博物院已调查的窑址

Notes：▲ Kiln sites

▲ Kilns that have been investigated by the Palace Museum

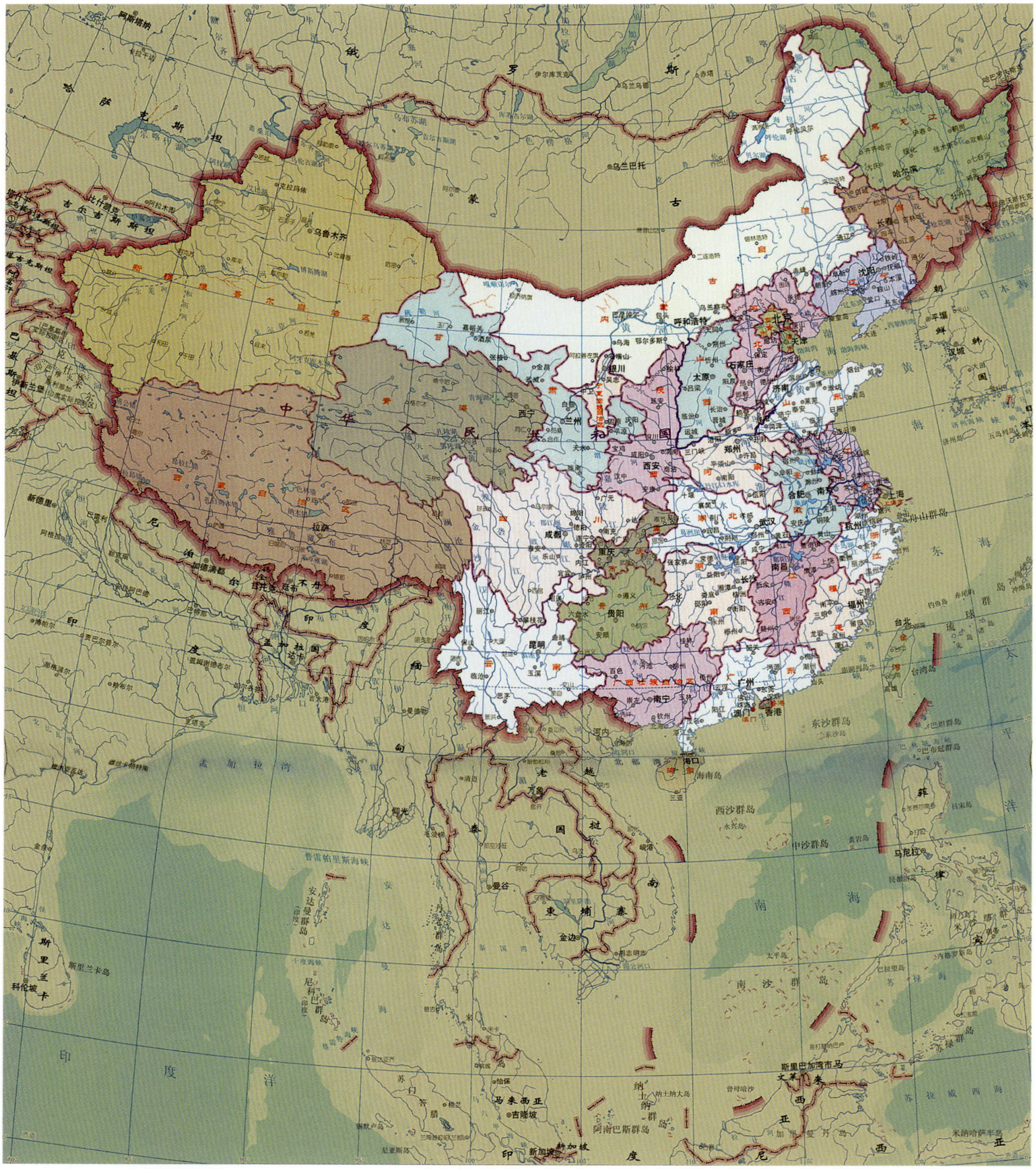

北京

门头沟 ▲
密云 ▲

河北

隆化 ▲
曲阳 ▲
井陉 ▲
临城 ▲
内丘 ▲
邯郸 ▲
彭城 ▲
临水 ▲
磁县 ▲
贾壁 ▲

河南

安阳 ▲
林州 ▲
鹤壁 ▲
浚县 ▲
淇县 ▲
辉县 ▲
焦作 ▲
修武 ▲
新乡 ▲
博爱 ▲
陕县 ▲
新安 ▲
宜阳 ▲
巩义 ▲
荥阳 ▲
密县 ▲
登封 ▲
禹县 ▲
汝州 ▲
宝丰 ▲
郏县 ▲
鲁山 ▲
内乡 ▲
南阳 ▲
邓州 ▲
唐河 ▲

山东

德州 ▲
武城 ▲
临清 ▲
淄博 ▲
淄川 ▲
临淄 ▲
泰安 ▲
宁阳 ▲
泗水 ▲
曲阜 ▲
临沂 ▲
枣庄 ▲

山西

天镇 ▲
大同 ▲
浑源 ▲
广灵 ▲
左云 ▲
怀仁 ▲
朔县 ▲
河曲 ▲
保德 ▲
神池 ▲
代县 ▲
定襄 ▲
静乐 ▲
兴县 ▲
临县 ▲
交城 ▲
文水 ▲
汾阳 ▲
榆次 ▲
孝义 ▲
盂县 ▲
平定 ▲
寿阳 ▲
和顺 ▲
左权 ▲
介休 ▲
灵石 ▲
隰县 ▲
汾西 ▲
霍县 ▲
蒲县 ▲
临汾 ▲
翼城 ▲
乡宁 ▲
浮山 ▲
吉县 ▲
曲沃 ▲
长子 ▲
襄垣 ▲
沁源 ▲
长治 ▲
长子 ▲
壶关 ▲
高平 ▲
阳城 ▲
晋城 ▲
河津 ▲
夏县 ▲

陕西

旬邑 ▲
耀州 ▲
白水 ▲
澄城 ▲
富平 ▲
麟游 ▲

甘肃

武威 ▲
兰州 ▲
华亭 ▲
天水 ▲

内蒙

赤峰 ▲
林东 ▲

宁夏

灵武 ▲

辽宁

辽阳 ▲

安徽

萧县 ▲
淮南 ▲
霍山 ▲
庐江 ▲
繁昌 ▲
枞阳 ▲
泾县 ▲
绩溪 ▲
歙县 ▲
休宁 ▲

江西

景德镇 ▲
乐平 ▲
婺源 ▲
横峰 ▲
弋阳 ▲
铅山 ▲
贵溪 ▲
九江 ▲
靖安 ▲
奉新 ▲
铜鼓 ▲
上高 ▲
丰城 ▲
金溪 ▲
南丰 ▲
广昌 ▲
萍乡 ▲
永丰 ▲
吉安 ▲
宁都 ▲
于都 ▲
赣州 ▲
大余 ▲
寻乌 ▲
定南 ▲
龙南 ▲
全南 ▲

江苏

宜兴 ▲

浙江

长兴 ▲
吴兴 ▲
德清 ▲
余杭 ▲
萧山 ▲
杭州 ▲
临安 ▲
绍兴 ▲
上虞 ▲
诸暨 ▲
嵊县 ▲
宁波 ▲
鄞县 ▲
慈溪 ▲
余姚 ▲
奉化 ▲
象山 ▲
浦江 ▲
义乌 ▲
东阳 ▲
永康 ▲
兰溪 ▲
金华 ▲
武义 ▲
仙居 ▲
临海 ▲
黄岩 ▲
台州 ▲
温岭 ▲
龙游 ▲
衢州 ▲
常山 ▲
江山 ▲
缙云 ▲
丽水 ▲
遂昌 ▲
龙泉 ▲
云和 ▲
庆元 ▲
永嘉 ▲
乐清 ▲
温州 ▲
文成 ▲
瑞安 ▲
泰顺 ▲
苍南 ▲

福建

浦城 ▲
光泽 ▲
崇安 ▲
松溪 ▲
政和 ▲
邵武 ▲
建阳 ▲
建瓯 ▲
顺昌 ▲
南平 ▲
柘荣 ▲
周宁 ▲
福安 ▲
霞浦 ▲
屏南 ▲
宁德 ▲
罗源 ▲
闽侯 ▲
闽清 ▲
福州 ▲
福清 ▲
连江 ▲
泰宁 ▲
建宁 ▲
将口 ▲
宁化 ▲
三明 ▲
大田 ▲
沙县 ▲
长汀 ▲
连城 ▲
永定 ▲
德化 ▲
永春 ▲
安溪 ▲
南安 ▲
同安 ▲
泉州 ▲
晋江 ▲
仙游 ▲
莆田 ▲
厦门 ▲
华安 ▲
长泰 ▲
漳州 ▲
南靖 ▲
龙海 ▲
平和 ▲
漳浦 ▲
云霄 ▲
诏安 ▲
东山 ▲

广东

梅县 ▲
大埔 ▲
五华 ▲
兴宁 ▲
潮州 ▲
饶平 ▲
潮安 ▲
揭阳 ▲
揭西 ▲
揭东 ▲
普宁 ▲
惠来 ▲
海丰 ▲
陆丰 ▲
紫金 ▲
龙川 ▲
惠州 ▲
龙门 ▲
博罗 ▲
惠东 ▲
广州 ▲
乐昌 ▲
仁化 ▲
韶关 ▲
始兴 ▲
乳源 ▲
南雄 ▲
英德 ▲
肇庆 ▲
封开 ▲
高要 ▲
郁南 ▲
佛山 ▲
南海 ▲
三水 ▲
高明 ▲
鹤山 ▲
恩平 ▲
新会 ▲
信宜 ▲
高州 ▲
茂名 ▲
廉江 ▲
遂溪 ▲
吴川 ▲
雷州 ▲
深圳 ▲
澄海 ▲
海康 ▲

海南

澄迈 ▲
东方 ▲
万宁 ▲
陵水 ▲

广西

桂林 ▲
全州 ▲
兴安 ▲
灵川 ▲
临桂 ▲
永福 ▲
钟山 ▲
藤县 ▲
容县 ▲
北流 ▲
柳州 ▲
桂平 ▲
田东 ▲
宾阳 ▲
邕宁 ▲
东兴 ▲
浦北 ▲
合浦 ▲
大新 ▲
百色 ▲

湖北

武昌 ▲
鄂城 ▲

湖南

岳阳 ▲
汨罗 ▲
湘阴 ▲
常德 ▲
益阳 ▲
长沙 ▲
浏阳 ▲
醴陵 ▲
衡阳 ▲
衡东 ▲
衡山 ▲
衡南 ▲
祁东 ▲
耒阳 ▲
常宁 ▲
沅陵 ▲
怀化 ▲
武冈 ▲
新宁 ▲
祁阳 ▲
蓝山 ▲
新田 ▲
道县 ▲
零陵 ▲
郴县 ▲
永兴 ▲
汝城 ▲

四川

广元 ▲
成都 ▲
郫县 ▲
灌县 ▲
大邑 ▲
新津 ▲
彭县 ▲
邛崃 ▲
绵阳 ▲
江油 ▲
乐山 ▲

重庆

南岸 ▲
奉节 ▲

云南

玉溪 ▲
禄丰 ▲
建水 ▲

窑址标本目录

河北

贾壁窑

磁州窑

邢窑

定窑

井陉窑

隆化窑

List of Plates

Hebei Province

Jiabi Kiln

Cizhou Kiln

Xing Kiln

Ding Kiln

Jingxing Kiln

Longhua Kiln

窑址标本

Plates

河北

河北省是宋代著名白瓷定窑的所在地，北方民间瓷窑的代表磁州窑也在这里，30 年来故宫博物院等单位对定窑、磁州窑、邢窑、井陉窑等进行过多次调查，河北省文物工作队做了多次发掘，取得了一定收获。

Hebei Province

Hebei province is the place where locates the Ding kiln, a famous white glaze porcelain kiln in Song dynasty. Cizhou kiln, which best represents the civilian kilns in northern China, is also in the province. Over the past three decades, experts from the Palace Museum had conducted a dozen of investigations and at the mean time, the Working Force for Cultural Relics of Hebei province and other institutions had excavated the ruin of Ding kiln, Cizhou kiln, Xing kiln, Jingxing kiln and other kilns in the province. Achievements in many aspects were made during the investigations and excavations.

河北窑址分布图
The Distribution Map of Kilns in Hebei Province

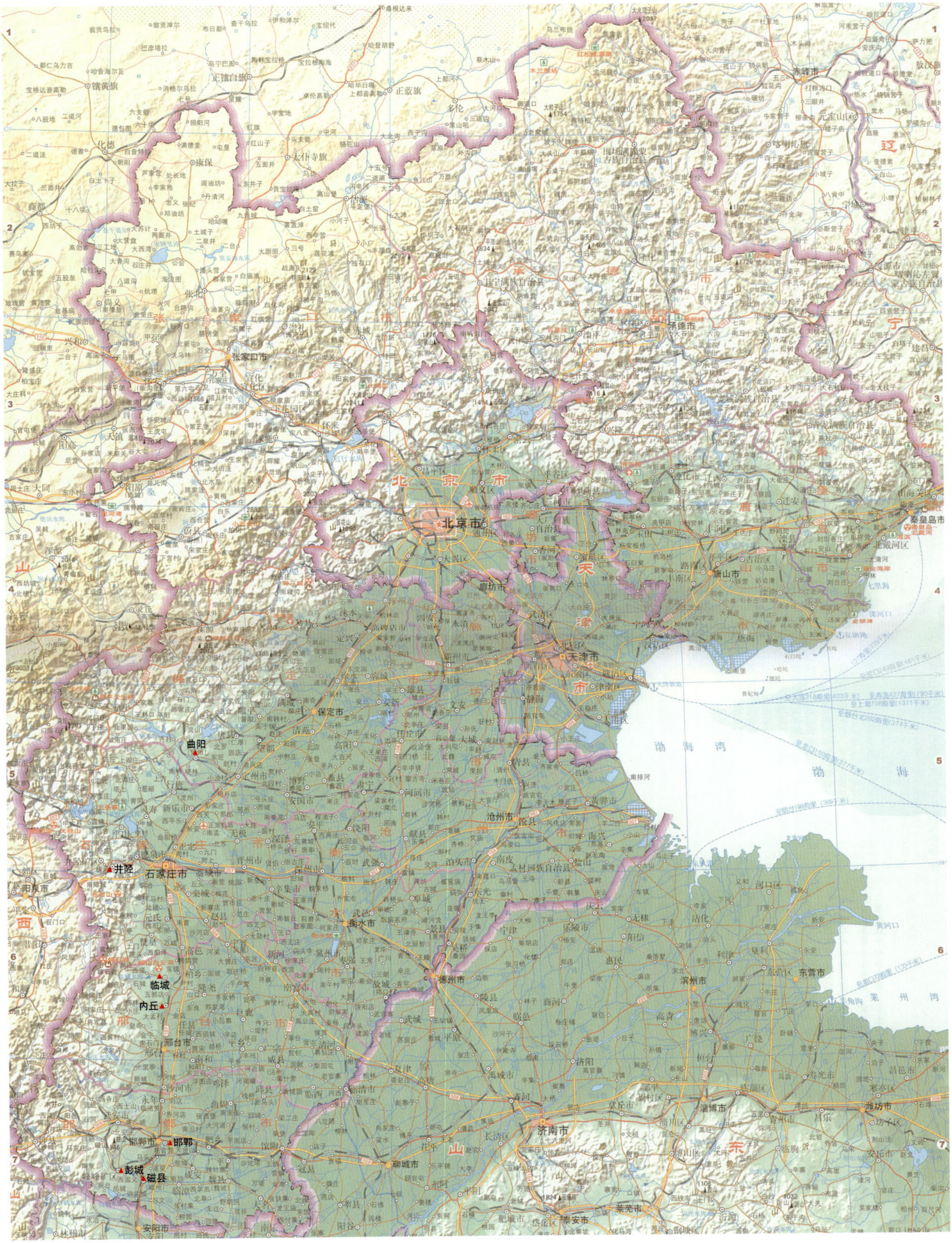
北京市
天津市
石家庄市
保定市
沧州市
衡水市
德州市
济南市
唐山市
承德市
张家口市
秦皇岛市
廊坊市
邢台市
邯郸市
聊城市
滨州市
东营市
淄博市
潍坊市
赤峰市
安阳市
泰安市
莱芜市
曲阳
井陉
临城
内丘
邯郸
彭城
磁县
渤海湾
渤海
莱州湾

贾壁窑

故宫博物院的部分专家和学者于20世纪50年代对贾壁窑进行了调查。

窑址在北贾壁村，隋代青瓷窑。遗物有高足盘、碗、钵、洗等标本。装饰花纹仅发现划刻波浪纹一种。胎厚重，施釉厚而透明，垂釉现象比较普遍，在器皿下部集成黑色玻璃珠是它们的特征。碗有大小数式，多深形敞口，小平底，中心微内凹。河南安阳隋卜仁墓等出土的青瓷，有可能是贾壁窑烧造的产品。

Jiabi Kiln

Experts from the Palace Museum made an investigation into Jiabi kiln in the 1950s. The ruin of the kiln is located in Beijiabi Village, Cixian County. It was a celadon kiln of Sui dynasty. Parts of stemmed plate, bowl, alms bowl, washer, etc. had been found at the ruin of the kiln. Incised wave design is the only way of decoration found on celadon. The bodies of celadon are thick thus heavy. Thick, transparent glaze were applied, thus, glaze flows were quite common. Black grass balls turned from glaze drops accumulating at the low part of the wares after firing is a distinguishing characteristic. Bowls vary in sizes, usually deep-shaped and with spreading mouth, small flat bottom whose center is concave a bit. The celadon unearthed from Bu Ren tomb of Sui dynasty in Anyang City, Henan Province is most likely from Jiabi kiln.

1 **隋　青釉罐标本**

Sui dynasty

Specimen of green glaze jar

附图

隋　青釉弦纹盘口瓶

高 32.5 厘米　口径 6.6 厘米

足径 9.2 厘米

故宫博物院藏

Illustration

Sui dynasty Green glaze vase with dish-shaped mouth and strings

Height 32.5cm, mouth diameter 6.6cm, foot diameter 9.2cm

Collected by the Palace Museum

瓶盘口，细颈，溜肩，鼓腹，下腹弧收，圈足外撇。灰白胎，外施青绿釉至腹部，流釉现象明显。肩、腹部刻划弦纹。

此瓶造型规矩，口部周正硬朗，肩部饱满圆润。

2 隋 青釉碗标本

Sui dynasty

Specimens of green glaze bowl

3　隋　青釉碗标本

Sui dynasty

Specimens of green glaze bowl

4　隋　青釉高足盘标本
Sui dynasty
Specimen of green glaze plate with high stem

5　隋　青釉杯标本
Sui dynasty
Specimen of green glaze cup

6　隋　青釉洗标本
Sui dynasty
Specimen of green glaze washer

7　隋　青釉绳纹钵标本
Sui dynasty
Specimen of green glaze alms bowl
with rope design

8　隋　青釉划花水波纹钵标本

Sui dynasty

Specimens of green glaze alms bowl with incised wave design

9　隋　窑具标本
Sui dynasty
Specimen of kiln furniture

10　隋　窑具标本
Sui dynasty
Specimens of kiln furniture

磁州窑

故宫博物院部分专家和学者于20世纪60年代、70年代、80年代、90年代和2005年对该窑进行了调查。

磁州窑为宋代北方民间著名瓷窑之一，窑址主要在磁县贾壁、观台、东艾口、冶子村、彭城及临水等地。窑址范围广大，遗物丰富。烧制品种、装饰方法多种多样。其中以白地黑花最具代表性。白地黑花首先是在坯胎上施白色化妆土，然后用黑彩绘画纹饰，有些精品在黑彩上再划出花脉叶筋，最后施透明釉。花纹与地子黑白对比强烈，花纹生动，题材来自民间，具有浓郁的生活气息。

Cizhou Kiln

Experts from the Palace Museum made several investigations into Cizhou kiln in the 1960s, 1970s, 1980s, 1990s and in 2005. Cizhou kiln was one of the famous civilian kilns in northern China in Song dynasty. The ruins of Cizhou kiln were mainly found in Jiabi, Dongaikou, Yezicun, Linshui and Pengcheng, etc. Cixian County. Kiln sites were widespread across the county. A great number of porcelains or parts were collected. Cizhou kiln is rich in porcelain varieties and in decorative techniques. The most representative way of decoration is white glaze with design of black patterns. The making procedures of the ware are as follow: first, white engobe is applied to cover the body; then, decorates the body with patterns in black. For some of the first class quality wares with design of floral patterns, the decoration is so fine that the veins of leaves or flowers can be clearly seen; and finally transparent glaze is applied. Striking contrast of black and white, vivid patterns, folk themes, reflection of virtual life, all these contribute to the decoration style of Cizhou ware.

磁州（观台）窑遗址
Ruin of Cizhou kiln at Guantai Town

磁州（观台）窑遗址瓷片遗存
Pileup of porcelain parts at the ruin of Cizhou kiln at Guantai Town

磁州（冶子）窑遗址
Ruin of Cizhou kiln at Yezi Town

磁州（彭城富田）窑窑炉遗址
Ruin of Cizhou kiln at Futian, Pengcheng Town

磁州（彭城盐店）窑窑炉遗址
Ruin of Cizhou kiln at Yandian, Pengcheng Town

磁州（彭城盐店）窑窑炉遗址
Ruin of Cizhou kiln at Yandian, Pengcheng Town

彭城外景图（1941 年摄）
A bird's-eye view of Pengcheng Town (photographed in 1941)

11　**宋　白釉瓜棱罐标本**
Song dynasty
Specimen of white glaze melon-shaped jar

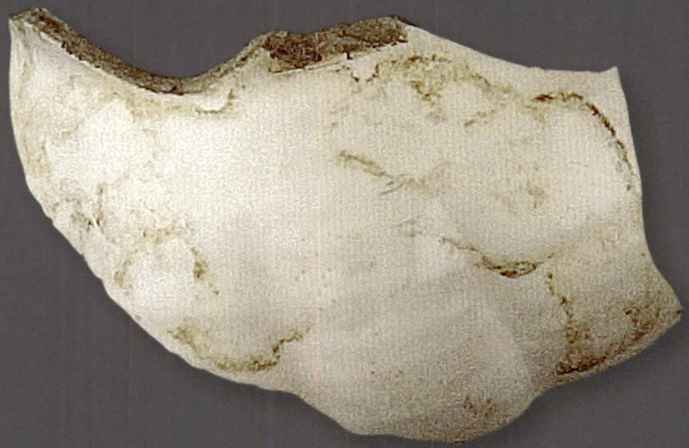

12　**宋　白釉壶标本**
Song dynasty
Specimen of white glaze pot

13　**宋　白釉供器标本**
Song dynasty
Specimen of white glaze sacrificial ware

14　**宋　白釉碗标本**
Song dynasty
Specimens of white glaze bowl

15　**宋　白釉花式碗标本**
Song dynasty
Specimen of white glaze flower-shaped bowl

16 **宋　白釉印花菊瓣纹盘标本**
Song dynasty
Specimen of white glaze plate with stamped chrysanthemum design

17 **宋　白釉刻花莲瓣纹碗标本**
Song dynasty
Specimen of white glaze bowl with incised lotus-petal design

18 **宋　白釉划花花卉纹枕标本**
Song dynasty
Specimen of white glaze pillow
with incised floral design

19 **宋　白釉划花水波纹枕标本**
Song dynasty
Specimen of white glaze pillow
with incised wave design

20 **宋 白釉划花人物纹枕标本**
Song dynasty
Specimen of white glaze pillow with incised figure design

21 **宋 白釉划花碗标本**
Song dynasty
Specimen of white glaze bowl with incised design

22　宋　珍珠地划花花叶纹枕标本

Song dynasty

Specimen of pillow with incised floral design over pearl-pattern ground

附图

宋

珍珠地划花花卉纹腰圆形枕

高 12 厘米　长 25.8 厘米
宽 18.4 厘米
故宫博物院藏

Illustration
Song dynasty
Oval pillow with incised floral design over pearl-pattern ground

Height 12cm, length 25.8cm,
width 18.4cm
Collected by the Palace Museum

枕腰圆形，枕面装饰珍珠地缠枝牡丹纹，枕侧饰划花花叶纹。

珍珠地划花装饰唐代开始出现，宋代较为流行。目前已发现河北、河南、山西等地瓷窑均有烧制。

23　宋　**珍珠地划花花叶纹枕标本**

Song dynasty

Specimen of pillow with incised floral design over pearl-pattern ground

附图

宋

珍珠地划花“长命”铭如意形枕

高 15.5 厘米　长 30.2 厘米

宽 29 厘米

故宫博物院藏

Illustration

Song dynasty

Pillow with incised design over pearl-pattern ground and with inscription *Chang Ming*

Height 15.5cm, length 30.2cm, width 29cm

Collected by the Palace Museum

枕面如意形，椭圆形平底。枕面装饰珍珠地，图案中央刻写“长命枕壹只”五字。

24　宋　珍珠地划花花叶纹枕标本

Song dynasty

Specimen of pillow with incised floral design over pearl-pattern ground

附图

宋　珍珠地划花牡丹纹腰圆形枕

高 9 厘米　长 22 厘米
宽 14 厘米
故宫博物院藏

Illustration
Song dynasty
Oval pillow with incised peony design over pearl-pattern ground

Height 9cm, length 22cm,
width 14cm
Collected by the Palace Museum

枕腰圆形，枕面装饰珍珠地折枝牡丹纹。花叶饱满，占据整个枕面，隙地满饰细密的珍珠纹。

25 宋 白釉剔花花卉纹瓶标本

Song dynasty

Specimens of white glaze vase with cut floral decoration

26 宋 白釉剔花花卉纹瓶标本

Song dynasty

Specimens of white glaze vase with cut floral decoration

27 宋 白釉剔花枕标本

Song dynasty

Specimen of white glaze pillow with cut decoration

28 **宋　白釉剔花兔纹枕标本**
Song dynasty
Specimen of white glaze pillow with cut rabbit decoration

附图

宋　白釉剔花兔纹八方形枕

长 26.4 厘米
河北省文物总店藏

Illustration
Song dynasty
White glaze octagonal pillow with cut rabbit decoration

Length 26.4cm
Collected by the Flag Antique Shop of Hebei Province

枕八方形，四沿突出， 枕侧八个棱角处装饰有八条竹节状凸起，背面有一个通气孔，素底。枕面白釉剔刻兔纹图案。枕有墨书“政和八年八月二十三日记之”。政和八年为 1118 年。

29　宋　白釉剔花花卉纹缸标本
Song dynasty
Specimens of white glaze vat with cut floral decoration

30　宋　白地黑花婴戏纹枕标本
Song dynasty
Specimen of white glaze pillow with design of black patterns of children at play

31　宋　白地黑花荷叶纹枕标本
Song dynasty
Specimen of white glaze pillow with design of black lotus-leaf patterns

32　宋　白地黑花牡丹纹枕标本
Song dynasty
Specimen of white glaze pillow with
design of black peony palterns

附图

北宋
白地黑花折枝牡丹纹如意形枕

高 19.4 厘米　长 36.5 厘米
宽 30 厘米
日本静嘉堂文库美术馆藏

Illustration
Northern Song dynasty
White glaze Ruji-shaped pillow with design of black patterns of disconnected sprays of peony

Height 19.4cm, length 36.5cm, width 30cm
Collected by Seikado Bunko Art Museum, Japan

枕呈叶形，中间凹，两侧及后侧枕面上翘，下有不规则的方形台座。是磁州窑北宋时期流行的枕式之一。

此枕采用剔花装饰，其方法是先施白色化妆土，再施黑釉，刻划出牡丹花叶纹，然后把花纹以外的黑釉剔掉，露出白色化妆土，最后施透明釉。以白色底衬托黑色花纹。此形枕除装饰牡丹纹以外，还有猫、熊等纹饰。

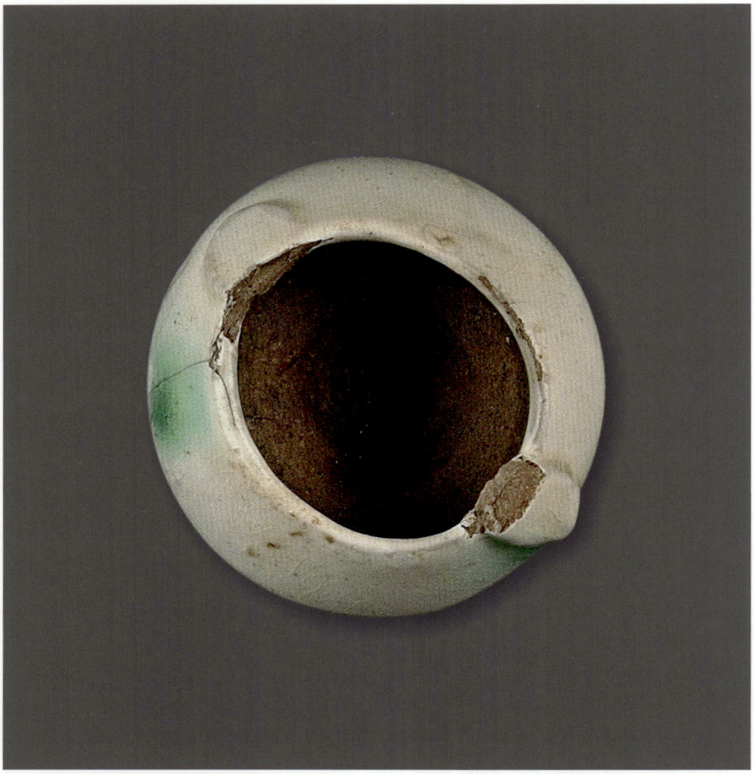

33　宋　白釉绿彩水盂标本
Song dynasty
Specimen of white glaze water container with green color design

34　宋　黑釉剔花瓶标本
Song dynasty
Specimen of black glaze vase with cut decoration

附图

宋　黑釉剔花牡丹纹梅瓶

高 33 厘米
日本五岛美术馆藏

Illustration
Song dynasty　Black glaze prunus vase with cut peony decoration

Height 33cm
Collected by the Gotoh Art Museum, Japan

瓶小口，短颈，圆肩，下腹内收。口施白釉，肩部刻划莲瓣纹，腹部通体黑釉剔刻牡丹纹，近足处刻划菊瓣纹。图案线条流畅，古朴，自然。

腹部黑釉剔花的做法是先施化妆土，再施釉彩，然后剔划出花纹，并把花纹以外的地子剔掉，以白色来衬托黑花，最后罩透明釉。

35　宋　黑釉剔花卷枝纹瓶标本

Song dynasty

Specimen of black glaze vase with cut branch scrolls design

36　宋　黑釉剔花花卉纹瓶标本

Song dynasty

Specimens of black glaze vase with cut floral decoration

37　宋　黑釉剔花牡丹纹瓶标本

Song dynasty

Specimens of black glaze vase with cut peony decoration

38　宋　黑釉剔花牡丹纹瓶标本

Song dynasty

Specimen of black glaze vase with cut peony decoration

附图

宋　黑釉剔花牡丹纹梅瓶

高 40.2 厘米

日本永青文库藏

Illustration

Song dynasty　Black glaze prunus vase with cut peony decoration

Height 40.2cm

Eisei Bunko, Tokyo

瓶小口、短颈，圆肩，下腹内敛。口施白釉，外壁肩、胫处刻划黑釉菊瓣纹饰，腹部剔刻牡丹纹。

39　宋　黑釉剔花卷枝纹带字枕标本

Song dynasty

Specimen of black glaze pillow with cut branch scrolls decoration and Chinese characters

40　宋　黑釉剔花花鸟纹枕标本

Song dynasty

Specimen of black glaze pillow with cut bird and flowers decoration

附图

宋　黑釉剔花花鸟纹如意形枕

长 30 厘米

日本多摩中央信用金库藏

Illustration

Song dynasty　Black glaze Ruyi-shaped pillow with cut bird and flowers decoration

Length 30cm

Collected by the Tama Shinkin Central Bank, Japan

枕面如意形，椭圆形平底枕箱。枕面黑釉剔花折枝花卉绶带鸟图案。

41　宋　黑釉剔花花卉纹缸标本
Song dynasty
Specimen of black glaze vat with cut floral decoration

42　宋
黑釉剔花开光花卉纹缸标本
Song dynasty
Specimens of black glaze vat with cut floral decoration in reserved panels

43　宋（金）　白地黑花枕标本

Song dynasty (Jin dynasty)

Specimens of white glaze pillow

with design of black patterns

44　宋（金）　白地黑花枕标本

Song dynasty (Jin dynasty)

Specimens of white glaze pillow with design of black patterns

附图

宋（金）　白地黑花竹纹“张家造”款八方形枕

高 10.5 厘米　长 28.3 厘米
宽 19.8 厘米
故宫博物院藏

Illustration
Song dynasty (Jin dynasty)
White glaze octagonal pillow with design of black bamboo patterns and inscription *Zhang Jia Zao*

Height 10.5cm, length 28.3cm,
width 19.8cm
Collected by the Palace Museum

枕八方形，边沿突出，背面有一通气孔，素底。枕面以白地黑花画竹纹，枕面边缘饰有黑彩边框，枕壁画缠枝唐草纹。底戳印“张家造”款识。

宋代磁州窑枕的数量猛增，这源于人们对其清凉去热物理特性的认识。北宋张耒《谢黄师是惠碧瓷枕》诗云：“巩人作瓷坚且青，故人赠我消炎蒸。持之入室凉风生，脑寒发冷泥丸惊。”枕上还常带有“某家造”、“某家枕”等商标式的款识，其中以张家作坊产品最多，延续时间亦最长。

45 宋（金） 白地黑花枕标本

Song dynasty (Jin dynasty)
Specimen of white glaze pillow with design of black patterns

附图

宋（金） 白地黑花诗文如意形枕

高 13.2 厘米　长 31 厘米
宽 22 厘米
故宫博物院藏

Illustration
Song dynasty (Jin dynasty)
White glaze Ruyi-shaped pillow with design of black patterns and verse lines

Height 13.2cm, length 31cm, width 22cm
Collected by the Palace Museum

枕如意形，枕箱随形，平底。枕面饰白地黑花诗句图案，边饰采用如意形、波浪形条带装饰，枕壁为卷草纹。

46　宋（金）　**白地黑花花卉纹枕标本**

Song dynasty (Jin dynasty)

Specimen of white glaze pillow with design of black floral patterns

附图

宋（金）

白地黑花折枝牡丹纹八方枕

高 12 厘米　长 32 厘米

宽 23 厘米

故宫博物院藏

Illustration

Song dynasty (Jin dynasty)

White glaze octagonal pillow with design of black pattern of disconnected spray of peony

Height 12cm, length 32cm, width 23cm

Collected by the Palace Museum

枕呈八方形，中心内凹。施白釉，素底。枕边棱随形涂绘出八方形开光，枕面中心先以黑彩绘折枝花纹一朵，再以竹木或金属工具划出花瓣、叶脉等细节，装饰效果黑白分明，对比强烈。

47 宋（金） 白地黑花花卉纹枕标本

Song dynasty (Jin dynasty)

Specimens of white glaze pillow with design of black floral patterns

附图

宋（金）
白地黑花喜鹊登枝纹腰圆形枕

高 12.7 厘米　长 31 厘米
宽 22.7 厘米
磁州窑博物馆藏

Illustration
Song dynasty (Jin dynasty)
White glaze oval pillow with design of black patterns of magpie on branch

Height 12.7cm, length 31cm, width 22.7cm
Collected by the Museum of Cizhou Kiln

枕腰圆形，边缘刻划双线装饰，枕面以黑彩绘折枝花鸟，鸟呈回首状，两侧为花枝。

在磁州窑瓷枕中，以花鸟题材为主题的纹饰比较常见，有枯枝啄木鸟、喜鹊梅花、喜鹊枯枝、竹雀、水鸟花草等组合。

48 宋（金）

白地黑花花卉纹枕标本

Song dynasty (Jin dynasty)

Specimen of white glaze pillow with design of black floral patterns

49 宋（金）

白地黑花竹叶纹枕标本

Song dynasty (Jin dynasty)

Specimen of white glaze pillow with design of black bamboo patterns

附图

元　白地黑花竹雀纹如意形枕

高 13 厘米　长 29 厘米
宽 22.5 厘米

Illustration
Yuan dynasty
White glaze Ruyi-shaped pillow with design of black patterns of bird and bamboo

Height 13cm, length 29cm, width 22.5cm

枕面出沿，略呈如意形，外周有三组如意形开光装饰，主题纹饰绘简洁的竹雀纹，色有浓淡变化，竹纹色重，雀鸟笔画纤细而色淡，与竹纹形成鲜明对比。枕侧绘卷枝纹。

50 宋（金） 白地黑花诗文枕标本

Song dynasty (Jin dynasty)

Specimens of white glaze pillow with design of black patterns and verse lines

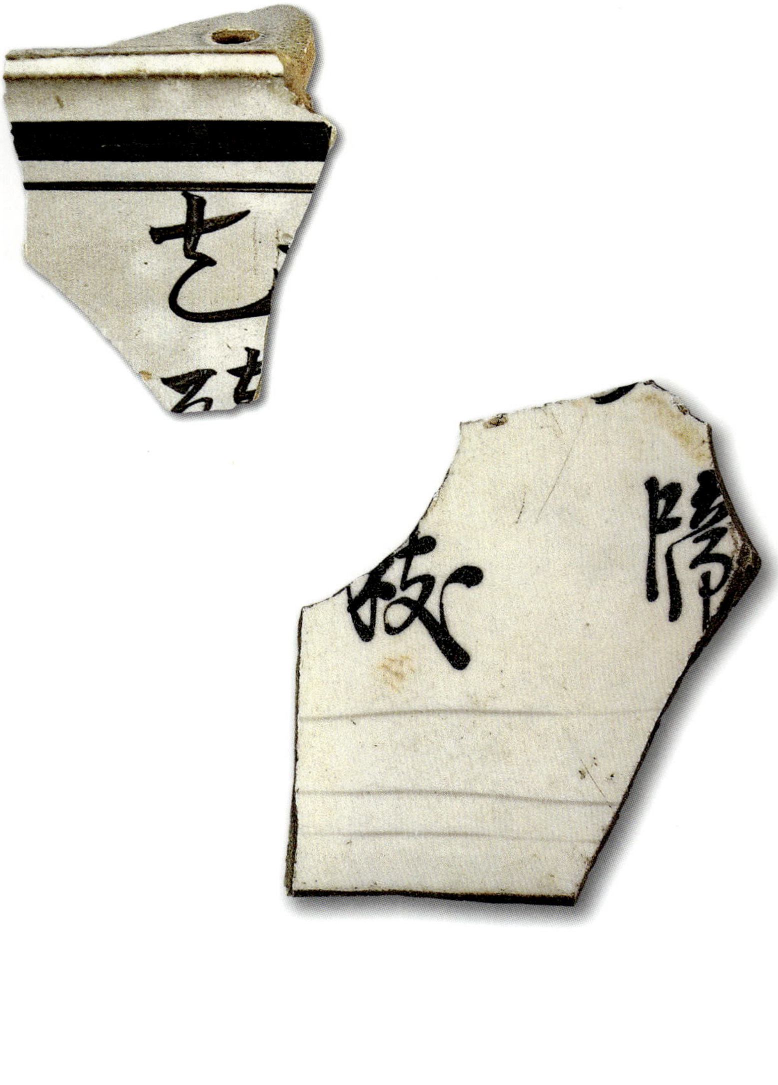

51 宋（金） 白地黑花诗文枕标本

Song dynasty (Jin dynasty)

Specimen of white glaze pillow with design of black patterns and verse lines

附图

宋（金） 白地黑花诗文腰圆形枕

高 13 厘米 长 31 厘米

宽 22 厘米

故宫博物馆院藏

Illustration

Song dynasty (Jin dynasty)

White glaze oval pillow with design of black patterns and verse lines

Height 13cm, length 31cm, width 22cm

Collected by the Palace Museum

枕椭圆形。施白釉，素底。枕面白地黑花开光内草书诗句“明知空手去，刚惹业随身”，周围装饰缠枝花草纹。

文字装饰是磁州窑极富特色的一类，内容既有表达吉祥寓意的民间俗语、警句、对联等，也有不少名人诗词。以楷书、行楷、行书、行草为主，风格多样，天真活泼，带有民间书写的便捷灵动性。

52 宋（金） 白地黑花水鸟纹枕标本

Song dynasty (Jin dynasty)

Specimen of white glaze pillow with design of black bird patterns

附图

宋（金）

白地黑花仙鹤纹如意形枕

高 13 厘米　长 32 厘米

宽 23 厘米

磁州窑博物馆藏

Illustration

Song dynasty (Jin dynasty)

White glaze Ruyi-shaped pillow with design of black pattern of crane

Height 13cm length 32cm width 23cm

Collected by the Museum of Cizhou Kiln

枕呈如意形，前低后高，两侧微上翘。枕边多层如意形开光装饰，枕面主题纹饰绘一回首仙鹤立于水塘芦苇边。画面简约生动。枕侧绘卷枝纹。底素胎，长方形边框内戳印“张家造”款识。边框上覆荷叶，下托荷花。

53 宋（金） **白地黑花鹭鸶纹枕标本**

Song dynasty (Jin dynasty)

Specimen of white glaze pillow with design of black octagonal patterns

附图

宋（金）

白地黑花飞鹤纹八方形枕

高 8.3 厘米 长 21.1 厘米

宽 13.5 厘米

故宫博物院藏

Illustration

Song dynasty (Jin dynasty)

White glaze octagonal pillow with design of black crane

Height 8.3cm, length 21.1cm,

width 13.5cm

Collected by the Palace Museum

枕呈八方形，中心内凹。施白釉，枕面以黑彩在八方形开光内绘飞鹤一只。底部露胎，中心戳印“张家造”三字款。

54　宋（金）　白地黑花鹭鸶纹枕标本

Song dynasty (Jin dynasty)

Specimen of white glaze pillow with design of black octagonal patterns

附图

金　白地黑花鹭鸶纹八方形枕

高 17 厘米　长 27 厘米
宽 17.8 厘米
磁州窑博物馆藏

Illustration
Jin dynasty
White glaze octagonal pillow with design of black pattern of egret

Height 17cm, length 27cm, width 17.8cm
Collected by the Museum of Cizhou Kiln

枕呈八方形，面出沿。外周有宽窄两条线纹边饰，中心主题纹绘一鹭鸶在水塘芦苇边散步觅食。画面写意，形象生动。枕侧光素无纹饰。

55 宋（金） 白地黑花芦雁纹枕标本

Song dynasty (Jin dynasty)

Specimen of white glaze pillow with design of black wild goose patterns

附图

金

白地黑花芦雁纹八方形枕

高 11 厘米　长 28.9 厘米

宽 18.1 厘米

邯郸市峰峰矿区文保所藏

Illustration

Jin dynasty

White glaze octagonal pillow with design of black patterns of reed and wild goose

Height 11cm, length 28.9cm, width 18.1cm

Collected by the Institute of Cultural Relics Preservation of Fengfengkuangqu, Handan City

枕八方形，枕面出沿，前低后高，两侧微翘。外周有宽窄两条边线开光，中心绘一只口衔芦草的大雁。画面简洁，自然生动。枕侧装饰卷枝纹。底有戳印款“张家造”，款外有长方形边框。

56 **宋（金）　白地黑花动物纹枕标本**

Song dynasty (Jin dynasty)

Specimen of white glaze pillow with black zoomorphic design

附图

宋（金）
白地黑花狮纹腰圆形枕

高 10 厘米　长 23.5 厘米
宽 18.3 厘米
故宫博物院藏

Illustration
Song dynasty (Jin dynasty)
White glaze oval pillow with design of black lion patterns

Height 10cm, length 23.5cm, width 18.3cm
Collected by the Palace Museum

枕腰圆形，以白地黑花图案装饰，枕边为四瓣如意形开光，中心画狮子戏球图案，枕壁为缠枝唐草纹，是典型的磁州窑风格作品。

57　宋（金）　白地黑花击角球纹枕标本

Song dynasty (Jin dynasty)

Specimen of white glaze pillow with design of black patterns of children at play

附图

金　白地黑花婴戏纹八方形枕

高 12.9 厘米　长 30 厘米
宽 21 厘米
磁州窑博物馆藏

Illustration
White glaze octagonal pillow with design of black pattern of egret

Height 12.9cm, length 30cm, width 21cm
Collected by the Museum of Cizhou Kiln

枕八方形，枕面出沿，前低后高，两侧微翘。外周有宽窄两条边线开光，主题纹饰绘一孩儿放风筝，形象可爱生动。枕侧绘卷枝纹。底有长方形边框，上覆荷叶，下托荷花，框内有“张家造”款识。

58　宋（金）　白地黑花“张家造”款枕标本

Song dynasty (Jin dynasty)

Specimens of white glaze pillow with design of black patterns and *Zhang Jia Zao* inscription

附图

元
白地黑花仕女游春图长方形枕

高 14.1 厘米　长 39.1 厘米
宽 17.2 厘米
故宫博物院藏

Illustration
Yuan dynasty
White glaze rectangular pillow with design of black patterns of beauties' outing in spring

Height 14.1cm, length 39.1cm, width 17.2cm
Collected by the Palace Museum

枕长方形，前低后高，面出沿，枕面四周有边线装饰。中心开光内绘主题纹饰仕女游春，画面有五六个女子及二个男子在山水景物间。开光外以花卉填满隙地空间。前后侧面绘开光竹雀纹，开光外填满花卉。两侧为莲花。底部有长方形边框，边框上覆荷叶，下托莲花。框内上方有“古相”，下有“张家造”款识。

元代磁州窑烧制的这种长方形枕数量较多，多采用开光装饰，多以山水、人物故事为主要题材。

59 宋（金） 白地黑花“张家造”款枕标本

Song dynasty (Jin dynasty)

Specimens of white glaze pillow with design of black patterns and *Zhang Jia Zao* inscription

60 宋（金） **白地黑花“张家造”款枕标本**

Song dynasty (Jin dynasty)

Specimen of white glaze pillow with design of black patterns and *Zhang Jia Zao* inscription

附图

元

白地黑花岸边观鱼图长方形枕

高 14 厘米　长 31.8 厘米

宽 15.4 厘米

故宫博物院藏

Illustration

Yuan dynasty

White glaze rectangular pillow with design of black patterns of fish-watching

Height 14cm, length 31.8cm, width 15.4cm

Collected by the Palace Museum

枕长方形，前低后高面出沿。枕面四周有边线装饰，中心开光内绘主题纹饰岸边观鱼，开光外隙地绘满花卉。枕前后两面开光内绘折枝花卉，开光外填满卷枝纹。两侧绘莲花纹。底部长方框内有“张家造”戳印款。

61　宋（金）　白地黑花“张家造”款枕标本

Song dynasty (Jin dynasty)

Specimens of white glaze pillow with design of black patterns and *Zhang Jia Zao* inscription

附图

宋（金）
白地黑花“宜男小枕”铭八方形枕

高 7.4 厘米　长 20.3 厘米
宽 12 厘米
故宫博物院藏

Illustration
Song dynasty (Jin dynasty)
White glaze octagonal pillow with design of black patterns and *Yi Nan Xiao Zhen* inscription

Height 7.4cm, length 20.3cm, width 12cm
Collected by the Palace Museum

枕八方形，边沿突出，背面有一个通气孔，素底。枕面以白底黑花书“宜男小枕”四字，枕面边缘饰有黑彩边框，枕壁无纹饰，底戳印“张家造”款识。

62　宋（金）　白地黑花“张家造”款枕标本

Song dynasty (Jin dynasty)

Specimens of white glaze pillow with design of black patterns and *Zhang Jia Zao* inscription

63　**宋（金）**

白地黑花花鸟纹洗标本

Song dynasty (Jin dynasty)

Specimen of white glaze washer with design of black patterns of birds and flowers

64　**宋（金）**

白地黑花牡丹纹盆标本

Song dynasty (Jin dynasty)

Specimen of white glaze pot with design of black peony patterns

65　宋（金）　白釉点褐彩钵标本

Song dynasty (Jin dynasty)

Specimens of white glaze alms bowl with brown dots

附图

宋（金）　白釉点褐彩钵

高 7.5 厘米　口径 11.5 厘米
足径 6 厘米
故宫博物院藏

Illustration
Song dynasty (Jin dynasty)
White glaze alms bowl with brown dots

Height 7.5cm, mouth diameter 11.5cm,
foot diameter 6cm
Collected by the Palace Museum

钵圆口内敛，直壁，圈足。内外施白釉，釉不到底，外壁装饰褐彩梅花形图案。

66 宋（金） 白釉点褐彩钵标本

Song dynasty (Jin dynasty)

Specimens of white glaze alms bowl with brown dots

67 宋（金） 白地褐花缸标本

Song dynasty (Jin dynasty)

Specimen of white glaze vat with design of brown patterns

68 宋（金） 白地褐花花卉纹缸标本

Song dynasty (Jin dynasty)

Specimens of white glaze vat with design of brown floral patterns

69 宋（金） 黑釉碗标本
Song dynasty (Jin dynasty)
Specimen of black glaze bowl

70 宋（金） 黑釉俑标本
Song dynasty (Jin dynasty)
Specimen of black glaze figurine

71 宋（金） 黑地划花水波纹枕标本

Song dynasty (Jin dynasty)

Specimens of black glaze pillow with incised wave design

72　宋（金）　黑地划花水波纹枕标本

Song dynasty (Jin dynasty)

Specimens of black glaze pillow with incised wave design

附图

金　白地黑花水波纹如意形枕

高13.2厘米　长31厘米
宽23厘米
磁县冶子村出土
磁县博物馆藏

Illustration
Jin dynasty
White glaze Ruji-shaped pillow
with design of black wave patterns

Height 13.2cm, length 31cm, width 23cm
Unearthed at Yezicun Village, Cixian County
Collected by the Cixian Museum

枕如意形，枕面边缘及枕侧为线纹及卷草纹。枕面主题纹饰为黑地水波纹。

此种类型的装饰除如意形枕外还有八方形枕。

73　宋（金）　黑釉酱彩器盖标本
Song dynasty (Jin dynasty)
Specimen of black glaze cover with dark brown color design

74　宋（金）　黑釉酱彩碗标本
Song dynasty (Jin dynasty)
Specimen of black glaze bowl with dark brown color design

附图

金至元　黑釉酱彩碗

高 4 厘米　口径 14 厘米
足径 5.5 厘米
故宫博物院藏

Illustration
From Jin dynasty to Yuan dynasty
Black glaze bowl with dark brown color design

Height 4cm, mouth diameter 14cm,
foot diameter 5.5cm
Collected by the Palace Museum

碗撇口，宽唇，斜弧壁，圈足。里外均施黑釉酱彩。

黑釉酱彩是北方宋金元时期各瓷窑普遍采用的装饰，有点、条、斑块状形式，磁州窑元代以条形彩较为常见。

75 宋（金） 黑釉酱彩碗标本

Song dynasty (Jin dynasty)

Specimen of black glaze bowl with dark brown color design

附图

元　黑釉酱彩碗

高 8.2 厘米　口径 17.2 厘米
足径 6.6 厘米
磁州窑博物馆藏

Illustration
Yuan dynasty
Black glaze bowl with decoration of dark brown color

Height 8.2cm, mouth diameter 17.2cm, foot diameter 6.6cm
Collected by the Museum of Cizhou Kiln

碗直口，厚唇，斜直壁，浅圈足。足外跟部平削一刀。碗内外施黑釉，内壁上饰两周短条形酱彩，外近足部露胎。

76 宋（金） 黑釉酱彩碗标本

Song dynasty (Jin dynasty)

Specimens of black glaze bowl with dark brown color design

77 **宋（金） 褐釉剔花瓶标本**

Song dynasty (Jin dynasty)

Specimens of brown glaze vase with cut decoration

78　宋（金）　绿釉剔花牡丹纹瓶标本

Song dynasty (Jin dynasty)

Specimen of green glaze vase with cut decoration

附图

金　绿釉剔花缠枝牡丹纹梅瓶

高 14 厘米　口径 3.6 厘米
足径 7.8 厘米
英国大英博物馆藏

Illustration
Jin dynasty
Green glaze prunus vase with cut design of interlocking peony

Height 14cm, mouth diameter 3.6cm, foot diameter 7.8cm
Collected by the British Museum, UK

梅瓶小口，短颈，丰肩，长腹，圈足。工艺采用先施化妆土，然后剔刻缠枝牡丹，最后罩绿釉。

磁州窑剔花装饰有白釉、黑釉、绿釉等，制作工艺较为复杂。

79 宋（金） 绿地黑花花卉纹瓶标本

Song dynasty(Jin dynasty)

Specimen of green glaze vase with design of black floral patterns

附图

宋（金） 绿地黑花花卉纹梅瓶

高 32 厘米 口径 3 厘米
底径 7.6 厘米
故宫博物院藏

Illustration
Song dynasty (Jin dynasty)
Green glaze prunus vase with design of black floral patterns

Height 32cm, mouth diameter 3cm,
bottom diameter 7.6cm
Collected by the Palace Museum

瓶小口，短颈，圆肩，下腹内敛，素底内凹。通体施绿釉，釉面平润。釉下画四层纹饰，肩部画两层水波纹，腹部的主题图案为缠枝花卉纹，胫部为折枝花草纹。

磁州窑以白地黑花为代表，绿地黑花是在白地黑花的基础上施以透明的绿釉，是磁州窑器物中比较罕见的品种。

80 **宋（金） 绿地黑花花卉纹瓶标本**

Song dynasty(Jin dynasty)

Specimen of green glaze vase with design of black floral patterns

附图

宋（金） 绿地黑花鱼藻纹梅瓶

高 38.5 厘米 口径 3 厘米

底径 9 厘米

故宫博物院藏

Illustration

Song dynasty (Jin dynasty)

Green glaze prunus vase with design of black patterns of fish and aquatic plants

Height 38.5cm, mouth diameter 3cm, bottom diameter 9cm

Collected by the Palace Museum

瓶小口，短颈，圆肩，下腹内敛，素底内凹。通体施绿釉，釉面平润。釉下画五层纹饰，肩部画一层水波纹，腹部的主题图案为鱼藻纹，胫部为三周水波纹。

81　宋（金）　绿地黑花枕标本
Song dynasty (Jin dynasty)
Specimens of green glaze pillow with design of black patterns

82　宋（金）　绿地黑花枕标本
Song dynasty (Jin dynasty)
Specimen of green glaze pillow with design of black patterns

附图

金　绿地黑花诗文八方形枕

高 12 厘米　长 30 厘米　宽 20 厘米
磁县冶子村出土
磁县博物馆藏

Illustration
Jin dynasty
Green glaze octagonal pillow with design of verse lines and black patterns

Height 12cm, length 30cm, width 20cm
Unearthed at Yezicun Village, Cixian County Collected by the Cixian Museum

枕八方形，上下出沿，背部有通气孔。枕面主题纹饰为“蜂飞花下至，鹤引水边行”五言诗二句。枕侧绘卷草纹。通体施绿釉。

83　宋（金）

素胎褐花花卉纹枕标本

Song dynasty (Jin dynasty)

Specimen of unglazed pillow with design of brown floral patterns

84　金

白釉划花“忍”字枕标本

Jin dynasty

Specimen of white glaze pillow with incised Chinese character *Ren* design

85　金　**白釉划花花卉纹碗标本**

Jin dynasty

Specimens of white glaze bowl with incised floral design

86　金　白釉划花荷莲纹碗标本

Jin dynasty

Specimens of white glaze bowl with incised lotus design

87　金　白釉划花荷莲纹碗标本

Jin dynasty

Specimen of white glaze bowl with incised lotus design

附图

金　白釉划花花卉纹碗

高 8.5 厘米　口径 24 厘米
足径 6.8 厘米
故宫博物院藏

Illustration
Jin dynasty
White glaze bowl with incised floral design

Height 8.5cm, mouth diameter 24cm,
foot diameter 6.8cm
Collected by the Palace Museum

碗敞口，深弧壁，圈足。灰白胎，施白色化妆土，碗内壁刻划大朵花卉图案。花卉以外采用篦划纹作为图案的地子，衬托出白色的朵花纹样，碗心内有五支烧痕迹。

88 金 白釉划花莲花纹碗标本

Jin dynasty

Specimen of white glaze bowl with incised lotus design

附图

金　白釉划花荷莲纹碗

高 8.5 厘米　口径 24 厘米
足径 6.8 厘米
故宫博物院藏

Illustration
Jin dynasty
White glaze bowl with incised lotus design

Height 8.5cm, mouth diameter 24cm,
foot diameter 6.8cm
Collected by the Palace Museum

碗敞口，弧壁，圈足。灰白胎，施白色化妆土，碗内壁刻划莲花荷叶图案。花卉以外采用篦划纹作为图案的地子，衬托出白色的莲花纹样。碗心内有五个条形支烧痕迹。

此碗是金代磁州窑的代表性器物。

89 金 白釉划花花卉纹盆标本

Jin dynasty

Specimens of white glaze pot with incised floral design

90 金 白地黑花花卉纹瓶标本

Jin dynasty

Specimen of white glaze vase with design of black floral patterns

91　金　白地黑花花卉纹瓶标本

Jin dynasty

Specimen of white glaze vase with design of black floral patterns

附图

金　白地黑花花卉纹梅瓶

高 39.4 厘米　口径 3 厘米
足径 9 厘米
故宫博物院藏

Illustration
Jin dynasty
White glaze prunus vase with design of black floral patterns

Height 39.4cm, mouth diameter 3cm, foot diameter 9cm
Collected by the Palace Museum

瓶小口，短颈，圆肩，下腹内敛，瓶身修长。口施白釉。外壁白釉黑花绘有五层装饰，瓶腹的主题图案为花卉纹。表现出磁州窑绘画风格潇洒飘逸的艺术效果。

92　金　白地黑花花卉纹瓶标本

Jin dynasty

Specimen of white glaze vase with design of black floral patterns

附图

金　白地黑花花卉纹梅瓶

高 46.8 厘米　口径 4 厘米
足径 10.3 厘米
故宫博物院藏

Illustration
Jin dynasty
White glaze prunus vase with design of black floral patterns

Height 46.8cm, mouth diameter 4cm, foot diameter 10.3cm
Collected by the Palace Museum

瓶小口，短颈，圆肩，下腹内敛，瓶身修长。口施白釉，外壁白釉黑花绘画莲瓣纹、唐草纹和若干弦纹。瓶腹的主题图案为花卉纹，花朵丰腴，花叶细长，图案充满瓶腹，花叶与花朵主次分明，黑白对比强烈。

93　金　白地黑花花卉纹玉壶春瓶标本

Jin dynasty

Specimen of white glaze pear-shaped vase with flaring lip and with design of black floral patterns

附图

金至元　白地黑花牡丹纹瓶

高 25.5 厘米　口径 6.5 厘米
足径 6 厘米
故宫博物院藏

Illustration
From Jin dynasty to Yuan dynasty
White glaze vase with design of black peony patterns

Height 25.5cm, mouth diameter 6.5cm, foot diameter 6cm
Collected by the Palace Museum

瓶侈口，翻沿，长颈，溜肩，圈足。外壁施白釉至下腹，圈足无釉。黑彩装饰分为两层，肩颈部为花叶纹，腹部为牡丹纹。两层装饰之间及边饰分别绘粗细不等的弦纹，构图明快疏朗，格调质朴清新。

94　金　**白地黑花罐标本**

Jin dynasty

Specimen of white glaze jar with design of black patterns

95　金　**白地黑花花卉纹罐标本**

Jin dynasty

Specimen of white glaze jar with design of black floral patterns

附图

金　白地黑花花卉纹罐

高 11.3 厘米　口径 9.7 厘米
足径 6.9 厘米
故宫博物院藏

Illustration
Jin dynasty White glaze jar with design of black floral patterns

Height 11.3cm, mouth diameter 9.7cm, foot diameter 6.9cm
Collected by the Palace Museum

罐圆唇，敛口，深腹，下腹圆收，圈足。灰白胎，细密坚致。白釉泛灰，光润，施釉近底足。外壁以黑彩绘折枝花卉纹几组，笔触洗练概括，线条流畅奔放。

96　金　白地黑花花卉纹器盖标本

Jin dynasty

Specimen of white glaze cover with design of black floral patterns

附图

金　白地黑花花卉纹盖缸

高 7.3 厘米　口径 11.6 厘米

足径 5.5 厘米

故宫博物院藏

Illustration

Jin dynasty

White glaze jar with cover and design of black floral patterns

Height 7.3cm, mouth diameter 11.6cm, foot diameter 5.5cm

Collected by the Palace Museum

器盖微隆，器身圆唇，直口，弧腹，圈足。灰白胎，细密坚致，外壁施白釉至下腹。盖面及器身均以黑彩折枝花卉纹装饰，边饰弦纹，笔触洗练概括，线条流畅奔放。

97　金　白地黑花飞鸟纹钵（缸）标本

Jin dynasty

Specimen of white glaze alms bowl (vat) with design of black bird patterns

98　金　白釉点褐彩碗标本

Jin dynasty

Specimen of white glaze bowl with brown dots

99　金

里白釉划花外黑釉碗标本

Jin dynasty

Specimen of bowl of white glaze with incised design inside and black glaze outside

100　金　里白釉划花花卉纹外黑釉碗标本
Jin dynasty
Specimen of bowl of white glaze with incised floral design inside and black glaze outside

101　金　里白釉划花鱼纹外黑釉碗标本

Jin dynasty

Specimen of bowl of white glaze with incised fish design inside and black glaze outside

102　金　白地黑花酱黄釉花卉纹虎形枕标本

Jin dynasty

Specimen of white glaze tiger-shaped pillow with design of black and dark yellow floral patterns

附图

金
白地黑花酱黄釉芦雁纹虎形枕

高 10.7 厘米　长 36 厘米
宽 14 厘米
故宫博物院藏

Illustration
Jin dynasty
White glaze tiger-shaped pillow with design of black and dark yellow patterns of reeds and wild geese

Height 10.7cm, length 36cm, width 14cm
Collected by the Palace Museum

枕虎形，眼、鼻、口等装饰十分清晰，虎鼻为枕的通气孔。虎身酱黄釉黑色条纹，虎背饰白地黑花芦雁纹。

此枕形象逼真，有辟邪、镇宅的寓意。

103　金　白地黑花酱黄釉花卉纹虎形枕标本

Jin dynasty

Specimen of white glaze tiger-shaped pillow with design of black and dark yellow floral patterns

附图

金

白地黑花酱黄釉花鸟纹虎形枕

高 11.7 厘米　长 36 厘米

宽 16.5 厘米

故宫博物院藏

Illustration

Jin dynasty　White glaze tiger-shaped pillow with design of black and dark yellow birds and flowers

Height 11.7cm, length 36cm, width 16.5cm

Collected by the Palace Museum

枕虎形，眼、鼻、口等装饰十分清晰，虎鼻为枕的通气孔。虎身酱黄釉黑色条纹，虎背饰白地黑花花鸟纹。

104 **金 钧釉瓶标本**
Jin dynasty
Specimen of Jun glaze vase

105 **金 钧釉器盖标本**
Jin dynasty
Specimen of Jun glaze cover

106　金　钧釉碗标本

Jin dynasty

Specimens of Jun glaze bowl

107　**金　黄釉盏托标本**
Jin dynasty
Specimen of yellow glaze saucer

108　**金　黄釉镂空器标本**
Jin dynasty
Specimen of yellow glaze ware in openwork

109　金　**绿釉划花枕标本**

Jin dynasty

Specimen of green glaze pillow with incised design

附图

金　绿釉诗文腰圆形枕

高 9.8 厘米　长 29 厘米

宽 20.5 厘米

故宫博物院藏

Illustration

Jin dynasty　Green glaze oval pillow with poetry design

Height 9.8cm, length 29cm, width 20.5cm

Collected by the Palace Museum

枕腰圆形。枕面施绿釉，枕壁施釉不到底，底素胎无釉。枕面四周刻划瓜果，中间刻“咏瓜”二字及诗文：“绿叶追风长，黄花向日开。香因风里得，甜向苦中来。”

110　金　三彩划花兔纹枕标本
Jin dynasty
Specimen of pillow with decoration in three colors and with incised rabbit design

附图

金　三彩划花兔纹长方形枕

高 10.3 厘米　面径 36.8×17 厘米
底径 36×14.5 厘米
故宫博物院藏

Illustration
Jin dynasty　Rectangular pillow with decoration in three colors and with incised rabbit design

Height 10.3cm, face size 36.8×17cm, bottom size 36×14.5cm
Collected by the Palace Museum

枕长方形，微有弧度。枕面施绿、黄、白三种釉色，枕壁施釉不到底，底素胎无釉。枕面刻划一只小兔、花草，剔刻缠枝花图案。

111　金　三彩划花鱼纹枕标本

Jin dynasty

Specimen of pillow with decoration in three colors and with incised fish design

附图

金　三彩划花花卉纹腰圆形枕

高 10 厘米　面径 40 × 25 厘米
底径 39 × 24 厘米
故宫博物院藏

Illustration
Jin dynasty　Oval pillow with decoration in three colors and with incised floral design

Height 10cm, face size 40×25cm,
bottom size 39×24cm
Collected by the Palace Museum

枕腰圆形。枕面施绿、黄、白三种釉色，枕壁施釉不到底，底素胎无釉。枕面划刻盆花纹，枕侧划卷枝纹。

112　金

素胎印花开光花卉纹枕标本

Jin dynasty

Specimen of unglazed pillow with stamped floral design in reserved panels

113　金　素胎划花卷枝纹枕标本

Jin dynasty

Specimen of unglazed pillow with incised branch scrolls design

114　金　素胎划花花卉纹枕标本
Jin dynasty
Specimen of unglazed pillow with incised floral design

115　金　素胎划花荷莲纹枕标本
Jin dynasty
Specimen of unglazed pillow with incised lotus design

116　金　素胎划花水波纹枕标本
Jin dynasty
Specimen of unglazed pillow with incised wave design

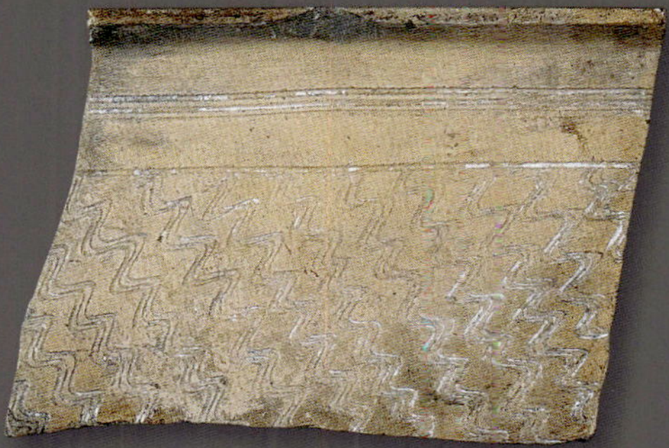

117　金　素胎划花鸟纹枕标本

Jin dynasty

Specimen of unglazed pillow with incised bird design

118　金　素胎炉标本

Jin dynasty

Specimen of unglazed burner

119　**金　红绿彩碗标本**

Jin dynasty

Specimens of bowl with decoration in red and green

120　金　红绿彩花卉纹盘标本

Jin dynasty

Specimen of plate with floral decoration in red and green

121　金　红绿彩羊形器标本

Jin dynasty

Specimen of sheep figure with decoration in red and green

122　金　红绿彩牛首俑标本
Jin dynasty
Specimen of ox-headed figure
with decoration in red and green

123　金　红绿彩人物俑标本
Jin dynasty
Specimens of figure with decoration in red and green

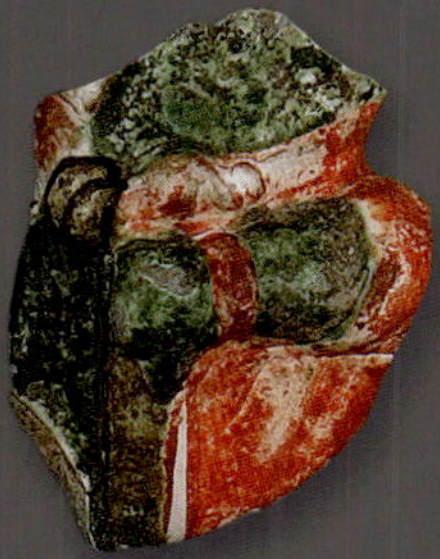

124 金 红绿彩人物俑标本

Jin dynasty

Specimens of figure with decoration in red and green

附图

金　三彩官人俑

高 21.6 厘米
邯郸市峰峰矿区文保所藏

Illustration
Jin dynasty　Figure of official with decoration in three colors

Height 21.6cm
Collected by the Institute of Cultural Relics Preservation of Fengfengkuangqu, Handan City

像头戴官帽，蓄八字胡和长须，身披红袍，双手作揖状。帽及衣均饰花纹，色彩以红色为主，兼黑、黄、绿彩。

125 **金 红绿彩人物俑标本**

Jin dynasty

Specimens of figure with decoration in red and green

附图

金　三彩仕女俑

高 11.8 厘米
河北省文物研究所藏

Illustration
Jin dynasty　Figure of beauty with decoration in three colors

Height 11.8cm
Collected by the Research Institute of Cultural Relics of Hebei Province

女俑坐姿，双袖合，五官、眉发及衣领着黑彩。身穿红袍，衣边饰绿彩。金代三彩以红、绿彩为主，又称“红绿彩”，有的加饰黄、黑彩。器物有人物、动物俑及碗、盘等日用器。

126　**金　红绿彩人物俑标本**

Jin dynasty

Specimens of figure with decoration in red and green

附图

金　红绿彩观音

高 4.7 厘米　底径 2 厘米
故宫博物院藏

Illustration
Jin dynasty　Guanyin with decoration in red and green

Height 4.7cm, bottom diameter 2cm
Collected by the Palace Museum

观音坐像，头束发髻，披斗笠式袈裟。通体白釉，釉上施红绿彩，并以黑彩勾勒五官。

这类小件观音像在宋代比较流行，南北方窑都有烧造，有各种釉色，各种造型，可能是用制作大件器物的下脚料随意捏塑，所以做工一般较粗糙。

127　元　白地黑花“仁和馆”铭瓶标本

Yuan dynasty

Specimen of white glaze vase with black color design and inscription of *Ren He Guan*

附图

元
白地黑花牡丹纹"仁和馆"铭四系瓶

高 25.5 厘米　口径 3.5 厘米
足径 6 厘米
故宫博物院藏

Illustration
Yuan dynasty White glaze vase with four handles and with design of black peony patterns and inscription of *Ren He Guan*

Height 25.5cm, mouth diameter 3.5cm, foot diameter 6cm
Collected by the Palace Museum

瓶圆口，短颈，长圆腹，圈足。颈肩处饰有四系。外壁一面白釉黑花绘牡丹纹，另一面墨书"仁和馆"三字，腹下半部及足施褐釉。

此瓶为酒器，当时叫"经瓶"。宋袁文《翁牖闲评》卷六载："今人盛酒，大瓶谓之京瓶，乃用京师京字，意谓此瓶出自京师，误也。京字当用经籍之经字，普安人以瓦壶小颈、环口、修腹，受一斗可以盛酒者名曰经，则知经瓶者当用此经字也。"

128　元　**白地褐花花卉纹罐标本**

Yuan dynasty

Specimen of white glaze jar with design of brown floral patterns

附图

元　白地褐花龙凤纹罐

高 27.5 厘米　口径 19.5 厘米
足径 12.3 厘米
故宫博物院藏

Illustration
Yuan dynasty
White glaze jar with design of brown patterns of dragon and phoenix

Height 27.5cm, mouth diameter 19.5cm, foot diameter 12.3cm
Collected by the Palace Museum

罐直口，短颈，圆肩，下腹内敛，暗圈足。内施白釉，外壁白釉褐花两层装饰，肩饰缠枝菊花纹，腹饰龙凤纹。

元代磁州窑大型器物流行，因此也出现了较大面积的彩绘装饰。画面构图多采用分层装饰，每层以弦纹间隔，器物内底、腹部等醒目位置多为主题装饰，口沿、颈、肩、胫等部位常分布辅助装饰。

129 元 白地褐花花卉纹罐标本

Yuan dynasty

Specimen of white glaze jar with design of brown floral patterns

附图

元 白地褐花菊花纹罐

高 22 厘米 口径 15 厘米
足径 11 厘米
故宫博物院藏

Illustration
Yuan dynasty
White glaze jar with design of brown chrysanthemum patterns

Height 22cm, mouth diameter 15cm,
foot diameter 11cm
Collected by the Palace Museum

罐直口，短颈，圆肩，下腹内敛，暗圈足。内施白釉，外壁白地褐花两层菊花装饰。

130　**元　白地褐花花卉纹罐标本**

Yuan dynasty

Specimen of white glaze jar with design of brown floral patterns

附图

元

白地褐花菊花纹“至正十一年”铭罐

高 9.6 厘米　口径 6.7 厘米

足径 6 厘米

故宫博物院藏

Illustration

Yuan dynasty　White glaze jar with design of brown chrysanthemum patterns and inscription of *Zhi Zheng Shi Yi Nian*

Height 9.6cm, mouth diameter 6.7cm, foot diameter 6cm

Collected by the Palace Museum

罐直口，短颈，圆肩，下腹内敛，暗圈足。内施白釉，外壁白釉褐花两层装饰，肩部有“至正拾壹年七月廿九日小河东陈家亲造”铭，腹饰折枝菊花纹。

此器是一件带有元代纪年的标准器。

131　元　白地褐花枕标本

Yuan dynasty

Specimen of white glaze pillow with design of brown patterns

附图

元

白地黑花山水人物纹长方形枕

高 14 厘米　面径 31.5×15 厘米

底径 30.6×10.3 厘米

故宫博物院藏

Illustration

Yuan dynasty

White glaze rectangular pillow with design of black patterns of landscape and figure

Height 14cm, face size 31.5×15cm, bottom size 30.6×10.3cm

Collected by the Palace Museum

枕长方形，枕面及四壁采用白地黑花装饰。枕面在菱形开光内画山水人物图案，四角饰花卉纹和枕面的图案相互呼应。枕的四壁同样采用菱形开光的装饰技法，开光内画有花卉图案。

132　元　**白地褐花花卉纹碗标本**

Yuan dynasty

Specimens of white glaze bowl with design of brown floral patterns

133 元

白地褐花"王"字碗标本

Yuan dynasty

Specimen of white glaze bowl with design of brown patterns and Chinese character *Wang*

134 元

白地褐花"王"字碗标本

Yuan dynasty

Specimen of white glaze bowl with design of brown patterns and Chinese character *Wang*

附图

元　白地黑花“王”字碗

高8厘米　口径17厘米
足径7厘米
磁州窑博物馆藏

Illustration
Yuan dynasty
White glaze bowl with design of black patterns and Chinese character *Wang*

Height 8cm, mouth diameter 17cm, foot diameter 7cm
Collected by the Museum of Cizhou Kiln

碗敞口，深腹，圈足。胎体较厚，施白色化妆土。釉色白中泛黄。褐彩装饰，碗心有双圈，双圈内书一“王”字，俗称“王”字碗，是元代的典型器物。

135　元　**白地褐花牡丹纹盘标本**

Yuan dynasty

Specimen of white glaze plate with design of brown peony patterns

136　元　**白地褐花花卉纹盆标本**

Yuan dynasty

Specimens of white glaze pot with design of brown floral patterns

137　元　白地褐花鸟纹盆标本

Yuan dynasty

Specimen of white glaze pot with design of brown bird patterns

附图

元　白地黑花云凤纹罐

高 22.5 厘米　口径 13.2 厘米

足径 12.5 厘米

故宫博物院藏

Illustration

Yuan dynasty

White glaze jar with design of black cloud and phoenix patterns

Height 22.5cm, mouth diameter 13.2cm, foot diameter 12.5cm

Collected by the Palace Museum

罐圆唇，直口，短颈，溜肩，鼓腹，下腹弧收成足。褐黄胎，较粗硬。乳白釉，光泽弱，外施釉近底足。外壁以黑褐彩装饰，颈部、腹部各绘弦纹三道，中间绘凤鸟和云朵纹。

138　元　钧釉碗标本
Yuan dynasty
Specimen of Jun glaze bowl

139　元　孔雀绿釉人物纹盘标本
Yuan dynasty
Specimen of peacock green glaze plate with figure design

140　元　孔雀绿釉花卉纹盘标本
Yuan dynasty
Specimen of peacock green glaze plate with floral

141 **宋至元 窑具标本**
From Song dynasty to Yuan dynasty
Specimen of kiln furniture

142 **宋至元 窑具标本**
From Song dynasty to Yuan dynasty
Specimen of kiln furniture

邢窑

故宫博物院的部分专家和学者于20世纪50年代、60年代、80年代、90年代及2002年、2005年分别调查了该窑的临城瓷窑沟、南程、射兽、祁村、内丘窑址。

邢窑为唐代的著名瓷窑，创烧于北朝，延续烧造至金元时期。窑址主要分布在河北内丘、临城、祁村等地。印证了《国史补》有关“内丘白瓷瓯”的记载。出土的精、粗两种白釉器物，精者胎釉洁白如雪，不施化妆土，称之白如雪，并非过誉。有碗、托子、皮囊壶、注子和罐等。一些碗、罐底刻“盈”字。粗者以各式碗为多，此外有注子、枕等器物。粗碗均施化妆土，外部施釉不到底，采用叠烧法，碗与碗之间垫以三角形支具，碗心多留有支烧痕。白釉器物中还有带褐彩装饰的。此外，还有黄釉、黑釉、褐黄釉及三彩。

邢窑作为一代名窑，其产品流通范围极其广泛，这从国内外出土的大量邢窑器物及标本可以得到证实。国内唐墓及遗址出土邢窑白瓷的有广东、福建、河北及陕西四省，国外出土邢窑白瓷的有伊拉克、埃及、巴基斯坦、日本、伊朗等国。

Xing Kiln

Experts from the Palace Museum made investigations into Xing kiln sites in Ciyaogou of Lincheng, Nancheng, Shexiu, Qicun and Neiqiu in the 1950s, 1960s, 1980s, 1990s, and in 2002, 2005 respectively. Xing kiln is a famous porcelain kiln in Tang dynasty. It started to fire in Northern dynasties and did not stop fire until Jin and Yuan dynasty. Kiln sites are mainly located in Neiqiu, Lincheng, Qicun, Hebei Province which well matches the historical records of white porcelain from Neiqiu. White glaze wares unearthed can be classified into two categories: fine or coarse. The body and glaze of fine ones are as white as snow, and no engobe are used. It is not overrated at all to use the phrase as white as snow to describe such white glaze ware of Xing kiln. Fine white glaze wares are bowls, saucers, bladder-shaped pots, cylindrical pots and jars, etc. The bottoms of some of the bowls and jars are with inscription of Chinese character, Ying. Coarse white glaze wares are mainly bowls of various types. There are also some coarse white glaze cylindrical pots and pillows. In the making of coarse white glaze bowls, engobe are applied, and the external glazing is incomplete. Glaze stops before reaching the bottoms of the wares. The bowls were put into kilns one next to the other with mouth toward the same direction. In between the bowls, triangular braces were used to separate each other, thus, spur-marks were left behind in the center of the bowls. The third white glaze ware is with brown color design. In addition, the kiln fired yellow glaze, black glaze, brown-yellow glaze and wares with decoration in three colors.

As a famous kiln, Xing kiln wares had a widespread distribution, which is confirmed by the great number of Xing kiln wares or specimens unearthed. White glaze wares were unearthed from tombs and ruins in Guangdong, Fujian, Hebei, Shaanxi and in Iraq, Egypt, Pakistan, Japan, Iran, etc.

邢窑内丘（西关村西）窑遗址保护碑
Monument for protecting the ruin of Xing kiln, west of Xiguan Village, Neiqiu County

邢窑内丘（西关村北）窑遗址保护碑
Monument for protecting the ruin of Xing kiln, north of Xiguan Village, Neiqiu County

143　隋　白釉碗标本
Sui dynasty
Specimens of white glaze bowl

144　隋　白釉碗标本
Sui dynasty
Specimen of white glaze bowl

附图

隋　白釉碗

高 8.35 厘米　口径 14 厘米
足径 6 厘米
邢台市顺德路出土
邢台市文物保管所藏

Illustration
Sui dynasty
White glaze bowl

Height 8.35cm, mouth diameter 14cm, foot diameter 6cm
Unearthed at Shunde Road, Xingtai City Collected by the Institute of Cultural Relics Preservation of Xingtai City

碗敞口，斜直腹，饼形实足，足心微凹，足外缘斜削一刀。灰白胎，釉下施化妆土，再施白釉，外施釉不到底，内满釉，里心有三个支烧痕。

145　隋　白釉钵标本
Sui dynasty
Specimen of white glaze alms bowl

146　隋　青釉瓶标本
Sui dynasty
Specimen of green glaze vase

附图

隋　白釉盘口瓶

高 28 厘米　口径 6.3 厘米
足径 8 厘米
内丘县城西关出土
邢窑博物馆藏

Illustration
Sui dynasty
White glaze vase with plate mouth

Height 28cm, mouth diameter 6.3cm,
foot diameter 8cm
Unearthed at Chengxiguan, Neiqiu County
Collected by the Museum of Xing Kiln

瓶盘口，长颈，长圆腹，饼形实足。灰白胎，外施白釉不到底，釉色泛青，开冰裂纹片。

147　隋　青釉带系罐标本

Sui dynasty

Specimen of green glaze jar with handles

附图

隋　青釉三系罐

高 27.5 厘米　口径 7 厘米
足径 10.7 厘米
磁窑沟隋墓出土
临城县文物保管所藏

Illustration
Sui dynasty　Green glaze jar with three handles

Height 27.5cm, mouth diameter 7cm,
foot diameter 10.7cm
Unearthed from Sui tomb at Ciyaogou
Collected by the Institute of Cultural Relics Preservation of Lincheng County

罐直口微内收，平肩，长圆腹，饼形足微外展。肩有三个双条形系，系高出口沿。上施青釉不到底。

148　隋　青釉碗标本

Sui dynasty

Specimen of green glaze bowl

149　隋　青黄釉高足盘标本

Sui dynasty

Specimen of greenish yellow glaze plate with high stem

附图

隋　青釉高足盘

高 4.7 厘米　口径 7.6 厘米
足径 4.5 厘米
邢窑博物馆藏

Illustration
Sui dynasty
Green glaze plate with high stem

Height 4.7cm, mouth diameter 7.6cm,
foot diameter 4.5cm
Collected by the Museum of Xing Kiln

盘心坦平，口外侈，转折处出棱一道，下承以喇叭状高圈足，足出边。施青釉不到底，釉面有开片。

150　隋　黄釉碗标本

Sui dynasty

Specimens of yellow glaze bowl

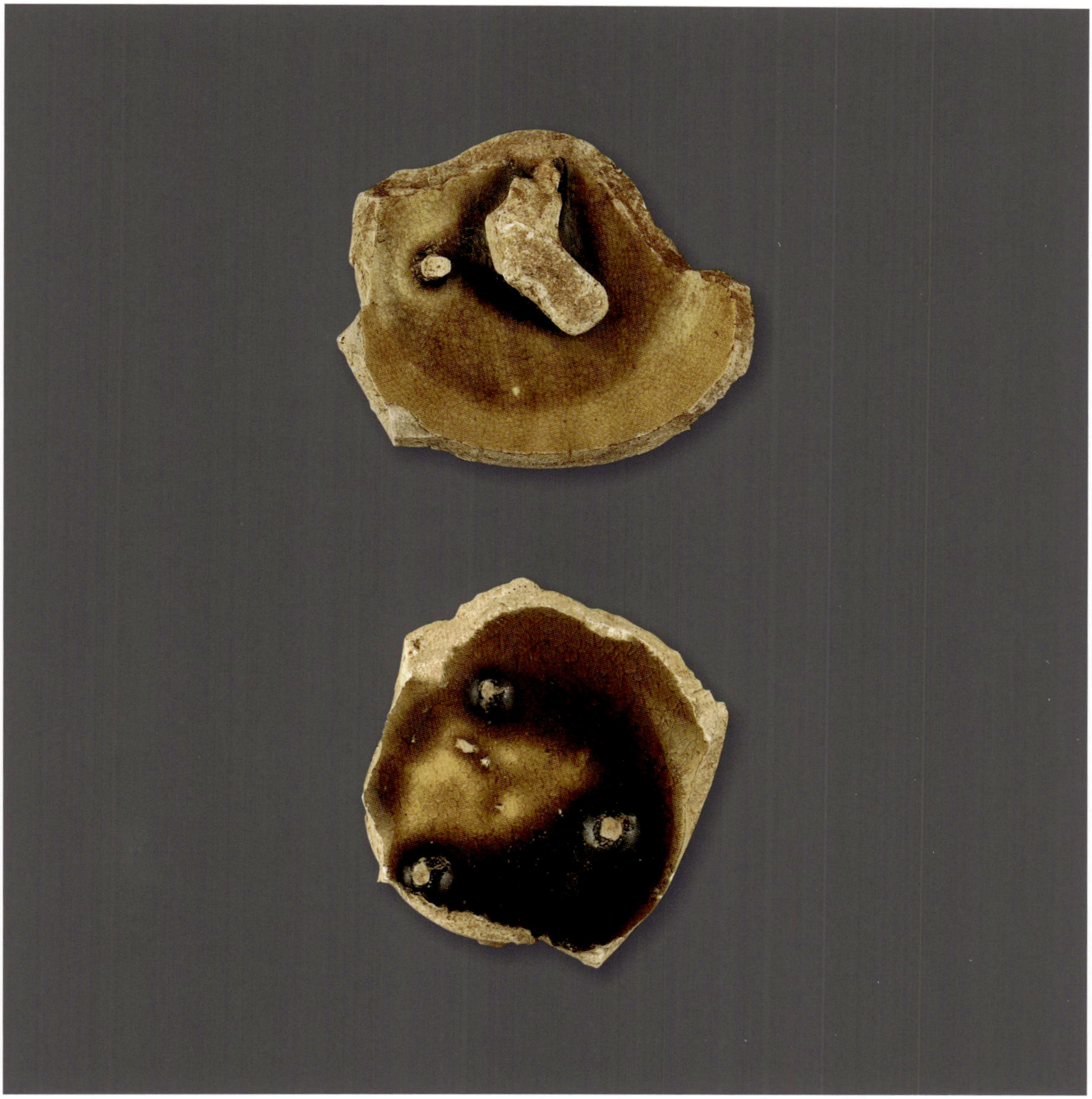

151　隋　黄釉碗标本

Sui dynasty

Specimen of yellow glaze bowl

附图

隋　黄釉碗

高 7.3 厘米　口径 13.8 厘米
足径 6.2 厘米
邢台市顺德路出土
邢台市文物保管所藏

Illustration
Sui dynasty
Yellow glaze bowl

Height 7.3cm, mouth diameter 13.8cm, foot diameter 6.2cm
Unearthed at Shunde Road, Xingtai City Collected by the Institute of Cultural Relics Preservation of Xingtai City

敞口，斜直腹，饼形实足，足心微凹，足外缘斜削一刀。釉下施化妆土，再施黄釉，外施釉不到底，内满釉，里心积釉较厚，有三个支烧痕。

152 **隋　黄釉钵标本**

Sui dynasty

Specimen of yellow glaze alms bowl

153　唐　白釉罐标本
Tang dynasty
Specimen of white glaze jar

附图

唐　白釉罐

高 13 厘米　口径 7.4 厘米
底径 6.1 厘米
故宫博物院藏

Illustration
Tang dynasty　White glaze jar

Height 13cm, mouth diameter 7.4cm,
bottom diameter 6.1cm
Collected by the Palace Museum

罐圆口，短颈，圆腹，平底。通体施白釉，釉色白中泛青。

154　唐　青釉弦纹罐标本

Tang dynasty

Specimen of green glaze jar with design of string

155　唐　黑釉碗标本

Tang dynasty

Specimen of black glaze bowl

156 **唐 黑釉钵标本**

Tang dynasty

Specimen of black glaze alms bowl

附图

唐 酱釉钵

高 9.7 厘米 口径 9 厘米
底径 5.9 厘米
邢窑博物馆藏

Illustration
Tang dynasty
Dark brown glaze alms bowl

Height 9.7cm, mouth diameter 9cm,
bottom diameter 5.9cm
Collected by the Museum of Xing Kiln

钵敛口，方唇，圆腹，平底。造型浑圆饱满。内施淡黄釉，外施酱釉，釉有多处垂流。

157　唐　窑具标本

Tang dynasty

Specimens of kiln furniture

158　唐　窑具标本

Tang dynasty

Specimens of kiln furniture

邢窑临城（南沟子）窑遗址保护碑
Monument for protecting the ruin of Xing kiln, Nangouzi, Lincheng County

邢窑临城（祁村）窑遗址及保护碑
Monument for protecting the ruin of Xing kiln, Qicun, Lincheng County

159　唐　白釉瓶（壶）标本
Tang dynasty
Specimen of white glaze vase (pot)

附图

唐　白釉壶

高 17.7 厘米　口径 7.5 厘米
足径 6.8 厘米
故宫博物院藏

Illustration
Tang dynasty　White glaze pot

Height 17.7cm, mouth diameter 7.5cm,
foot diameter 6.8cm
Collected by the Palace Museum

壶口微外撇，斜颈，圆肩，弧腹，饼形足。一侧有一短流，另一侧为一曲柄。施白釉，外壁施釉不到底。

此器胎质洁白细腻，釉色莹润，是一件典型的河北邢窑产品。

160　**唐　白釉壶标本**

Tang dynasty

Specimen of white glaze pot

附图

唐　白釉壶

高 10.5 厘米　口径 2.5 厘米

足径 5.3 厘米

故宫博物院藏

Illustration

Tang dynasty　White glaze pot

Height 10.5cm, mouth diameter 2.5cm, foot diameter 5.3cm

Collected by the Palace Museum

壶敛口，短颈圆腹，圈足。肩一侧有短流，对应一侧为壶柄，柄上端饰装饰结。

此壶造型小巧，釉质白润，是河北邢窑唐代产品。

161 唐 白釉盒标本
Tang dynasty
Specimen of white glaze box

162 唐 白釉碗标本
Tang dynasty
Specimens of white glaze bowl

163 唐 白釉碗标本

Tang dynasty

Specimens of white glaze bowl

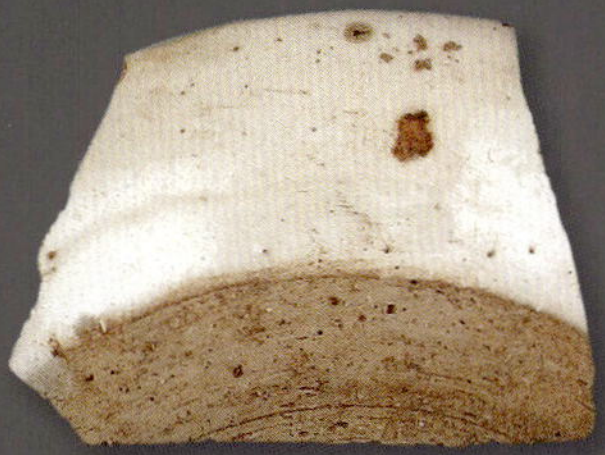

164　唐　白釉碗标本

Tang dynasty

Specimens of white glaze bowl

165 **唐　白釉玉璧底碗标本**

Tang dynasty

Specimens of white glaze bowl with foot in shaped of jade *Bi*

166　唐　白釉玉璧底碗标本

Tang dynasty

Specimens of white glaze bowl with foot in shape of jade *Bi*

附图

宋　白釉玉璧底碗

高 4.7 厘米　口径 15.6 厘米
足径 6.7 厘米
故宫博物院藏

Illustration
Song dynasty　White glaze bowl with foot in shape of jade *Bi*

Height 4.7cm, mouth diameter 15.6cm, foot diameter 6.7cm
Collected by the Palace Museum

碗撇口，斜壁，玉璧形底，通体施白釉，釉色白中泛青。

167 **唐　白釉玉璧底碗标本**

Tang dynasty

Specimens of white glaze bowl with foot in shape of jade *Bi*

168 **唐　白釉刻花莲瓣纹碗标本**

Tang dynasty

Specimen of white glaze bowl with incised lotus-petal design

169　唐　里白釉外黑釉碗标本
Tang dynasty
Specimen of bowl of white glaze inside
and black glaze outside

170　唐　里白釉外酱釉碗标本
Tang dynasty
Specimen of bowl of white glaze inside
and dark brown glaze outside

171 唐 黑釉罐标本
Tang dynasty
Specimen of black glaze jar

172 唐 黑釉碗标本
Tang dynasty
Specimen of black glaze bowl

173 唐 黑釉钵标本
Tang dynasty
Specimen of black glaze alms bowl

174　**唐　黑褐釉钵标本**

Tang dynasty

Specimens of black and brown glaze alms bowl

175 **唐　黄釉碗标本**

Tang dynasty

Specimen of yellow glaze bowl

176　**金　白釉碗标本**

Jin dynasty

Specimens of white glaze bowl

177　金　白釉印花花卉纹碗标本

Jin dynasty

Specimens of white glaze bowl with stamped floral design

附图

北宋　白釉印花双鱼纹盘

高 3.5 厘米　口径 16.7 厘米
临城县射兽砖厂出土
临城县文物保管所藏

Illustration　Northern Song dynasty
White glaze plate with stamped design of pair fish

Height 3.5cm, mouth diameter 16.7cm
Unearthed at Sheshou Brick-making Yard, Lincheng County
Collected by the Institute of Cultural Relics Preservation of Lincheng County

盘敞口，浅腹，圈足。通体施白釉，口无釉，釉色微泛灰色。碗内采用印花装饰，内口印回纹一周，内壁印荷花、荷叶纹，底心印海水双鱼纹。

178 金 白釉印花花卉纹碗标本

Jin dynasty

Specimens of white glaze bowl with stamped floral design

179　**金　白釉划花莲瓣纹器盖标本**

Jin dynasty

Specimen of white glaze cover with incised lotus-petal design

180　金　白釉点褐彩朵花纹碗标本
Jin dynasty
Specimens of white glaze bowl with brown splashes

附图

宋（金）　白釉褐彩折腰盘

高 3.2 厘米　口径 16.2 厘米
底径 6 厘米
临城县山下家族墓出土
临城县文物保管所藏

Illustration
Song dynasty (Jin dynasty)
White glaze waisted plate with brown color decoration

Height 3.5cm, mouth diameter 16.2cm, bottom diameter 6cm
Unearthed from Shanxia family tombs, Lincheng County
Collected by the Institute of Cultural Relics Preservation of Lincheng County

盘敞口，折底。灰褐色胎，施白色化妆土，外罩透明釉。器里满釉，外施釉不到底。内壁绘褐色草叶纹。

181 **唐 白釉罐标本**

Tang dynasty

Specimen of white glaze jar

182 **唐　白釉“盈”字款罐标本**

Tang dynasty

Specimen of white glaze jar with inscription of Chinese character *Ying*

定窑

故宫博物院的部分专家和学者于20世纪50年代、70年代、80年代、90年代以及2000年、2005年对该窑进行了调查，窑址主要在河北省曲阳县涧磁村及东西燕山村。

定窑是宋代著名瓷窑之一，创烧于隋唐，北宋至金大为发展，延续烧瓷至元代。所烧器物以白釉为主，还兼烧少量黑釉、酱釉、绿釉及白地褐花等品种。唐代器物多光素无纹饰，宋代定窑形成了自己独特的风格，白釉器物胎质坚硬，釉色白中泛黄，釉面因垂釉而形成“泪痕”。装饰多采用划花、印花。白釉划花是定窑瓷器常见的装饰方法，在胎上划出各种纹饰，最常见的为萱草纹，此外有龙纹、鱼纹、荷花纹、叶纹等，划花线条自然流畅，具有较高的水平。在北宋中晚期至金代大量采用印花装饰，它直接取材于定州缂丝，纹样细腻成熟，纹饰清晰，花纹生动自然，代表了宋代印花装饰的最高水平。北宋时期，定窑一度为宫廷及官府烧制瓷器。故宫博物院收藏的龙纹盘即为宫廷烧造，有一些器物入宫后刻“奉华”、“风华”、“禁苑”、“德寿”等宋代宫殿名称。窑址出土的标本有刻“官”、“新官”、“会稽”、“尚食局”、“尚药局”、“五王府”等款识的，显然是为官府或某些机构而烧制。为提高产量定窑采用覆烧方法，器口无釉，文献称为“芒口”，是它的特征之一。此种烧制工艺对南北方瓷窑产生很大的影响。

Ding Kiln

Experts from the Palace Museum made investigations into Ding kiln sites in Jianci and Dongxiyanshan Village, Quyang County, Hebei Province in the 1950s, 1970s, 1980s, 1990s and in 2002, 2005 respectively. Ding kiln is a famous porcelain kiln in Song dynasty. It started to fire in Sui and Tang dynasty. Great developments were achieved during Northern Song dynasty and Jin dynasty. It did not stop fire until Yuan dynasty. Its main products are white glaze wares. It fired small amount of black glaze, dark brown glaze, green glaze, white glaze with brown color design, etc. Ding wares of Tang dynasty are usually without decoration. Ding kiln in Song dynasty formed its own unique style. The body of white glaze ware is hard, and the glaze is in yellowish white. Glaze accumulated in the low part of the ware. The phenomenon is called "tears". As to decoration of wares, incised and stamped design is frequently used. White glaze with incised design is a very popular variety among Ding kiln wares. A variety of patterns can be seen incised on the bodies of white glaze wares. The most common pattern is Hemerocallis. Other common patterns are dragon, fish, lotus, flora, etc. The lines of the patterns were incised naturally and smoothly by skilled workers. From middle or late Northern Song dynasty to Jin dynasty, a large number of wares were with stamped design which was inspired by the design of Dingzhou tapestry. Mature, delicate, clear, vivid, natural patterns represent the highest level of porcelain with stamped design in Song dynasty. During Northern Song dynasty, Ding kiln once fired porcelains for the imperial court and official organizations. For instance, the dragon plate collected by the Palace Museum, wares with inscription of palace names of Song dynasty, such as Fenghua, Deshou, Jinyuan, etc. were for the imperial court. And those unearthed parts from ruin of the kiln with inscription of Guan, Xinguan, Huiji, Shangshiju, Shangyaoju, Wuwangfu, etc. were obviously made for official organizations of the time. In order to enhance outputs, Ding kiln used upside-down firing technique. Hence, the rims of the wares are without glaze or “Mangkou” as literature called. It's a distinguishing characteristic of Ding kiln wares. Such firing technique had a significant impact on kilns in the North and South.

定窑遗址
Ruin of Ding kiln

定窑遗址保护厅
Hall for protecting the ruin of Ding kiln

定窑遗址瓷片遗存
Pileup of porcelain parts at the ruin of Ding kiln

定窑遗址瓷片、窑具遗存

Pileup of porcelain and kiln furniture parts at the ruin of Ding kiln

183 **隋 白釉碗标本**

Sui dynasty

Specimens of white glaze bowl

184　**隋　青釉高足盘标本**

Sui dynasty

Specimen of green glaze plate with high stem

185 **唐　白釉碗标本**

Tang dynasty

Specimen of white glaze bowl

186 **唐　白釉玉璧底碗标本**

Tang dynasty

Specimen of white glaze bowl with foot in shape of jade *Bi*

187　唐　白釉玉璧底碗标本

Tang dynasty

Specimens of white glaze bowl with foot in shape of jade *Bi*

附图

唐　白釉玉璧底碗

高 4.7 厘米　口径 16.4 厘米
足径 7.9 厘米
故宫博物院藏

Illustration
Tang dynasty　White glaze bowl with foot in shape of jade *Bi*

Height 4.7cm, mouth diameter 16.4cm, foot diameter 7.9cm
Collected by the Palace Museum

碗唇口，斜壁，玉璧形底。通体施白釉。

188　唐　黄釉壶标本

Tang dynasty

Specimen of yellow glaze pot

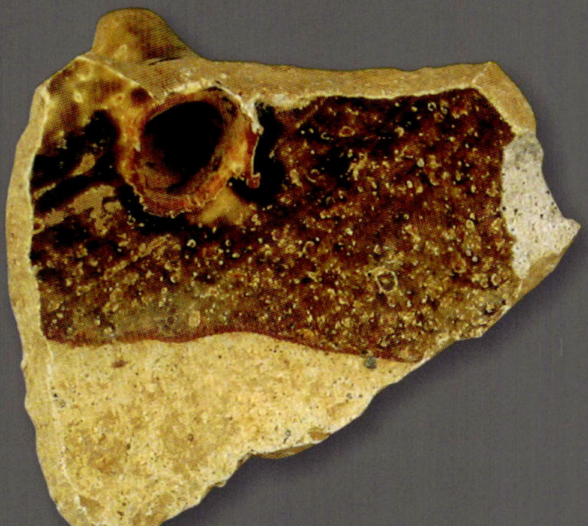

附图

唐　黄釉席纹壶

高 22.7 厘米　口径 7.1 厘米
底径 9.3 厘米
曲阳县文物保管所藏

Illustration
Tang dynasty　Yellow glaze pot with mat-impression design
Height 22.7cm, mouth diameter 7.1cm, bottom diameter 9.3cm
Collected by the Institute of Cultural Relics Preservation of Quyang County

壶直口微外展，短颈，圆唇，长腹，平底。肩一侧有短流，对称一侧为曲柄，流与柄间有双系。胎上施化妆土，再施黄釉，外釉施至下腹部。壶身装饰席纹，流上饰弦纹。

189　**五代 白釉壶标本**

Five Dynasties

Specimens of white glaze pot

附图

北宋　白釉壶

高 14 厘米　口径 6.1 厘米
定县博物馆藏

Illustration
Northern Song dynasty
White glaze pot

Height 14cm, mouth diameter 6.1cm
Collected by Dingxian County Museum

壶匜口，短颈，斜肩，圆腹，圈足。一侧为短流，一侧在肩与腹上方饰曲柄。盖镶入式，盖面隆起，小钮。施白釉，釉色微泛牙黄。

190　**五代 白釉碗标本**
Five Dynasties
Specimens of white glaze bowl

191　**五代至宋 白釉划花碗标本**
From Five Dynasties to Song dynasty
Specimen of white glaze bowl with incised design

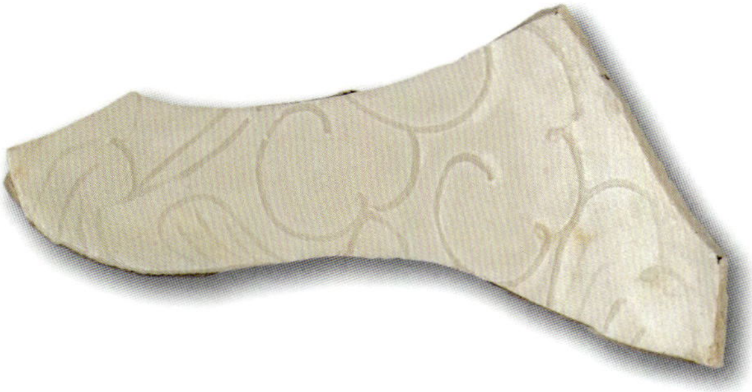

192　**宋　白釉瓶标本**

Song dynasty

Specimen of white glaze vase

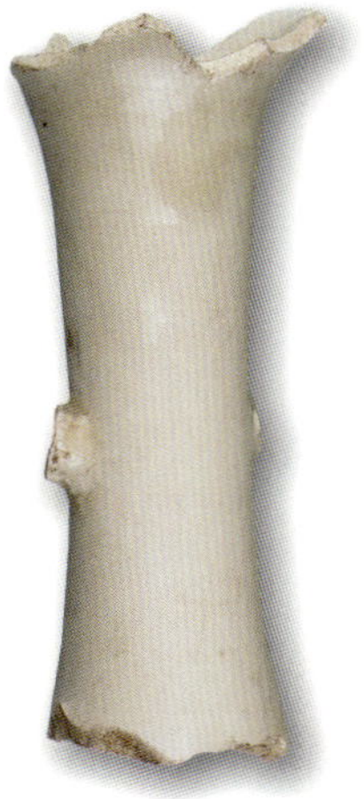

附图

宋　白釉划花花卉纹直颈瓶

高 22 厘米　口径 5.5 厘米

足径 6.4 厘米

故宫博物院藏

Illustration

Song dynasty　White glaze straight neck vase with incised floral design

Height 22cm, mouth diameter 5.5cm, foot diameter 6.4cm

Collected by the Palace Museum

瓶平口外翻，长直颈，圆腹，圈足。内、外施白釉，釉色微泛牙黄色。瓶颈无纹饰，瓶腹刻划花卉纹。

193 **宋 白釉瓶标本**

Song dynasty

Specimen of white glaze vase

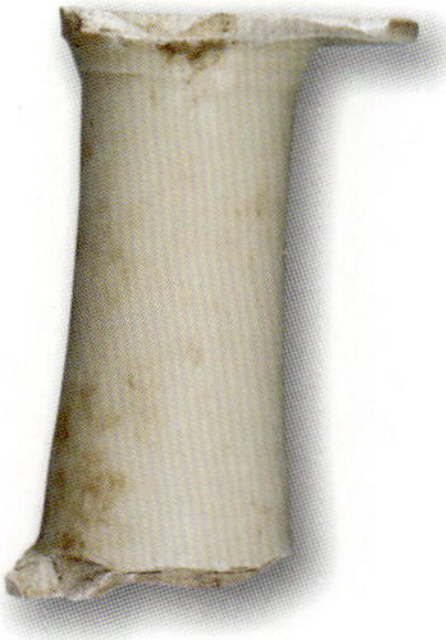

附图

宋 白釉刻花莲瓣纹龙首净瓶

高 15.8 厘米

定州静志寺北宋塔基出土

定州市博物馆藏

Illustration

Song dynasty White glaze dragon-head-shaped holy-water vase with incised lotus-petal design

Height 15.8cm

Unearthed from the tower base of Northern Song dynasty at the Jingzhi Temple in Dingzhou

Collected by Dingzhou Museum

瓶塔式盖，平口，长直颈，圆肩，长腹，下腹内敛，圈足微外撇。一侧饰龙形短流。施白釉，釉色微泛牙黄。肩、腹刻仰覆莲瓣纹、弦纹、唐草纹，纹饰清晰自然。

194 **宋　白釉龙首壶标本**

Song dynasty

Specimen of white glaze dragon-head-shaped pot

附图

宋　白釉刻花莲瓣纹龙首净瓶

高 60.9 厘米
定州静志寺北宋塔基出土
定州市博物馆藏

Illustration

Song dynasty　White glaze dragon-head-shaped holy-water vase with incised lotus-petal design

Height 60.9cm
Unearthed from the tower base of Northern Song dynasty at the Jingzhi Temple in Dingzhou
Collected by Dingzhou Museum

瓶塔式盖，平口，长直颈，圆肩，长腹，下腹内敛，圈足微外撇。一侧饰龙形短流。施白釉，釉色微泛牙黄。口、颈部分别饰莲瓣及弦纹，肩、腹刻莲瓣纹及唐草纹。

195　宋　白釉炉标本
Song dynasty
Specimen of white glaze burner

196　宋　白釉盒标本
Song dynasty
Specimens of white glaze box

197 **宋 白釉盒标本**

Song dynasty

Specimen of white glaze box

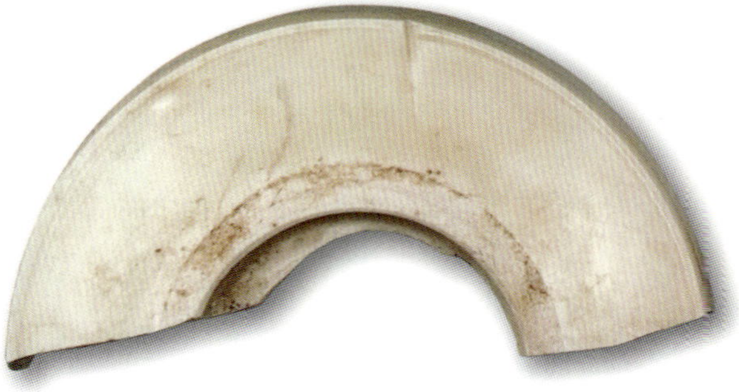

附图

北宋 白釉盒

高 4.3 厘米 口径 9.8 厘米

底径 4.5 厘米

定州市博物馆藏

Illustration

Northern Song dynasty

White glaze box

Height 4.3cm, mouth diameter 9.8cm, bottom diameter 4.5cm

Collected by Dingzhou Museum

盒圆形扁式，盒面与侧间转折处有凹棱一道，盒底边饰弦纹。

盒为定窑唐宋时期常见器型之一，造型丰富。宋代盒造型与唐代相比，高度下降，口径增大，多为扁式。

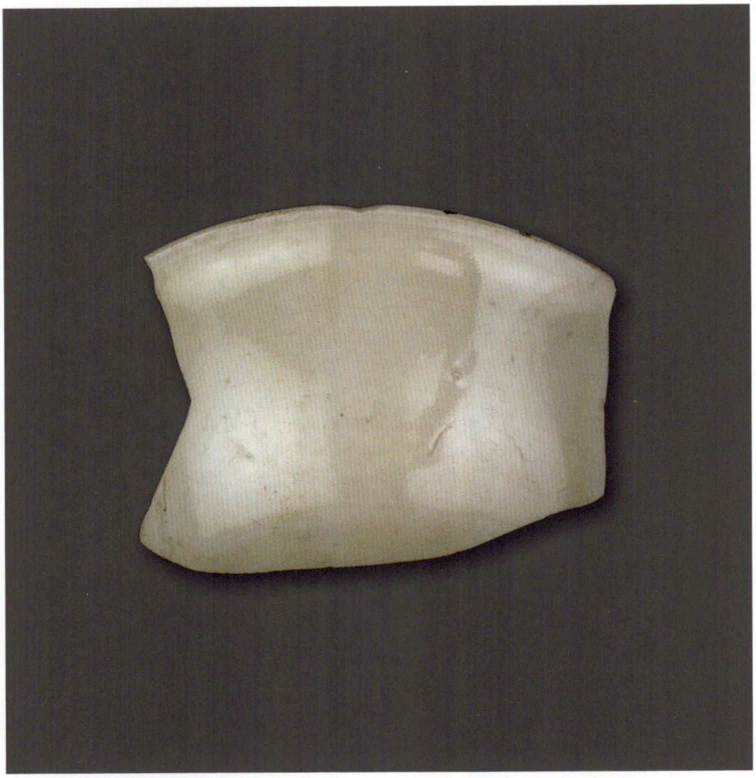

198　**宋　白釉花口碗标本**

Song dynasty

Specimen of white glaze bowl with flower rim

199　**宋　白釉花式碗标本**

Song dynasty

Specimen of white glaze flower-shaped bowl

200　宋　白釉盘标本
Song dynasty
Specimens of white glaze plate

201　宋　白釉花口盏标本
Song dynasty
Specimens of white glaze plate with flower rim

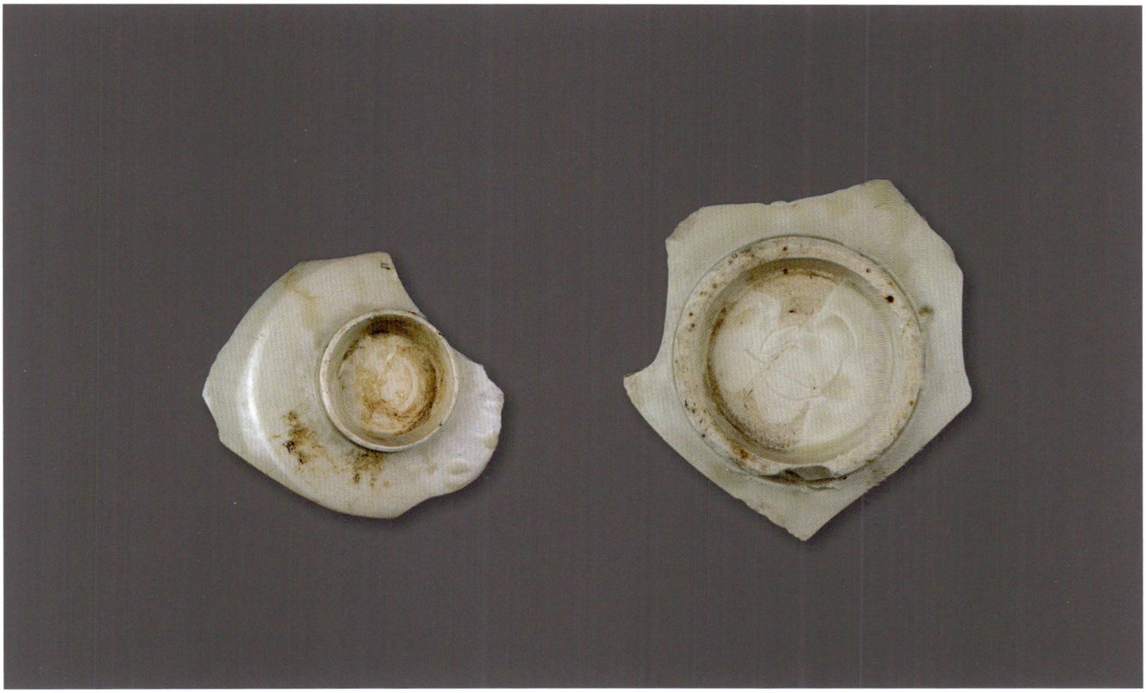

202　**宋　白釉围棋子标本**
Song dynasty
Specimen of white glaze Chinese chess

203　**宋　白釉印花盒标本**
Song dynasty
Specimen of white glaze box with stamped design

204　**宋　白釉印花花卉纹碗标本**
Song dynasty
Specimen of white glaze bowl with stamped floral design

附图

宋　白釉印花花鸟纹盘

高 5.5 厘米　口径 31 厘米
足径 12.5 厘米
故宫博物院藏

Illustration
Song dynasty　White glaze plate with stamped flower and bird design

Height 5.5cm, mouth diameter 31cm, foot diameter 12.5cm
Collected by the Palace Museum

盘敞口，浅弧壁，圈足。口镶铜釦，内、外施白釉，圈足内满釉，釉色微泛牙黄色。盘内印花花鸟纹图案。

205 宋 白釉印花花卉纹碗标本

Song dynasty

Specimens of white glaze bowl with stamped floral design

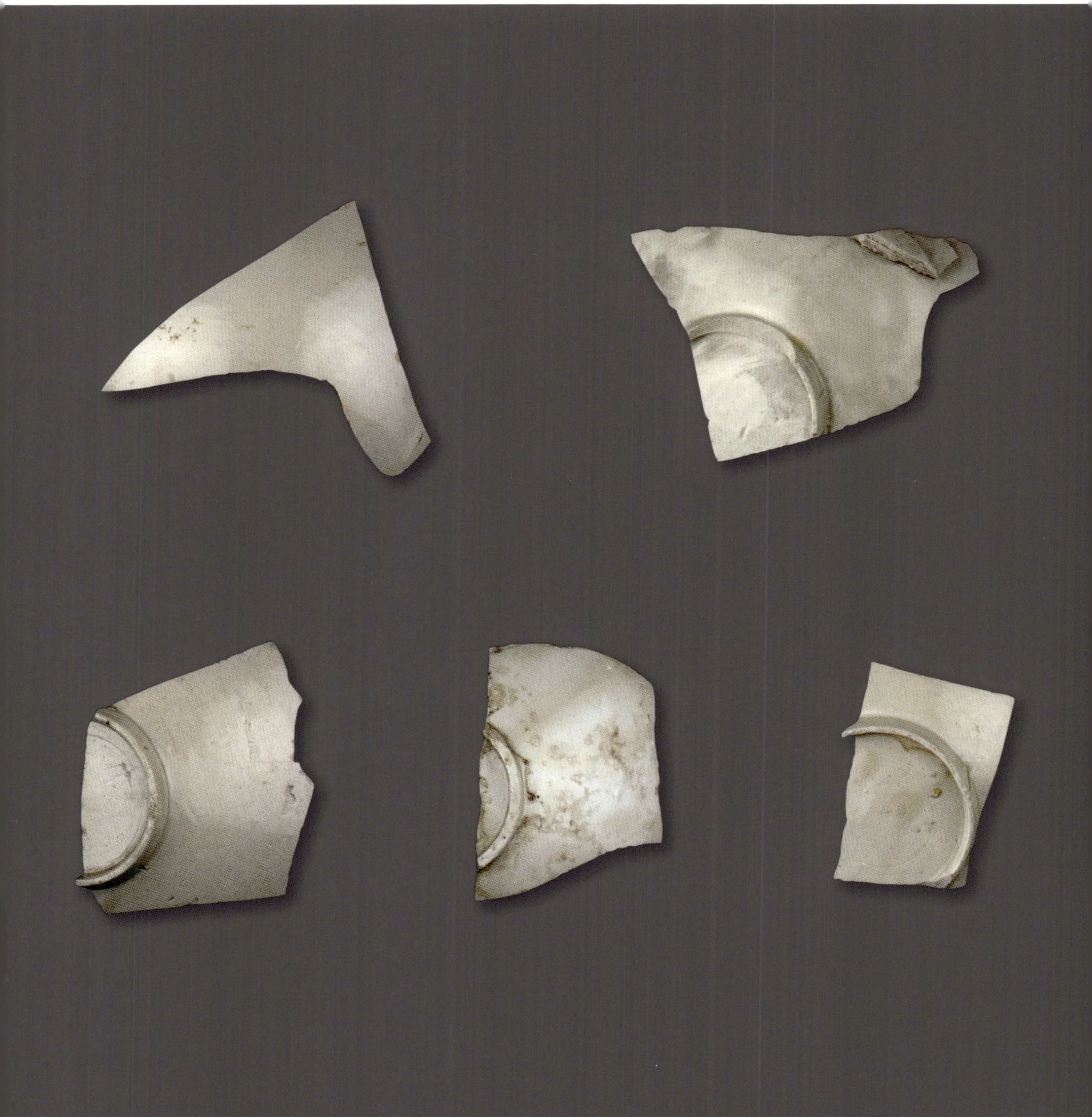

206　宋　白釉印花花卉纹碗标本

Song dynasty

Specimens of white glaze bowl with stamped floral design

207 宋 白釉印花龙纹碗标本

Song dynasty

Specimens of white glaze bowl with stamped dragon design

208 宋 白釉印花龙纹碗标本

Song dynasty

Specimens of white glaze bowl with stamped dragon design

209 宋 白釉印花龙纹碗标本
Song dynasty
Specimens of white glaze bowl with stamped dragon design

210　**宋　白釉印花凤纹碗标本**

Song dynasty

Specimen of white glaze bowl with stamped phoenix design

211　**宋　白釉印花鸳鸯纹碗标本**

Song dynasty

Specimen of white glaze bowl with stamped mandarin duck design

212 宋　白釉印花鱼纹碗标本

Song dynasty

Specimens of white glaze bowl with stamped fish design

213 宋　白釉印花莲池纹“慈福”铭碗标本

Song dynasty

Specimen of white glaze bowl with stamped design of lotus and pond and inscription of Chinese characters *Ci Fu*

214　宋　白釉印花龙纹盘标本

Song dynasty

Specimens of white glaze plate with stamped dragon design

附图

宋　白釉印花龙纹盘

高 4.7 厘米　口径 23 厘米
足径 10.8 厘米
故宫博物院藏

Illustration
Song dynasty　White glaze plate with stamped dragon design

Height 4.7cm, mouth diameter 23cm, foot diameter 10.8cm
Collected by the Palace Museum

盘敞口，浅弧壁，圈足。口镶铜釦。内、外施白釉，釉色微泛牙黄色。内壁模印龙纹图案。

215　宋　白釉印花鱼纹盘标本

Song dynasty

Specimen of white glaze plate with stamped fish design

216　宋　**白釉印花鱼纹盘标本**

Song dynasty

Specimen of white glaze plate with stamped fish design

217 宋 白釉印花鱼纹盘标本

Song dynasty

Specimens of white glaze plate with stamped fish design

附图

宋　白釉印花鱼纹洗

高 2.5 厘米　口径 13.8 厘米
足径 9.5 厘米
故宫博物院藏

Illustration
Song dynasty　White glaze washer with stamped fish design

Height 2.5cm, mouth diameter 13.8cm,
foot diameter 9.5cm
Collected by the Palace Museum

洗敞口，斜直壁，平底。口镶铜釦。内、外施白釉，釉色微泛牙黄色。内壁印花游鱼图案。

218　宋　白釉印花鱼纹盘标本

Song dynasty

Specimen of white glaze plate with stamped fish design

附图

宋　白釉印花鱼纹盘

高 6.2 厘米　口径 30.1 厘米

足径 12.3 厘米

故宫博物院藏

Illustration

Song dynasty　White glaze plate with stamped fish design

Height 6.2cm, mouth diameter 30.1cm, foot diameter 12.3cm

Collected by the Palace Museum

盘侈口，浅弧壁，圈足。口镶铜釦。胎质洁白，釉色牙黄。器里模印双鱼图案，形象生动传神。

219　宋

白釉印花“五王府”铭盘标本

Song dynasty

Specimens of white glaze plate with stamped design and inscription of Chinese characters *Wu Wang Fu*

220　宋

白釉印花荷莲纹“北苑”铭盘标本

Song dynasty

Specimen of white glaze plate with stamped lotus design and insrip-tion of Chinese characters *Bei Yuan*

221 宋 白釉印花花卉鱼纹“尚食局”铭盘标本

Song dynasty Specimens of white glaze plate with stamped floral and fish design and inscription of Chinese characters *Shang Shi Ju*

222 宋 白釉印花龙纹“尚食局”铭盘标本

Song dynasty Specimen of white glaze plate with stamped dragon design and inscription of Chinese characters *Shang Shi Ju*

223　宋　白釉印花凤纹“尚食局”铭盘标本

Song dynasty　Specimen of white glaze plate with stamped phoenix design and inscription of Chinese characters *Shang Shi Ju*

224　宋　白釉刻花钱纹炉标本

Song dynasty

Specimen of white glaze burner with incised cash pattern design

225　宋　白釉划花萱草纹罐标本

Song dynasty

Specimen of white glaze jar with incised tawny day lily design

226　宋　白釉划花花卉纹盖器标本

Song dynasty

Specimens of white glaze cover with incised floral design

227 **宋　白釉划花花卉纹碗标本**

Song dynasty

Specimens of white glaze bowl with incised floral design

228　**宋　白釉划花花卉纹碗标本**

Song dynasty

Specimens of white glaze bowl with incised floral design

229 **宋　白釉划花花卉纹碗标本**

Song dynasty

Specimen of white glaze bowl with incised floral design

附图

宋　白釉划花花卉纹碗

高 6.8 厘米　口径 19.2 厘米

足径 5.7 厘米

故宫博物院藏

Illustration

Song dynasty　White glaze bowl with incised floral design

Height 6.8cm, mouth diameter 19.2cm, foot diameter 5.7cm

Collected by the Palace Museum

碗敞口，浅弧壁，圈足。口镶铜釦。内、外施白釉，釉色微泛牙黄色。内壁刻划花卉纹。

230 **宋　白釉划花花卉纹碗标本**

Song dynasty

Specimens of white glaze bowl with incised floral design

231　**宋　白釉划花萱草纹碗标本**

Song dynasty

Specimens of white glaze bowl with incised tawing day lily design

232　宋　**白釉划花萱草纹碗标本**

Song dynasty

Specimens of white glaze bowl with incised tawing day lily design

附图

宋　白釉划花萱草纹葵口碗

高 6.8 厘米　口径 19.2 厘米
足径 5.7 厘米
故宫博物院藏

Illustration
Song dynasty
White glaze tawny day lily bowl with incised intertwined lotus design

Height 6.8cm, mouth diameter 19.2cm, foot diameter 5.7cm
Collected by the Palace Museum

碗撇口，呈六瓣，口镶铜釦，深弧壁，浅圈足。通体施白釉，釉色微泛黄。碗内刻莲花、慈姑等纹饰，线条流畅自然。

233　宋　白釉划花萱草纹碗标本
Song dynasty
Specimens of white glaze bowl with incised tawny day lily design

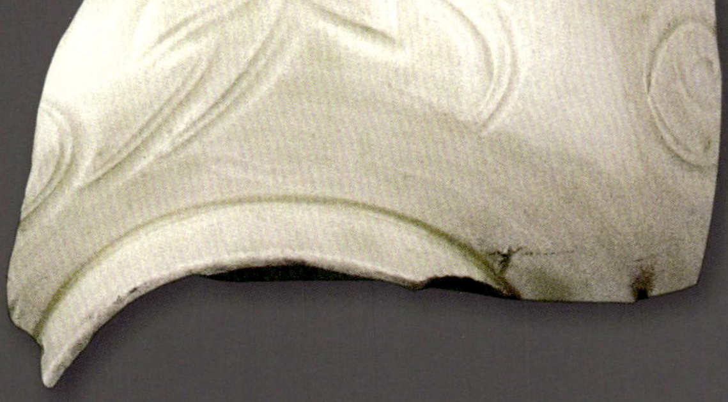

附图

北宋　白釉划花萱草纹温碗

高 13.3 厘米　口径 26 厘米
底径 14.5 厘米
故宫博物院藏

Illustration
Northern Song dynasty
White glaze warming bowl with incised tawny day lily design

Height 13.3cm, mouth diameter 26cm, bottom diameter 14.5cm
Collected by the Palace Museum

温碗敞口，深弧壁，圈足。口镶铜釦。内外施白釉。内外皆刻萱草纹，纹饰线条清晰流畅，刀法简洁大方。原本应有与之配套使用的注壶，用于温酒。

萱草，按《毛诗注疏》的解释，一名“宜男”，一名“忘忧草”，自古即是一种带有多重吉祥寓意的植物，宋代瓷器装饰中经常使用。

234　**宋　白釉划花莲瓣纹碗标本**
Song dynasty
Specimens of white glaze bowl with incised lotus-petal design

附图

宋　白釉划花莲瓣纹碗

高 15.6 厘米　口径 32.5 厘米
足径 16.4 厘米
故宫博物院藏

Illustration
Song dynasty　White glaze bowl with incised lotus-petal design

Height 15.6cm, mouth diameter 32.5cm, foot diameter 16.4cm
Collected by the Palace Museum

此碗硕大，直口微微内敛，深式，直壁，圈足。外壁刻划浅浮雕三层莲瓣纹。

235　**宋　白釉划花菊瓣纹碗标本**
Song dynasty
Specimen of white glaze bowl with incised chrysanthemum-petal design

236　**宋　白釉划花水波纹碗标本**
Song dynasty
Specimen of white glaze bowl with incised wave design

237　宋　白釉划花花卉纹盘标本

Song dynasty

Specimens of white glaze plate with incised floral design

238　宋　白釉划花花卉纹盘标本

Song dynasty

Specimen of white glaze plate with incised floral design

239　宋　白釉划花花卉纹盘标本

Song dynasty

Specimens of white glaze plate with incised floral design

240　宋　白釉划花萱草纹盘标本

Song dynasty

Specimens of white glaze plate with incised tawny day lily design

241 **宋 白釉划花荷莲纹盘标本**

Song dynasty

Specimen of white glaze plate with incised lotus design

242　**宋　白釉划花荷莲纹盘标本**

Song dynasty

Specimen of white glaze plate with incised lotus design

243　**宋　白釉划花荷叶纹盘标本**

Song dynasty

Specimen of white glaze plate with incised lotus-leaf design

244　宋　白釉划花海水纹盘标本

Song dynasty

Specimen of white glaze plate with incised wave design

245 **宋　白釉划花龙纹盘标本**

Song dynasty

Specimens of white glaze plate with incised dragon design

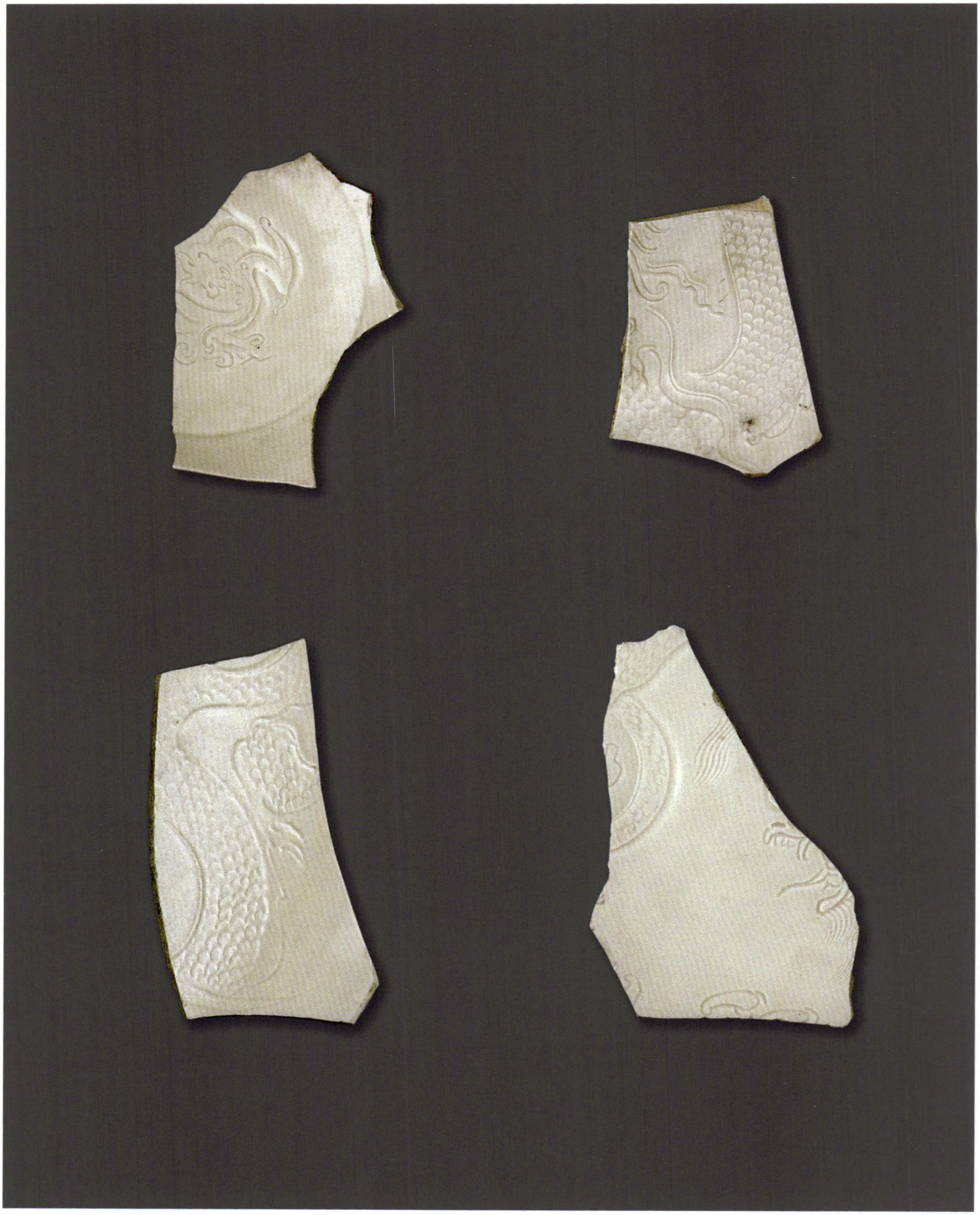

246 宋 白釉划花龙纹盘标本
Song dynasty
Specimen of white glaze plate
with incised dragon design

247 宋 白釉划花龙纹盘标本
Song dynasty
Specimen of white glaze plate
with incised dragon design

248　宋　白釉划花龙纹盘标本
Song dynasty
Specimen of white glaze plate
with incised dragon design

249　宋　白釉划花龙纹盘标本
Song dynasty
Specimen of white glaze plate
with incised dragon design

250　宋　白釉划花龙纹盘标本

Song dynasty

Specimens of white glaze plate with incised dragon design

251 宋 白釉划花龙纹盘标本

Song dynasty

Specimens of white glaze plate with incised dragon design

252 宋 白釉划花龙纹盘标本

Song dynasty

Specimens of white glaze plate with incised dragon design

253　宋　白釉划花龙纹盘标本

Song dynasty

Specimen of white glaze plate with incised dragon design

附图

宋　白釉划花蟠螭纹洗

高 5.5 厘米　口径 15.7 厘米
底径 13.7 厘米
故宫博物院藏

Illustration
Song dynasty
White glaze washer with incised interlaced-hydras design

Height 5.5cm, mouth diameter 15.7cm, bottom diameter 13.7cm
Collected by the Palace Museum

洗芒口，直壁，平底。内底心刻划蟠螭纹。

254　宋　白釉划花鱼纹盘标本

Song dynasty

Specimens of white glaze plate with incised fish design

附图

宋　白釉划花折枝莲纹盘

高1.2厘米　口径8.5厘米
足径6.3厘米
定州市博物馆藏

Illustration
Song dynasty
White glaze plate with incised design of disconnected spray of lotus

Height 1.2cm, mouth diameter 8.5cm, foot diameter 6.3cm
Collected by Dingzhou Museum

盘浅式，口外敞。通体满釉，口边无釉。盘里心刻划折枝莲花纹，纹饰线条简练。

255 宋 白釉划花鱼纹盘标本
Song dynasty
Specimen of white glaze plate with incised fish design

256 宋 里素胎刻花海水纹外白釉碗标本
Song dynasty
Specimen of bowl of unglazed inside with incised wave design and white glaze outside

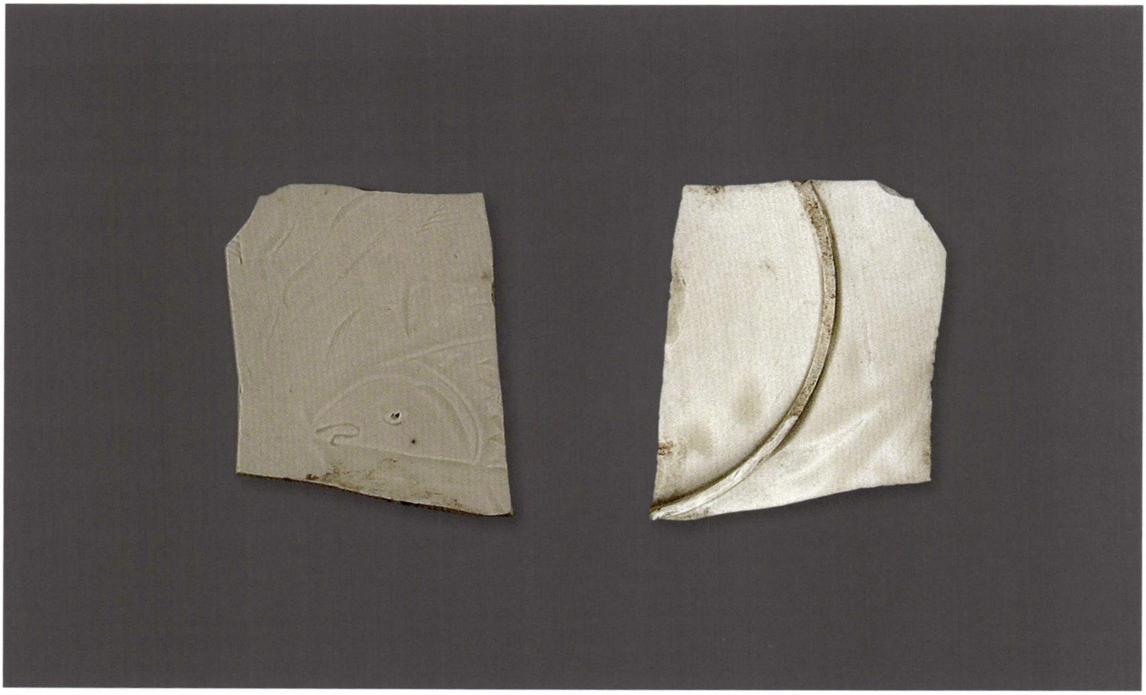

257　宋　里白釉外酱釉碗标本

Song dynasty

Specimens of bowl of white glaze inside and dark brown glaze outside

258 **宋 里白釉外酱釉碗标本**

Song dynasty

Specimen of bowl of white glaze inside and dark brown glaze outside

259 **宋 黑釉瓶标本**

Song dynasty

Specimens of black glaze vase

260　**宋　黑釉罐标本**
Song dynasty
Specimen of black glaze jar

261　**宋　黑釉壶标本**
Song dynasty
Specimen of black glaze pot

262　宋　黑釉炉标本
Song dynasty
Specimen of black glaze burner

263　宋　黑釉盒标本
Song dynasty
Specimen of black glaze box

264　宋　黑釉器盖标本
Song dynasty
Specimen of black glaze cover

265 宋 黑釉碗标本
Song dynasty
Specimen of black glaze bowl

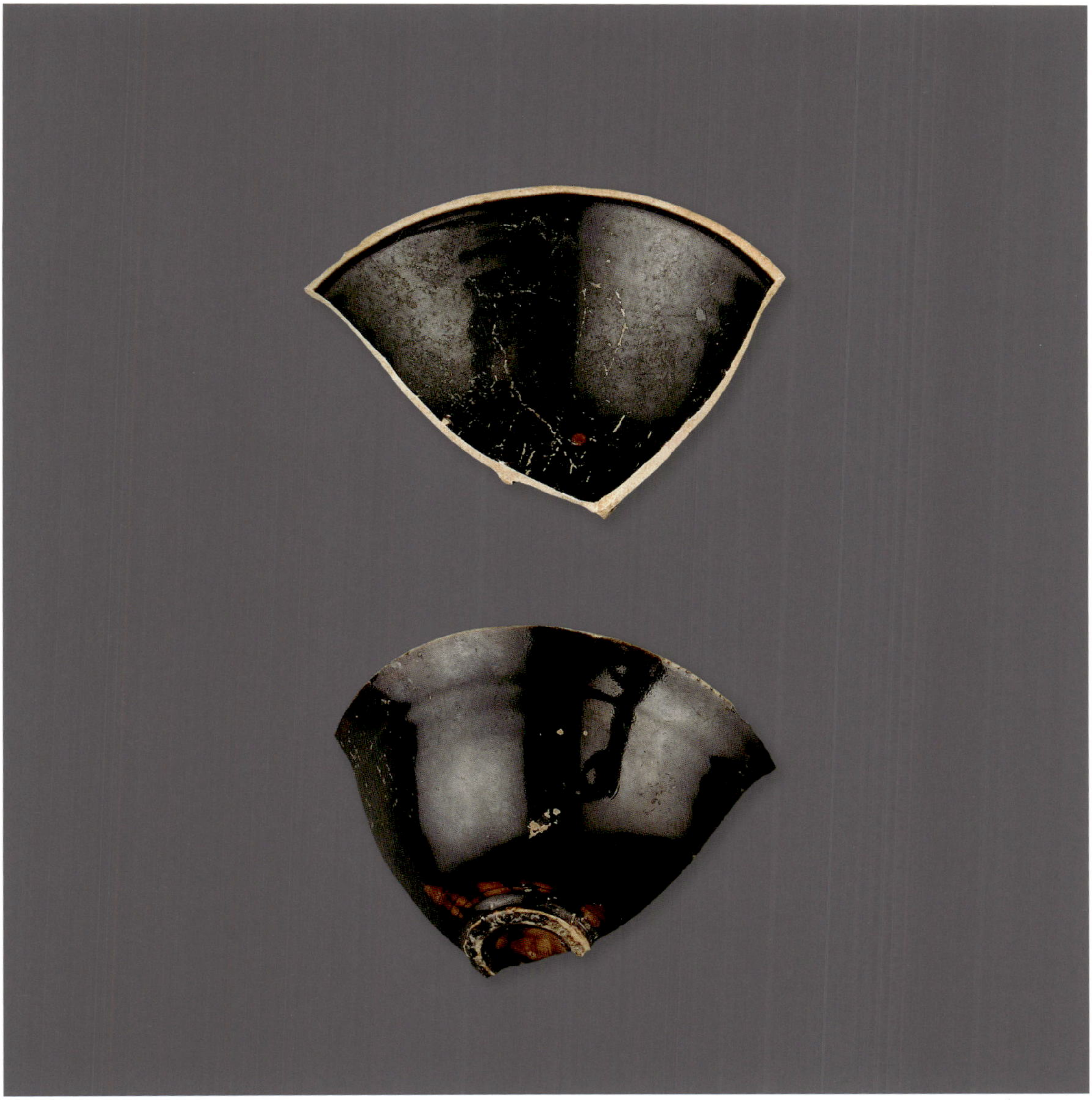

266　宋　黑釉碗标本

Song dynasty

Specimens of black glaze bowl

267 **宋　黑釉酱彩瓶标本**
Song dynasty
Specimen of black glaze vase with dark brown color design

268 **宋　黑釉酱彩瓶标本**
Song dynasty
Specimen of black glaze vase with dark brown color design

269 **宋　酱釉瓶标本**
Song dynasty
Specimen of dark brown glaze vase

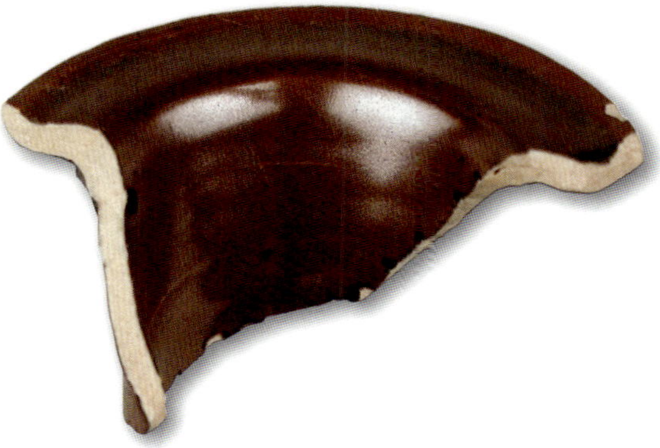

270 宋 酱釉器盖标本

Song dynasty

Specimen of dark brown glaze cover

附图

宋 酱釉带盖碗

通高 9.6 厘米 口径 12 厘米

足径 5.3 厘米

故宫博物院藏

Illustration

Song dynasty

Dark brown glaze bowl with cover

Overall height 9.6cm,
mouth diameter 12cm, foot diameter 5.3cm

Collected by the Palace Museum

盖碗直口，深腹，直壁，圈足。盖平边，盖面微微隆起，扁钮。胎质洁白，釉色为酱紫色，施釉到底边，足边无釉。

271 **宋 酱釉碗标本**

Song dynasty

Specimen of dark brown glaze bowl

272　**宋　酱釉盘标本**

Song dynasty

Specimen of dark brown glaze plate

附图

宋　酱釉葵瓣盘

高 3.5 厘米　口径 17.9 厘米

足径 5.9 厘米

故宫博物院藏

Illustration

Song dynasty　Dark brown glaze mallow-petal-shaped plate

Height 3.5cm, mouth diameter 17.9cm, foot diameter 5.9cm

Collected by the Palace Museum

盘六瓣花口，浅弧壁，折腰，圈足。胎质洁白，内外施酱釉，施釉不到底，足底心有釉。

273 **宋 酱釉印花牡丹纹碗标本**
Song dynasty
Specimen of dark brown glaze bowl with stamped peony design

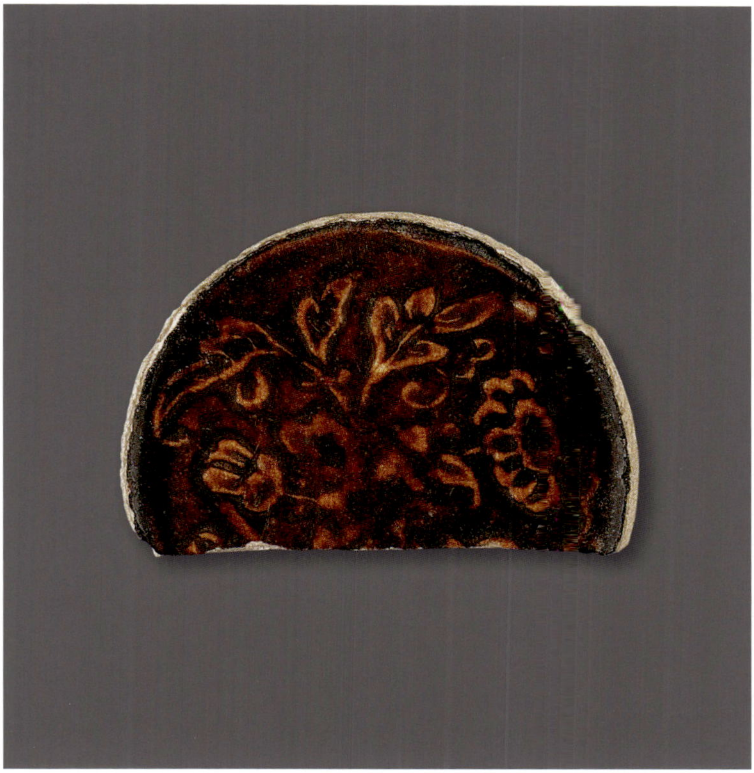

274 **宋 酱釉划花花卉纹盘标本**
Song dynasty
Specimen of dark brown glaze plate with incised floral design

275　宋　绿釉划花花卉纹枕标本

Song dynasty

Specimen of green glaze pillow with incised floral design

附图

宋（金）　绿釉剔花游鸭纹枕

高 9.8 厘米　长 31.5 厘米
宽 23.3 厘米
定州市南关出土
定州市博物馆藏

Illustration
Song dynasty (Jin dynasty)
Green glaze pillow with cut design of swimming ducks

Height 9.8cm, length 31.5cm,
width 23.3cm
Unearthed at Nanguan, Dingzhou City
Collected by Dingzhou Museum

枕腰圆形，前低后高，两边微上翘，底部有二个通气孔。采用剔花装饰，主题纹饰为莲池游鸭，边缘饰划刻的弦纹及水波纹，枕侧饰弦纹及剔花花叶纹。

276　宋　绿釉器标本

Song dynasty

Specimen of green glaze ware

277　宋　绿釉印花龙纹盘标本

Song dynasty

Specimen of green glate plate with design of stamped dragon

278 **宋　素胎刻花鸭纹碗标本**

Song dynasty

Specimen of unglazed bowl with incised duck design

279 宋（金） 白釉器盖标本
Song dynasty (Jin dynasty)
Specimens of white glaze cover

附图

宋（金）　白釉盖碗

高 9.4 厘米　口径 11 厘米
足径 5.3 厘米
故宫博物院藏

Illustration
Song dynasty (Jin dynasty)
White glaze bowl with cover

Height 9.4cm, mouth diameter 11cm
foot diameter 5.3cm
Collected by the Palace Museum

碗直口，直壁，圈足。盖平边，盖面微微隆起，扁钮。胎质洁白，釉色牙黄，光素无纹饰。

280 **宋（金） 白釉匜标本**

Song dynasty (Jin dynasty)

Specimens of white glaze ewer

附图

宋（金）　白釉匜

高3.5厘米　口径7.9厘米
底径3.7厘米
故宫博物院藏

Illustration
Song dynasty (Jin dynasty)
White glaze ewer

Height 3.5cm, mouth diameter 7.9cm,
bottom diameter 3.7cm
Collected by the Palace Museum

匜浅式，平底，一侧饰花式板沿，板沿下有一环柄。覆烧。胎质洁白，满釉，釉色牙黄。

281　宋（金）　白釉印花鸳鸯纹碗标本

Song dynasty (Jin dynasty)

Specimen of white glaze bowl with stamped mandarin duck design

282　宋（金）　白釉印花鱼纹盘标本

Song dynasty (Jin dynasty)

Specimens of white glaze plate with stamped fish design

283　**宋（金）　白釉刻花莲瓣纹缸标本**

Song dynasty (Jin dynasty)

Specimen of white glaze vat with incised lotus-petal design

附图

宋（金）　白釉莲瓣纹缸

高 11 厘米　口径 13.7 厘米
足径 6.4 厘米
定州市博物馆藏

Illustration
Song dynasty (Jin dynasty)
White glaze vat with incised lotus-petal design

Height 11cm, mouth diameter 13.7cm,
foot diameter 6.4cm
Collected by Dingzhou Museum

缸直壁芒口，深腹，圈足，盖失。腹部饰凸起的莲瓣纹装饰。

这种造型的器物在宋金时期很流行，河北、河南、山西、山东、陕西等地瓷窑都有烧造。除白釉以外，还有青釉。

284　宋（金）　白釉划花花卉纹花式碗标本

Song dynasty (Jin dynasty)

Specimens of white glaze flower-shaped bowl with incised floral design

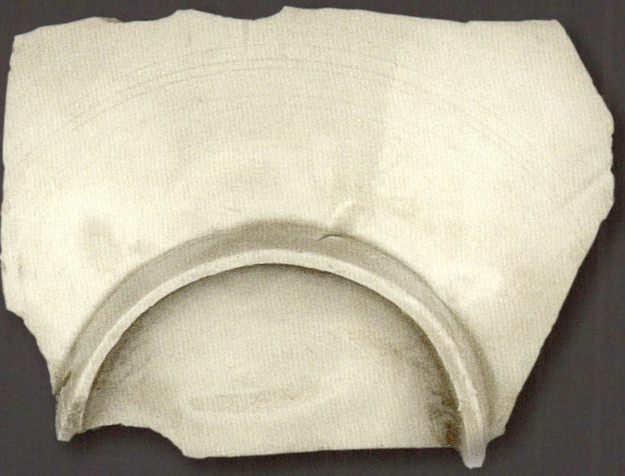

285　**金　白釉枕标本**
Jin dynasty
Specimen of white glaze pillow

286　**金　白釉划花枕标本**
Jin dynasty
Specimen of white glaze pillow with incised design

287　**金　白釉划花花卉纹盆标本**
Jin dynasty
Specimen of white glaze pot with incised floral design

288　金　白地黑花枕标本
Jin dynasty
Specimen of white glaze pillow with design of black patterns

289　金　白地黑花“李”字盘标本
Jin dynasty
Specimen of white glaze plate with design of black patterns and inscription of Chinese character *Li*

290　金　白地黑花“段”字盘标本
Jin dynasty
Specimen of white glaze plate with design of black patterns and inscription of Chinese character *Duan*

291　金　绿釉枕标本

Jin dynasty

Specimen of green glaze pillow

292　宋（金）　花卉纹印模标本

Song dynasty (Jin dynasty)

Specimen of seal with incised floral design

293　宋（金）匣钵标本
Song dynasty (Jin dynasty)
Specimen of kiln furniture

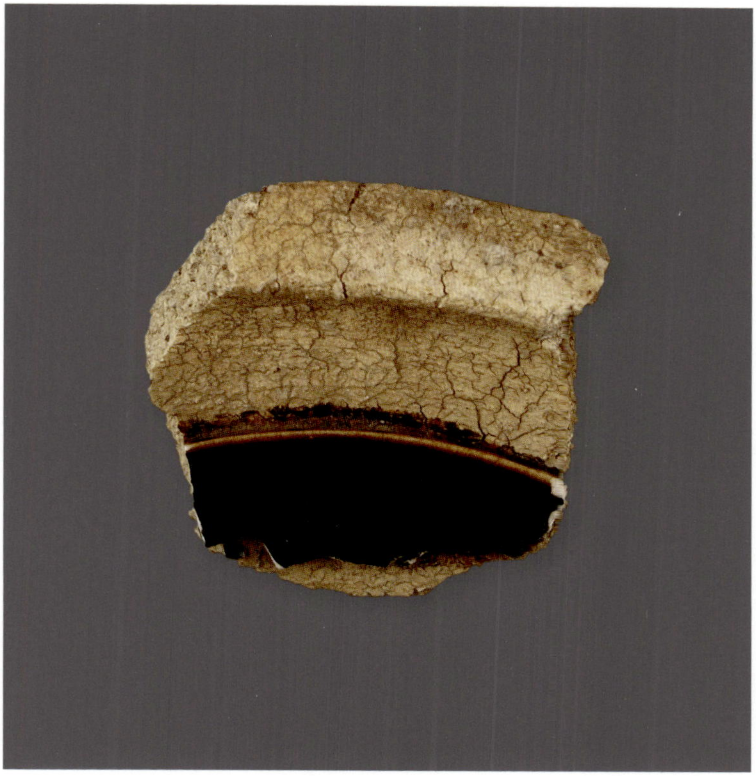

294　宋（金）窑具标本
Song dynasty (Jin dynasty)
Specimens of kiln furniture

井陉窑

故宫博物院的部分专家和学者于2002年、2005年对井陉窑进行了调查。关于井陉窑的文献有清代雍正八年刻本《井陉县志》、乾隆二十七年刻本《正定府志》以及民国二十三年铅印本《井陉县志》。三本志书在风俗、集市、物产条中分别记载井陉有陶冶，产瓷器，并于明代进贡瓷器。由此我们知道井陉窑明清两代生产瓷器。民国本的《井陉县志》陶冶编中记载了民国四年在井陉县高级小学校操场内出土刻有“天威军官瓶”的器物。

对窑址调查表明，井陉窑窑址范围较大，烧瓷时间始于唐，终于元，宋、金为兴盛时期。烧制具有定窑划花、印花风格的器物，以白釉器物为主，一般采用盘碗里心刮釉支烧，具有典型的金代风格。所烧器物从总体上看，略粗于定窑，但其精品与定窑难分伯仲。在传世或出土的具有定窑风格的器物中，应当有井陉窑的产品。文献中记载的“天威军官瓶”故宫博物院收藏有一件，胎质略红，釉失亮，造型同梅瓶，小口、溜肩、体瘦长，通体饰弦纹（又称瓦垅纹），肩部刻“天威军官瓶”五字，是文献中记载的井陉县高级小学校出土的器物，当是宋代井陉窑为天威军定烧的盛水用的容器。

Jingxing Kiln

Experts from the Palace Museum made investigations into Jingxing kiln in 2002 and 2005. The porcelain production of Jingxing kiln was documented in Annals of Jingxing County printed in the eighth year of Yongzheng's Reign, Qing dynasty and in the 23rd year of Republic of China, and in Annals of Zhengding Region printed in the twentieth year of Qianlong's Reign, Qing dynasty as well. According to the Annals, the kiln paid tributes to emperors of Ming dynasty. Thus, it is clear that Jingxing kiln continued to fire porcelains in Ming and Qing dynasty. Based on the Republic of China version of Annals of Jingxing County, a vase with inscription of five Chinese characters, Tian Wei Jiang Jun Ping, was unearthed from the playground of Senior Primary School, Jingxing County in 1915.

The investigations show that Jingxing kiln was once a large one. It started to fire in Tang dynasty and closed in Yuan dynasty. It reached its heyday in Song and Jin dynasty. It fired wares with incised or stamped design, very much the style of Ding kiln. White glaze is the main produce of Jingxing kiln. Glaze at the inside center of plates and bowls was usually scraped off and then fired with spurs, typical of style of Jin dynasty wares. In general, the quality of Jingxing kiln wares is slightly inferior to that of Ding kiln. With regard to first class Jingxing kiln wares, they are well in match with Ding kiln wares. Among the handed down or unearthed Ding kiln style utensils, there should be some from Jingxing kiln. The above mentioned vase with inscription of five Chinese characters, Tian Wei Jiang Jun Ping, on shoulder is now collected by the Palace Museum. It was fired for the Tianwei Army by Jingxing kiln in Song dynasty. It was a water container. The body is slightly reddish and glaze is no longer luminous. With small mouth, slanting shoulder and slender body and with design of strings across the whole body, the vase looks pretty much plum vase.

井陉窑遗址
Ruin of Jingxing kiln

井陉窑遗址
Ruin of Jingxing kiln

井陉窑遗址瓷片遗址
Pileup of porcelain parts at the ruin of Jingxing kiln

2005年井陉窑发掘现场
Scene of the 2005 excavation of Jingxing kiln

2005 年井陉窑发掘出土标本
Porcelain parts from the 2005 excavation of Jingxing kiln

295　金　白釉碗标本
Jin dynasty
Specimens of white glaze bowl

296　金　白釉碗标本
Jin dynasty
Specimens of white glaze bowl

297　金　白釉碗标本

Jin dynasty

Specimen of white glaze bowl

298　金　白釉花式碗标本

Jin dynasty

Specimens of white glaze flower-shaped bowl

299　**金　白釉刻花折沿器标本**

Jin dynasty

Specimen of white glaze ware with everted flange and with incised design

300　**金　白釉划花碗标本**

Jin dynasty

Specimen of white glaze bowl with incised design

301　金　里白釉外酱釉碗标本

Jin dynasty

Specimens of bowl of white glaze inside and dark brown glaze outside

302　金　酱釉碗标本

Jin dynasty

Specimen of dark brown glaze bowl

隆化窑

故宫博物院的部分专家和学者于20世纪80年代调查此窑。

窑址在河北省隆化县，属元代瓷窑遗址。已发现元代烧制磁州窑系的白地黑花器以及钧窑系的钧釉器物。白地黑花器物以大件缸、罐器为主，器物胎体厚重，胎质较粗，白釉泛黄，彩呈褐色；钧釉器物以碗为主，胎质粗，釉色为灰蓝色，较暗淡。此外还烧制白釉、黑釉器物。

Longhua Kiln

Experts from the Palace Museum made an investigation into Longhua kiln in the 1980s. The ruin of the kiln is located in Longhua County, Hebei Province. It was a porcelain kiln of Yuan dynasty. White glaze with design of black patterns, sorts of Cizhou wares, and Jun glaze, sorts of Jun kiln wares, of Yuan dynasty had been found at the ruin of the kiln. White glaze wares with design of black patterns are mainly large vats and jars with thick and heavy bodies which are relatively coarse. The white glaze looks yellowish or even brown. Jun glaze wares are mainly bowls. The bodies of the bowls are coarse, too. The glaze of Jun wares is gray-blue, relatively dark. In addition, the kiln fired white and black glaze wares.

303　元　白地黑花罐标本

Yuan dynasty

Specimens of white glaze jar with design of black patterns

304　**元　白地黑花花卉纹罐标本**

Yuan dynasty

Specimens of white glaze jar with design of black flroal patterns

305　元　白地黑花碗标本

Yuan dynasty

Specimens of white glaze bowl with design of black patterns

306　元　里白釉外酱釉碗标本

Yuan dynasty

Specimens of bowl of white glaze inside and dark brown glaze outside

307　元　钧釉碗标本

Yuan dynasty

Specimens of Jun glaze bowl

窑址考察论文选

Selected Thesis on Kiln Investigation

河北磁县贾壁村隋青瓷窑址初探

冯先铭

1959年6月上旬，有机会与陈万里先生一道去磁州窑所在地——峰峰，峰峰现属邯郸市，该市于彭城镇设陶瓷研究所，致力于古磁州窑的恢复工作。我们在陶瓷研究所附属的瓷厂工作告一段落以后，想利用很短的时间调查一下彭城镇附近的古瓷窑址。了解后，决定去距镇12.5公里的磁县青碗窑村和距镇17.5公里的磁县贾壁村。

青碗窑不见于记载，顾名思义是以烧青釉碗而得名的。从地理方位及以往墓葬出土物情况推测，安阳一带出土的青釉碗可能是青碗窑的产品，两地的距离只有30余公里，因之对于青碗窑寄予很大的希望。

6月10日早晨与陈先生、陶研所叶广成及正在瓷厂领导同学辅导生产的工艺美术学院梅健鹰、梁任生先生同去调查。青碗窑在彭城镇西12.5公里，步行7.5公里抵宿凤后，乘马车上张庄岭，沿岭南行约3.5公里，再西行1.5公里即至青碗窑乡。通过调查判明青碗窑是烧制元钧釉系统器皿的一个瓷窑，遗址面积不大，碎片标本不多，时已下午4时许，陈万里先生等乃先返回彭城镇，我与叶广成骑车同往贾壁村探查，结果发现隋代青瓷窑址一处。原来希望在青碗窑解决的问题，不想竟在北贾壁村解决了。

贾壁窑未见于文献记载，近人著作中曾提到它是北朝的窑。贾壁村距青碗窑乡5公里，由青碗窑乡沿河道北行，河道干涸，雨季来临山洪暴发时始有水，因干涸时久，农民多不知其名，即以地名名之。贾壁村分为北、中、南三个部分，据南贾壁农民反映，过去中贾壁与北贾壁之间农民翻地经常掘出古瓷片，北贾壁距南贾壁只有一公里，乃急乘车去北贾壁探访。北贾壁四面环山，河东岸有贾壁中学，数年前学生于河西岸取土时掘出过大量青瓷碎片，学校曾把掘出的瓷片办了一个小型展览，以启发同学与农民热爱祖国文物。到贾壁中学后，承王校长热情介绍并亲自引导我们到窑址所在地——寺沟口去实地调查。

寺沟口在河西岸，与贾壁中学隔河相望，窑址就在寺沟口西约70米的沟北山坡上，田间散布着为数不少的青釉瓷片与窑具。遗址长达20米，据王校长说约一米以下有大量瓷片，当时正值雹雨方停，田间一片泥泞，举足即陷入泥中，只稍事采集了一些散布于地面的标本即返回学校。

这次调查共采集青瓷碎片及窑具70件。青瓷碎片计分三种器型——碗、高足盘和钵形器。

一 器物分类

1．碗类

可分为三式：

Ⅰ式。口内敛，平底足，底心微凹入。胎厚重，多黑色斑点。碗里满釉，外部只施半釉，釉呈青褐色，透明，胎中黑点明显露出，垂釉处聚如圆珠，透明如玻璃，口下有弦纹一道。高 9.8 厘米，口径 14 厘米，底径 6.8 厘米。

Ⅱ式。口与碗身垂直，腰以下始收敛，平底，底心亦微凹入，施釉方法、釉色与胎土特点与Ⅰ式碗相同。这种碗采集得最多，高 5.5～5.8 厘米，口径 7.8～8.3 厘米，底径 3.6～3.8 厘米。

Ⅲ式。口微内敛，平底，底足上窄而下稍宽，底心亦微凹入。碗里满釉，外部施釉过半，釉呈淡青绿色，较Ⅰ式、Ⅱ式碗薄，无垂釉现象。胎较Ⅰ式、Ⅱ式碗也薄，胎土细洁无黑色斑点。高 7 厘米，口径 9.6 厘米，底径 4.2 厘米。

上述三种碗轮旋都很规整，碗底与足相接处都有一条深深的轮旋纹。碗里都聚有较厚的釉，聚釉处都呈深褐色。碗心都有三个支烧痕，小碗中也有不带支烧痕的，那是烧时放在最上面的，里面不再套放其他器物。

2．高足盘类

大型高足盘。只采集到一件，为盘心及高足的上部。胎土多黑色斑点，釉呈深褐色，高足部分釉不到底。

中型高足盘。采集到两件，都为盘沿之一部分。口沿外撇，盘心平坦。胎土多黑斑点，釉青褐色。一件盘心有支烧痕。

3．钵形器

共采集到两件，一件口内敛，口沿旋平。两件胎都厚重，器里都划有纹饰，一件划水波纹两道，纹外各划弦纹两条；一件划花瓣纹，纹外亦各划弦纹两条。这两种纹饰还保留有汉晋的风格，在洗、罐等器皿上时常可以看到。两件器里部都施满釉，外部施釉仅及口下，一件釉色与Ⅰ式碗相同，另一件与Ⅲ式碗相同。

4. 窑具

共分为四种：

齿形支烧具。地面散布极多，计有大小两种，大的五齿，支烧钵形器皿时所用；小的四齿，支烧Ⅰ式碗时所用，地面散布的四齿形具与Ⅰ式碗底黏结在一起的也不少。

三叉形支具。为支烧Ⅱ式、Ⅲ式小碗的支具，这种支具陶土较齿形支具为细洁，与Ⅲ式碗胎色一致。

垫饼。扁圆形，土质稍粗，为放于筒形支具上的一种支具。

筒形支具。有大小两种，用耐火土制成，为瓶或罐等立体器皿的支具。

二 收获

隋代近 40 年，就中国陶瓷发展的悠久历史来说，只不过是短暂的一瞬。但它处于上继南北朝下启唐代的一个继往开来阶段，因之这一段时间是相当重要的。

多年来流传于世的不少隋瓷，都被划入了唐瓷的范畴。一直到 1929 年河南安阳殷墟发现了卜仁墓葬以后，由于墓志上有确切的年代，因而使我们知道了出土的几件青瓷的相对时代，隋瓷的面貌才初步揭示出来为人所知，通过这几件瓷器也解决了以往安阳出土与它同型的不少瓷器的时代问题，安阳因而成为我国主要隋瓷出土地点之一。在山东曲阜，也出土了不少隋瓷，造型及胎釉特征有与安阳完全属于同一类型的。这两处隋墓出土的青瓷，胎釉与南方系统显然不同，一致认为它们同属于北方的青瓷系统，但对于它们的产地与窑口，多年来一直悬而未决。

近几年来，长江以南也陆续发现了一些隋代墓葬，长沙与武昌近郊隋墓中也出土有不少青瓷。长沙出土的瓷器与安阳不同，胎釉都很细洁，器身装饰有精美的花纹，似属于南方青釉系统。武昌近郊周家大湾发现的一座隋墓出土有青釉四系大尊与小碗等数件瓷器，胎釉又属于北方系统。这两地隋墓的发现，丰富了我们对于隋代瓷器的知识，同时也出现了一些新的问题，那就是长沙出土的南方系统的隋瓷是哪个窑出品的，窑址又在哪里？而武昌出土属于北方系统的隋瓷又是哪个窑的产品，窑址又在哪里？

贾壁村窑址的探查，初步解决了上述各地出土隋瓷中一部分的窑口问题。

安阳卜仁墓出土的青黄釉高足大盘[1]与本文前述采集高足大盘造型、胎土特点完全相同，釉色前者呈青黄色，后者呈青褐色，稍有不同，但这在青釉瓷器中是比较普遍的现象，这种现象在早期晋瓷、越窑及龙泉窑瓷器中都屡见不鲜。安阳出土的另一件高足盘[2]也与本文前述采集中型高足盘为同一类型。另一隋墓出土的小碗[3]与本文前述Ⅱ式、Ⅲ式两碗完全相同。因之可以肯定这三件出土物的具体窑口问题。

曲阜隋墓出土有一件双系瓶（此瓶近由山东省博物馆支援给北京历史博物馆展览），瓶身上的几条粗弦纹装饰，胎土中的黑点、青褐色釉以及垂釉的透明圆珠等特点，也告诉我们它是贾壁窑的产品。

武昌周家大湾隋墓出土的青釉四系大尊，肩部刻划有一周花纹，它与本文前述采集钵形器的花瓣纹极相似，它的釉色呈淡青绿色，与本文Ⅲ式碗相同；同墓出土的另一件小碗，其胎釉也与比碗一样。因此也认为这两件器物是贾壁窑的产物。

这次调查适值霉雨，地面泥泞难行，调查是比较粗糙的，采集的标本也较少，对于贾壁窑的烧制品种与上下时限就很难得到比较全面的认识。好在这只是初探，仅将初步调查所得提出，希有关单位能对它进行一次彻底的清理，这将是很有价值的。

（原载《考古》1959年第10期）

注释：

1 宋伯胤:《卜仁墓中的隋代青瓷器》图3,《文物参考资料》1958年第8期。

2 宋伯胤:《卜仁墓中的隋代青瓷器》图7左,《文物参考资料》1958年第8期。

3［日］小山富士夫:《支那青瓷史稿》图42上。

Abstract of a Preliminary Study on the Celadon Kiln Ruin of Sui Dynasty at Jiabi Village, Cixian County, Hebei Province

Feng Xianming

The investigation into the ruin of Jiabi kiln was made in 1959. The kiln site is located at the entrance of a valley near Jiabicun Temple, Pengcheng Town, 17.5 km away from Cixian County. The porcelain parts were distributed along a slope, 70m west to the entrance of the valley. The kiln ruin was about 20m in length along the slope. From the ruin, specimens of green glaze wares and kiln furniture were collected. The green glaze wares can be divided into three categories: bowl, alms bowl and plate with high stem. There are three types of bowls. Basically, the bowls are with grabbing or straight mouth, deep body, pie-shaped concave bottom. Transparent glaze was applied to the bowls with full glaze inside and semi glaze outside. In the center of the bowl, there are three spur-marks. The bodies of alms bowls are thick, thus heavy. They have incurving lips. Glaze was fully applied. One of the alms bowls is with incised wave design and the other with incised flower design. Plate with high stem differs in size, but all have a flat center and glaze are not fully applied. Some of the plates have spur-marks in the center. Jiabi kiln has clear characteristics of the Sui dynasty based on the specimens and kiln furniture found. The discovery of the kiln site adds new information on kilns of Sui dynasty and helps to identify the source of some of the unearthed artifacts.

磁州窑遗址调查

李辉柄

磁州窑是我国古代北方民间著名的瓷窑之一，在中国陶瓷发展史上占据着比较重要的地位。然而，由于磁州窑的文献记载很少，更由于真正代表磁州窑风格的窑址一直未搞清楚，所以人们对磁州窑的概念是不够清晰的。

据明代曹昭的《格古要论》记载："古磁器出河南彰德府磁州，好者与定器相似，但无泪痕，亦有划花、绣花，素者价高于定器，新者不足论也。"对磁州窑的研究，仅依据这一记载是不够的。必须进行遗址的调查来加以印证。

过去曾经把一些不属于磁州窑的作品，特别是把白地黑花的器物一概划入磁州窑，后来由于河南修武当阳峪窑、禹县扒村窑、汤阴鹤壁集窑以及山西介休窑等遗址的陆续发现，使我们知道烧制磁州窑的典型器——白地黑花器物的窑口除了磁州窑以外，还有其他瓷窑，于是在陶瓷研究者中间就流传开了一种"磁州窑型"或"磁州窑系"的新名称，用来概括这些地区与磁州窑密切相关的窑的作品。这种含混牵强的提法，在磁州窑的基本面貌尚未弄清楚以前是很自然的。后来又由于在河南修武当阳峪窑的遗址中发现了一些非常精致的白地黑花的器物碎片，而这种碎片在磁州窑的遗址中（磁县彭城镇遗址）却没有发现，据此有的学者把一些精致的器物，尤其是白地黑花的器物，全都划入河南修武当阳峪窑之列了。

十多年来随着我国考古事业的发展，窑址调查与发掘工作也广泛展开，从而解决了好多陶瓷发展史上的重要问题，对磁州窑的研究同时也有所进展。首先是对和磁州窑最密切相关的河南修武当阳峪窑和禹县扒村窑作了调查，其次对汤阴鹤壁集窑和山西介休窑也作了调查，对它们烧制情况有了一个初步的认识。对磁州窑的调查方面除了彭城镇以外，还调查了贾壁村、青碗窑村、冶子村、观台镇等遗址。今年 4 月故宫博物院派我和姚万卿同志前往磁县作了为时一个星期的调查，收获较大。这次调查邯郸市陶瓷公司、陶瓷研究所给予了大力支持，提供了许多方便，南响堂寺文物保管所还派了李长云同志一起参加调查。由于时间短，遗址分布地区又很广，就不免会带有一些片面性和局限性。现将此次调查结果报告如下。

一 磁州窑遗址情况

这次调查以邯郸市观台镇、东艾口村及磁县南部的冶子村为重点。三处窑址分布地区集中，都倚在漳河两岸，冶子村与观台镇隔河东西相峙，东艾口距观台只约5里，在漳河拐角处的南岸，形成了一个三角地带。

（一）观台镇遗址

遗址的范围非常广大，烧制器物的种类很多，计有白釉、黑釉、酱釉等单色釉的器物，还有白地绘黑花、白地绘划黑花、绿地黑花、白地绘酱花、白地绘划酱花、白釉剔花、白釉划花、褐色点彩、绿彩以及珍珠地、低温釉器物等十多种。其中以白釉、黑釉为最多，白釉划花也不少，珍珠地的器物比较少见。低温釉有绿釉、黄釉、三彩、红绿彩多种。其中以黄釉、绿釉的器物较多，红绿彩的器物较少。

1. 白釉

计有盘、碗、罐、瓶、水盂、印盒、各种玩具等，碗、盘的数量为最多。

（1）盘

有5式：

Ⅰ式。敞口，折腰，圈足。底中心微凸起，盘心有5个支钉烧痕。器内外施满釉，胎釉之间夹有一层白色化妆土，底足无釉。高3.6厘米，口径19厘米，足径5.7厘米。

Ⅱ式。敞口，口缘外部微凸出小唇，器身弧度大，圈足，足内较深，底中心平坦。高4.4厘米，口径16厘米，足径5.6厘米。

Ⅲ式。敞口，盘心有六组细砂粒支烧痕，圈足。高4厘米，口径16.7厘米，足径6.7厘米。

Ⅳ式。敞口，器身弧度小，折底，圈足，足内较深，底中心微凸起。高4.4厘米，口径17厘米，足径8厘米。

Ⅴ式。器型与Ⅳ式盘相同，圈足小，底中心平坦。高4.1厘米，口径15厘米，足径5.5厘米。

（2）碗

有16式：

Ⅰ式。浅形，敞口，器身压成花瓣形，圈足，底中心微凸起。高 5.6 厘米，口径 16 厘米，足径 8.2 厘米。

Ⅱ式。深形，敛口，口以下渐广，腹以下内收，器身弧度大，圈足，足内浅而底中心平坦。高 4.4 厘米，口径 8.1 厘米，足径 3.8 厘米。

Ⅲ式。口微敛，口以下弧线内收，碗心内凹一圈形，矮圈足。高 5.1 厘米，口径 13.4 厘米，足径 6.4 厘米。

Ⅳ式。浅形，唇口外撇，器身以 45 度角斜出，圈足，足内浅而底中心平坦。高 3.3 厘米，口径 10.6 厘米，足径 4 厘米。

Ⅴ式。浅形，敞口，口以下渐内收，器身弧度小，碗心有一圈细砂粒支烧痕，圈足。高 4.2 厘米，口径 14.4 厘米，足径 6.4 厘米。

Ⅵ式。敞口，口以下弧线内收，碗心凸起一圈形，圈足。高 4 厘米，口径 10 厘米，足径 3.7 厘米。

Ⅶ式。形同Ⅵ式，但足较瘦。高 4 厘米，口径 10.8 厘米，足径 3.7 厘米。

Ⅷ式。浅形，敞口，口以下弧线内收，矮圈足。高 4 厘米，口径 13.6 厘米，足径 4.9 厘米。

Ⅸ式。敞口，口以下弧线内收，碗心内凹一圈形，圈足，足内深而底中心平坦。高 6.2 厘米，口径 15 厘米，足径 6.2 厘米。

Ⅹ式。敞口微外撇，口以下弧线内收，碗心留有四组砂粒支烧痕，圈足。高 5.2 厘米，口径 14.4 厘米，口径 6.4 厘米。

Ⅺ式。敞口外撇，口以下微折弧线内收，圈足，底中心凸起。高 3.6 厘米，口径 9.8 厘米，足径 4 厘米。

Ⅻ式。敞口外撇，口以下渐内收，高圈足。高 5 厘米，口径 11.5 厘米，足径 3.6 厘米。

ⅩⅢ式。敞口，口以下弧线内收，圈足，足内较深而底中心微凸起。高 5.4 厘米，口径 14 厘米，足径 5.4 厘米。

ⅩⅣ式。敞口外撇，口以下弧线内收，碗心内凹一圈形，圈足。高 7.2 厘米，口径 22.4 厘米，足径 8.6 厘米。

ⅩⅤ式。敞口微内敛，碗内壁起线五条，碗心内凹一圈形，圈足。高 8.2 厘米，口径 22.2 厘米，足径 6.8 厘米。

ⅩⅥ式。深形，敞口，口边起弦纹一道，口以下弧线内收。高圈足，底中心微凸起。高 8 厘米，口径 16 厘米，足径 5.6 厘米。

（3）罐

有 5 式：

Ⅰ式。敞口外撇，短颈，颈以下渐广至腹部内收，腹部压成瓜棱形，圈足。足外部垂直，足内倾斜，底中心微凸起。器里留有明显的轮旋痕迹，施釉仅过口，器外施釉不到底，胎釉之间使用化妆土，底足露胎。高 12.9 厘米，口径 11.1 厘米，足径 6.5 厘米。

Ⅱ式。直口，口颈相连，口以下渐广至腹部内收，器里有明显的轮旋痕迹，圈足。足外部微向外撇，足内部倾斜，底中心凸起。高 8.7 厘米，口径 11.2 厘米，足径 8.4 厘米。

Ⅲ式。直口，口边凸起小唇，短颈，扁圆腹，颈腹交界处立对称双直系，圈足，足内外均外撇，底中心平坦。高 6.7 厘米，口径 11.2 厘米，足径 8.4 厘米。

Ⅳ式。直桶形，口折沿，沿上凸起鼓丁 12 个，直腹，腹中部微向内收，圈足。高 8.3 厘米，口径 10.6 厘米，足径 6.8 厘米。

Ⅴ式。敛口，口外边凸起弦纹一道，弦纹以下垂直，近底处暴敛，圈足，底中心微凸起。高 6.8 厘米，口径 11.8 厘米，足径 8.4 厘米。

（4）玩具

有壶、瓶、碗、碟、提篮等。

壶。均撇口，长颈，肩部一面立一短流，另一面立柄至颈部，圈足。最大者高 9 厘米，最小者高 6.5 厘米。

瓶。分敞口与敛口两种，均为细颈，圈足。最大者高 7.5 厘米，最小者高 6 厘米。

碗。均敛口，平底，最大者口径 4.6 厘米，最小者口径 3.5 厘米。

提篮。有大小之别，均为敛口，口沿立冲天绳系，平底，最大者高 5.5 厘米，最小者高 3.8 厘米。

2. 黑釉

计有碗、壶、瓶、罐、玩具等，除了壶、瓶不能复原外，其他都可分辨其整个造型。

（1）碗

有 4 式：

Ⅰ式。撇口，口以下内收，器壁弧度小，圈足，足内浅。器里满釉，有油滴斑点，器外施釉不到底，底足露胎。高 4 厘米，口径 11.2 厘米，足径 3.9 厘米。

Ⅱ式。敛口，口以下内收，器壁弧度小，圈足。器里满釉，器外施釉不到底，有垂釉现象，底足露胎。高 5.4 厘米，口径 12.8 厘米，足径 4.2 厘米。

Ⅲ式。敞口内敛，口以下内收，器壁较Ⅱ式碗为大，圈足。器里满釉，有酱色斑点，器外施釉不到底，有垂釉现象，底足露胎。高 5.6 厘米，口径 14.4 厘米，足径 5.1 厘米。

Ⅳ式。浅形，直口微内敛，口以下垂直，近底处弧度大，圈足。器里满釉，口边釉薄呈酱色，器外施釉不到底，底足露胎。高 3.4 厘米，口径 7.1 厘米，足径 3.7 厘米。

（2）壶

形制有两种：一种为直口，长颈，肩部一面有短流，另一面有柄；另一种在流柄之间的对称处再立双系，器里施釉仅过口，器外施釉不到底。

（3）罐

有 2 式：

Ⅰ式。广口微撇，口外边起弦纹两道，无颈，口以下渐广至腹部内收呈扁圆腹，圈足。器里满釉，器外施釉不到底，底足露胎。

Ⅱ式。直口微内敛，口外边凸起弦纹一道，弦纹以下内收，宽圈足。器里施满釉，器外施半载釉，有流釉现象，底足露胎。高 6.8 厘米，口径 11.9 厘米，足径 8.3 厘米。

（4）玩具

形制与白釉玩具相同。

3．白釉划花

此类器物在遗址中发现最多，器型多为盘、碗，其他器物未见。盘、碗的形式与白釉器物相同。划花都装饰在器里，器外光素。划花都很深刻流利，花纹清晰，在纹饰的空间都划细线条纹，用以突出主题纹饰。装饰题材有荷叶莲花、卷叶及水波浪纹多种，以荷叶莲花纹为最多。另有一种器物，外施黑釉，里为白釉划花。造型多为大碗，装饰题材除了荷叶莲花、卷叶及水波浪纹以外，还有鱼纹等。

4．白釉剔花

此类器物在遗址中发现得不多，器型计有罐、洗、盆、碗 4 种，其中可以复原的仅有罐、洗两种。

（1）罐

为敞口，无颈，口以下渐广至腹部内收，圆腹，圈足。腹部装饰以缠枝牡丹纹。器里外满釉，胎釉之间使用化妆土，底心满釉，足无釉。高 9.9 厘米，口径 13.7 厘米，足径 7.1 厘米。

（2）洗

为直口微内敛，口以下微广，近底处内收，平底。器身装饰以莲花瓣纹一周，器里外施满釉，底心无釉。高 3.6 厘米，口径 10 厘米，足径 9.8 厘米。

5．点彩

是用 3 点、4 点、5 点、7 点不等组成朵花安排在器物的上部及颈部。此种器物在遗址中发现不少，器型有瓶、壶、碗、灯、水盂等，其中以碗为最多，可以复原的也仅有碗一种。

碗为深形，直口微敛，口外边凸起一小唇，口以下渐广至腹部内收，圈足。足内外均垂直，底中心微凸起，腹部装饰以 5 点组成的朵花，器里满釉，器外施釉不到底，底足露胎。高 6.6 厘米，口径 11.5 厘米，足径 6.3 厘米。

6．绿彩

采集到的标本不多，器型有罐、灯、瓶、壶等。因多系残片，无法看出完整器型。绿彩多装饰在器物的口边及颈部。

7．绿地绘黑花

仅采集到两件标本，均为枕边残片，颜色鲜艳，绿黑分明。

8．白地绘黑花

标本采集得不多，器型以各种罐为多，枕和其他器物少见。装饰题材多为卷枝纹、片叶纹，也有凤凰、蝴蝶之类，都绘在器物的上半部。枕头的边饰都采用卷枝纹，枕面仅采集一件，上面绘花草蝴蝶等。

（1）罐

多系残片，除了一种直口罐以外，其他均无法辨别其完整器型。以罐的口部之不同可分为3式：

Ⅰ式。直口微外撇，口以下垂直，桶形，近底处内收，圈足。足内部浅，底中心平坦，器身装饰以片叶纹，器里施釉仅过口，器壁有明显的轮旋痕迹，器外光滑，近底处无釉，底足露胎。罐有盖，盖似碗形，圈形钮，盖面装饰以片叶纹，盖口合于罐口之内，盖面满釉，盖里无釉。通高18.2厘米，口径14.4厘米，足径10厘米。

Ⅱ式。敛口，口以下残缺，看不出其完整器型。纹饰除了片叶纹以外，还有凤凰、蝴蝶等，多装饰在罐的口部及腹部。器里施釉仅过口，器外施半截釉。

Ⅲ式。卷口，直颈，颈以下残缺。颈部装饰以片叶纹，器里施釉仅过口，器外施釉不到底。

（2）枕

多系残片，分枕面及枕边两种，能分辨其形状的有如意形、八角形、腰圆形枕3种。

9．白地绘划黑花

共采集到9件标本，其中瓶7件，枕面一件，盆底一件。

瓶。身绘划缠枝牡丹，瓶底都装饰以莲花瓣纹。器里无釉，有明显的轮旋痕迹。

枕。枕面装饰以缠枝花纹，上面还有“秋千”二字。

盆。底绘划重叠牡丹，周围以枝叶环绕，盆底无釉。这类器物制作非常精致，是磁州窑最具代表性的作品。

10．白地绘酱花

器物采集不多，又都系残件，无法看出其完整器型。残片反面无釉，有明显的轮旋痕迹。

11．白地绘划酱花

共采集到8件标本，多系梅瓶残片。瓶身都绘划缠枝牡丹纹，瓶底部装饰莲瓣纹。器里无釉，有明显的轮旋痕迹。

12．珍珠地划花

采集的标本较少，其中枕面5件，灯一件，因系残件，无法辨出其器型。

13．三彩

器物的烧制温度较低，胎质粗松，呈粉红色。在我们所采集的标本当中，绝大多数为未上釉的素胎，有釉的器物也不少。

14．素胎

计有大盆、香炉及各式枕等。

大盆。均为折沿，盆心印有各种花纹。

香炉。为长方形，敞口，口以下直线内收，平底。器里无纹饰，器外四面多用印花装饰，花纹均凸起，纹饰题材有水波浪纹、荷叶纹、鹭鸶纹等。

枕。有长方形、腰圆形两种，枕面多采用划花装饰，纹饰有缠枝花卉及兔纹等。

15. 其他

还有黄釉、绿釉、黄绿彩及红绿彩等。其中黄釉、绿釉的器物为多，以绿釉的器物最为精美，红绿彩较少，仅采集到一件瓷小人。黄釉的器物多为盏托，黄绿彩多为枕头，绿釉的器物有枕、罐及大小碗等。

（二）冶子村遗址

烧制的器物有白釉、黑釉、白釉划花、白釉刻花、白地绘黑花等。其中以白釉器物为最多，白釉划花次之，白地绘黑花的器物很少。

1. 白釉

计有碗、盘、盆 3 种器皿，其中以碗为最多。

（1）碗

共有 9 式：

Ⅰ式。与观台遗址中的Ⅸ式碗的形制相同。高 3.1 厘米，口径 10 厘米，足径 4.9 厘米。

Ⅱ式。浅形，敞口，口以下内收，器身弧度小，碗心凸起一圈形，圈足。高 3.3 厘米，口径 11.5 厘米，足径 4.5 厘米。

Ⅲ式。敞口，口以下直线内收，小圈足。高 3.8 厘米，口径 13.2 厘米，足径 3.3 厘米。

Ⅳ式。敞口，口以下弧线内收，圈足，足内深而中心微凸起。高 4.7 厘米，口径 12.1 厘米，足径 3.8 厘米。

Ⅴ式。与观台遗址中的Ⅵ式碗的形制相同。高 4.4 厘米，口径 10.4 厘米，足径 4.7 厘米。

Ⅵ式。敞口，口微折，口以下弧线内收，高圈足，足内深而中心平坦。高 5.5 厘米，口径 12.1 厘米，足径 4.5 厘米。

Ⅶ式。与观台遗址中的ⅩⅥ式碗的形制相同。高 6.9 厘米，口径 18.8 厘米，足径 6.6 厘米。

Ⅷ式。浅形，敞口外撇，口以下弧线内收，圈足，足内深而中心微凸起。高 5.1 厘米，口径 17.6 厘米，足径 6.6 厘米。

Ⅸ式。与观台遗址中的ⅩⅤ式碗在形制上相同。高 7.8 厘米，口径 21.7 厘米，足径 7 厘米。

（2）盘

有 2 式：

Ⅰ式。与观台遗址中的Ⅴ式盘的形制相同。高 4.3 厘米，口径 19.3 厘米，足径 7.6 厘米。

Ⅱ式。与观台遗址中的Ⅲ式盘的形制相同。高 3.9 厘米，口径 18.5 厘米，足径 7.3 厘米。

（3）盆

有大小之分，均为直口折沿，口以下直线内收，圈足，足内浅，中心平坦。器里施满釉，器外施釉不到底，底足无釉。最大者口径36.7厘米，最小者口径31厘米。

2. 黑釉

仅有碗一种，可分4式：

Ⅰ式。与观台遗址中的黑釉Ⅰ式碗的形制相同。高4.8厘米，口径11.8厘米，足径3.6厘米。

Ⅱ式。卷口，口以下弧线内收，圈足，足内浅，中心平坦。器里满釉，器外施釉不到底，有垂釉现象，底足露胎。高4.5厘米，口径10.6厘米，足径4厘米。

Ⅲ式。敞口微撇，口以下微内折弧线内收，圈足，足内浅，底中心微凸起，底足无釉。高5.5厘米，口径11.4厘米，足径4厘米。

Ⅳ式。敞口微撇，口以下内折直线内收，圈足，足内浅，底中心微凸起。高5厘米，口径12.2厘米，足径4.2厘米。

3. 白釉划花

计有盘、碗、大盆3种器皿，其中盘、碗所占比重较大。盘、碗的型、式与白釉器物相同。纹饰与观台遗址中的白釉划花基本相同，但多为缠枝荷叶莲花纹，碗心常用一开放莲花为装饰，像观台那样流利的卷叶纹，在冶子遗址中还未发现。

大盆的形式与白釉盆相同，器里划有各种花纹，器外光素无纹饰。

4. 白釉刻花

仅采集到5件标本，均为盘的残片，盘的形式与白釉盘相同，盘内均刻有缠枝花卉，盘外光素，盘心有支烧痕迹。

5. 白地绘黑花

仅采集到枕边及“张家枕”字样款各一件。枕为八角形，边装饰以卷枝纹。“张家枕”为阳文楷书。

（三）东艾口村遗址

采集的遗物共分白釉、白地绘黑花、白地绘酱花三类。

1. 白釉

器物多为各式碗、盘。

（1）碗

有8式：

Ⅰ式。与观台遗址中的Ⅳ式碗在形制上相同。高3.2厘米，口径9.4厘米，足径4.2厘米。

Ⅱ式。浅形，敞口，口以下弧线内收，圈足。高5.5厘米，口径17.3厘米，足径6.8厘米。

Ⅲ式。与Ⅰ式碗在形制上相同，只是近底处胎较薄，足微外撇。高4厘米，口径10.4厘米，足径4厘米。

Ⅳ式。敦子形，敞口，口以下弧线内收，圈足，足内深而中心平坦。高 7.2 厘米，口径 17.5 厘米，足径 7.7 厘米。

Ⅴ式。与冶子村遗址中的Ⅷ式碗的形制相同。高 5.2 厘米，口径 16.3 厘米，足径 6.5 厘米。

Ⅵ式。敞口，口以下弧线内收，圈足，足内深，底中心微凸起。高 7.7 厘米，口径 21.3 厘米，足径 7.4 厘米。

Ⅶ式。与Ⅵ式碗的形制相同。高 8.7 厘米，口径 23.5 厘米，足径 4.8 厘米。

Ⅷ式。与观台遗址中的XⅤ式碗的形制相同。高 7.5 厘米，口径 21.3 厘米，足径 6.8 厘米。

（2）盘

有 2 式：

Ⅰ式。与观台遗址中的Ⅲ式盘的形制相同。高 4 厘米，口径 15.5 厘米，足径 5.8 厘米。

Ⅱ式。敞口，口以下弧线内收，器里起线为花瓣形，圈足，足内深，底中心微凸起。高 4.4 厘米，口径 20 厘米，足径 6.8 厘米。

2. 白地绘酱花

仅采集到一件瓶身残片，上面绘折枝桃，颜色鲜艳，残片的反面无釉，而有轮旋痕迹。

3. 白地绘黑花

器物采集得较多，其中绝大多数为枕头残片，有"张家造"字样款的也采集到不少，分横、竖两种，均为阳文戳记，楷书。其次是罐的残片，其他形制的器物还未发现。

（3）枕

有 3 式：

Ⅰ式。为如意头形，枕边装饰以卷枝纹，在枕面与枕边的转折处绘有一周粗线波浪纹，枕面纹饰变化多端，题材有人物、花卉、鹭鸶、芦雁、竹子、水波浪等，另外还有诗文。

Ⅱ式。为腰圆形，枕边装饰卷枝纹一周，在枕面与枕边的转折处绘几条粗线纹，枕面纹饰富于变化，纹饰题材与如意形枕相同。

Ⅲ式。为八角形，枕边绘卷枝纹一周，枕面先绘出粗线黑边，主题纹饰安排在其间，纹饰题材同如意形枕。

（4）罐

有 3 式：

Ⅰ式。与观台遗址中的白地绘黑花Ⅰ式罐的形制相同。

Ⅱ式。与观台遗址中的白地绘黑花Ⅱ式罐的形制相同。纹饰除了片叶纹以外还有卷枝纹。

Ⅲ式。桶形，敛口，口以下垂直，近底处内收，圈足。足内浅，底中心平坦。器身绘卷枝纹一周。器里满施黑釉，有明显的轮旋痕迹。器外光滑，近底处无釉，底足露胎。罐有盖，盖似洗形，圈形钮，盖面装饰片叶纹三组，盖口合于罐口之外，盖面满釉，盖心无釉。通高 18.4 厘米，腹径 15 厘米 足径 11.6 厘米。

以上三处遗址在烧造技术与艺术风格上都大体相同。烧制器物都以白釉为主，器型以盘、碗为最多，形制也都大同小异。器里都为满釉，器外施釉不到底，胎釉之间使用化妆土，底足露胎。因系叠烧，器里都留有支钉烧痕。黑釉的器物以观台为多。东艾口较为少见。白地绘黑花枕三处都有发现，但以东艾口为最多。“张家造”字样款多出在东艾口，冶子村只找到一件，而在观台遗址中未发现。白地绘黑花盖罐，观台与东艾口都有，以东艾口为最多，冶子村不见有此物。白釉划花的器物以观台和冶子村为最多，几乎到处可以拾到，而在东艾口却拾到得很少。白釉刻花的器物只在冶子村采集到 5 件，在其他两个遗址中都未发现。观台的白地绘划黑花、白地绘划酱花、绿地黑花、白釉剔花以及珍珠地划花等在其他两个遗址中都未发现，而这些器物都代表了磁州窑的最高水平，因而观台遗址的进一步调查与发掘就具有重要的意义。

二 调查发现的几个新品种

多年来只知道磁州窑烧白地绘黑花器物和带“张家造”的瓷枕，这次调查新发现了几个品种，从而丰富了对它的了解。

1. 白地绘划黑花

陈万里先生在《谈当阳峪窑》[1]一文里称为“剔画法”，日本人称它为“搔落法”。其制法是先在敷好化妆土的胎胚上绘以花纹，再用一种工具划出花蕊与叶的茎脉，然后施釉烧制而成，所以在这里取名为白地绘划黑花。此种器物在这次调查中虽然只采集到 9 件，但足以看出磁州窑的艺术水平了。过去有些学者把这类风格的器物都放到修武当阳峪窑之列，这次调查证明这类器物中有些是磁州窑的作品。

2. 白地绘划酱花

制法跟白地绘划黑花相同，很可能是由于绘划黑花在窑内因火候关系而有某种变化所引起的，但它却出现了一种极不寻常的艺术效果，也应该是磁州窑的一种特殊品种，调查前是极少看到的。

3. 白釉剔花

制法是先在敷好化妆土的胎上用刀剔去花纹以外的部分，留出花纹，再在花纹上用一种工具划出花蕊及叶的茎脉，然后施釉烧制而成。这类器物中比较好的，过去也都把它划入修武当阳峪窑，这次调查虽然还未发现类似修武当阳峪窑的作品，但也证明了磁州窑确有剔花一类的品种。

4. 三彩

过去一般也把三彩的器物特别是三彩枕定为磁州窑，但在磁州窑过去未发现过烧制三彩器物的遗址。我们在这次调查中观台镇发现了一处专门烧低温陶器的遗址。除了绿釉、黄釉的器物和黄绿褐三色凸纹枕以外，釉上加红绿彩的器物也有发现。同时在我们所采集的标本中，大多数为未上釉的素胎，这十分可靠地说明了这类器物是先烧好素胎，然后施釉烧制而成。证明磁州窑除了烧制高温瓷器以外，还烧制低温三彩的器物。

5. 珍珠地划花

陈万里先生在《调查平原河北二省古代窑址报告》[2]里提到在冶子村发现有珍珠地划花的碎片，这次调查观台遗址时采集到了好几件，由此说明两窑都烧制这类器物。

6. “张家造”绘黑花枕

陈万里先生曾在观台镇发现过有“古相张家造”印章的瓷枕好几个。但此次我们在观台调查的过程中，却未发现一件“古相张家造”或“张家造”的标本，在冶子村倒有发现。另外在东艾口遗址，发现了大量的“张家造”瓷枕碎片和烧制瓷枕的匣钵残片，有的枕上还粘有匣钵，除此以外未发现其他器物。无疑这是一处专门烧瓷枕的窑址。在这里采集瓷枕残片200余件，而带“张家造”字样款的就有20余件。这一遗址的发现解决了不少宋墓出土瓷枕的窑口，如邢台宋墓出土“张家造”蝠鹿纹枕、曹演庄宋墓出土的绿釉黑字枕及另一题诗枕都是它的产品。曹演庄宋墓出土的带“张家枕”款的白釉绘黑蜻蜓枕及保定出土带“张家枕”款的钓鱼枕，都可能是冶子村的产品。

三 磁州窑的装饰特征

磁州窑的装饰方法有胎上划花、刻花、印花，釉下绘黑花、绘划黑花、珍珠地划花，釉上加红绿彩、点彩、绿彩等多种。其中以釉下绘黑花、釉下绘划黑花最为精致。装饰题材有卷叶、卷枝、片叶、缠枝牡丹、缠枝荷叶莲花、莲花瓣、水波浪、花蝶、鹭鸶、凤凰、小兔、芦雁、游鱼纹等，其中以缠枝牡丹、缠枝荷叶莲花、莲花瓣、卷枝、片叶纹最为普遍。

这些装饰手法和纹饰题材都表明磁州窑器物的装饰是富于变化的，而且每种装饰手法和题材收到了各自不同的艺术效果。磁州窑的纹饰既具有写实的特征，又给予了适当的夸张，使其收到了新鲜活泼、自然豪放的艺术效果。这表现出了民间瓷窑的一个基本特征。

代表磁州窑装饰特征的有划花、剔花、白地绘黑花、白地绘划黑花、珍珠地划花等。

胎上划花的方法多用来装饰白釉器物，以卷叶纹、缠枝荷叶莲花纹最为常见，游鱼纹较少。其特点是纹饰清晰，线条深刻流利，构图严谨。它的做法是先在胎上划出主要纹饰，然后在主纹的空间，根据需要划出横竖不同的细线条纹，这样处理并不显得烦琐，反而突出了主题。

釉下绘黑花的方法磁州窑运用得最为普遍，可说是主流，一般比较精致的器物如枕、瓶、罐等都采用这种手法。釉下绘黑花具有绘画的风格，在用笔上接受了在纸上绘画的方法，如鹭鸶纹枕四枕面上画的鹭鸶和芦草的形象逼真，取得了近于绘画的效果。其次在罐上的片叶、凤凰、蝴蝶纹等还具有浓厚的民间剪纸的风格。这种装饰由于它的纹饰是在釉下，所以色泽非常鲜艳，具有永不褪色的特点，尤其黑花衬托白地增强了艺术效果。

釉下绘划黑花是已发现的磁州窑所有器物中最精致、艺术价值最高的代表作品。它是绘瓷艺人们根据植物的特点，在釉下绘花的基础上创造出来的一种装饰方法，这体现了艺人们善于观察和把握植物的特征。我们常见到的白地绘划黑花的器物，以牡丹、莲花瓣等题材居多。这种装饰方法是在绘好了的黑花上用一种工具划出叶筋、花蕊以及花、叶的边，这就不同于绘黑花了，不仅有叶有花，而且有叶筋花蕊，同时花瓣与花瓣、叶与叶的间隔都显示出来了。虽然在一件器物上布满了植物的叶和花朵，但并不给人以杂乱无章的感觉。

珍珠地划花的器物在遗址中发现得并不多，但都很精致，我们所采集的标本中，以瓷枕残片为多。这种装饰比较复杂，据当地老艺人讲，它的装饰过程大体经过 4 道工序，一是在敷好了化妆土的坯上划出主题纹饰；二是用一种打戳的工具在主题纹饰的空间打满细小的圆圈；三是上一层色粉，再用力蹭擦，然后拂去色粉，这样在纹饰的凹处就蹭满了色粉；四是上釉入窑烧制。这种装饰既不同于胎上划花，又不同于釉下绘花，而是独具一格。

剔花的方法是在敷好化妆土的胎上，剔去花纹外的部分，留出花纹，再在花及叶上划花蕊、叶筋，然后施釉烧制。这种剔花装饰能使花纹凸起，给人以浮雕的感觉，再用划花的方法把花蕊和叶筋表现出来，这样处理的结果，就如用一支牡丹花缠绕在器物上一样。

四 磁州窑烧瓷历史

1918 年，在河北省巨鹿县所发现的宋大观二年的故城遗址中，就发现了有磁州窑的器物，器型除了盘、碗之外，还有枕与梅瓶等。其中最突出的有剔花与白地绘黑花的器物。特别值得注意的是枕头的底部有横排阳文“张家造”款，字体与我们在东艾口村遗址中所发现的相同。这不仅解决了巨鹿出土的枕头的窑口问题，而且为东艾口村遗址的时代找到了可靠的证据[3]。说明其上限要早于大观二年无疑，至于早到什么时间，根据与枕片同时出土的两枚铜钱来看，一枚为“祥符通宝”，另一枚为“天禧通宝”，这对确定遗址时代的上限有一定的参考价值。这种“张家造”字样款虽然在观台遗址中未找到，但类似这种白地绘黑花的枕片也有发现，在器型与装饰风格上都完全相同。此外在观台遗址中所发现的白地绘划黑花以及剔花的做法是与河南修武当阳峪窑紧密相连的。釉下珍珠地划花又和河南登封窑有着密切的关系。两窑盛烧瓷器的时代都是在北宋时期，因而观台遗址的上限也不会晚于北宋。在冶子村遗址调查中，我们还发现有“张家枕”字白地绘黑花枕一件，其形制和花纹装饰，都和东艾口相同。虽然这次未发现有珍珠地和白地绘划黑花的器物，但从烧制器物的特征看，却与观台、东艾口完全相同，例如冶子村的Ⅸ式碗与观台的ⅩⅢ式碗、东艾口的Ⅷ式碗完全相同，这种碗内起线作花瓣形，是北宋时最为常见的一种碗式。又如冶子村黑釉Ⅰ式碗和观台黑釉Ⅰ式碗在形制上也完全相同，这种敞口小矮圈足碗在宋代耀州窑中也是常见的。

另外我们在三处遗址中都拾到了一些晚于宋代的遗物，如带有“王”字、“马”字的碗等。

从上面这些情况来看，磁州窑遗址的烧瓷时限，应为北宋到元代。

五 磁州窑与邻近诸窑的关系

这次调查还不能将磁州窑与邻近诸窑的关系全面反映出来，但为今后进一步研究提供了一些线索，因此摘要提出以供大家参考。

烧制所谓“磁州窑风格”瓷器的瓷窑遍及于中原地区黄河南北各地，这些窑跟磁州窑都有一定的关系，其中尤以河南修武当阳峪窑、禹县扒村窑的关系最为密切。

白地黑花的器物是磁州窑的匠师们所创烧的，而又广泛地影响到邻近几个瓷窑，形成了北方民间瓷器的主流。禹县扒村窑无疑是受磁州窑的影响而大量烧制白地黑花瓷器的，但它又不同于磁州窑，具有自己的风格。常见的器型有梅瓶、大盆等，纹饰为莲花瓣纹、水藻纹、游鱼等。梅瓶的肩部与足部以莲花瓣为装饰，器身都装饰水藻纹。大盆常见的纹饰有水藻和莲花瓣纹，二者经常搭配在一起组成一幅完整的图案，盘心有时还装饰游鱼纹。磁州窑不见有水藻纹，莲花瓣的画法也不相同。扒村窑的纹饰都画得比较潦草，布局也很琐屑，经常在一件器物上画得满满的，给人以烦琐杂乱的感觉。扒村窑的胎质虽然接近磁州窑，但比较粗糙，含砂较多，胎与釉之间的化妆土常与胎结合得不够紧密，因而器物表面常发生暴釉的现象。

河南修武当阳峪窑是以烧制白地绘划黑花为其代表的。磁州窑虽然也烧制这类器物，但不是主流，一般地说在质量上也不如当阳峪窑，因此当阳峪窑的技术很可能影响磁州窑，但却经过磁州匠师们的加工，创造出了具有磁州窑特点的器物，虽然两窑烧制的这类器物相比有许多共同之处，但也有好些不同之点，最明显的有：

第一，胎质不同。当阳峪窑的胎近于缸瓦胎，质粗松，内含砂较多，吸水性也较强。磁州窑的胎为灰色胎，瓷质细而坚，吸水性弱。

第二，当阳峪窑的釉质多莹润透亮，光泽较强，釉层较薄，表面常有细密的小开片，化妆土也较白。所以一般地说，当阳峪窑的白地洁白如玉，黑花如漆。磁州窑的白地则微黄如象牙，黑花如墨。

第三，由于当阳峪窑的胎为缸瓦胎，吸水性较强，所以一般在器物的里面都有釉。磁州窑则胎坚，吸水性较弱，所以器里一般都无釉。

关于珍珠地划花器物的烧制窑口，据目前所知就有河南密县、登封、宝丰、鲁山、修武等窑，时代以密县、登封为最早，磁州窑受其影响，而在质量上又有所提高。密县、登封处于首创时期，所以釉质不甚光润，珍珠地的颜色也往往不易被掌握，常有发黑的现象，而磁州窑的这项技术，继承密县、登封两窑而在质量上较密县、登封为好。磁州窑的珍珠地器物不仅釉质光滑润泽，而且把珍珠地的赭红色完全地呈现了出来。

烧制白釉划花碗的也有三处窑，质量以观台最好，汤阴鹤壁集次之，禹县扒村最差。由北而南，即观台影响鹤壁集，再影响扒村。

这次调查，在原有工作的基础上，初步搞清楚了磁州窑的面貌及与邻近诸窑的关系。过去一向被认为是当阳峪窑的白地绘划黑花的器物，在磁州窑中也发现了。磁州窑白地绘黑花器物种类也得到了充分证据，特别是“张家造”枕遗址的被发现及白地酱花、白釉剔花、绿地黑花、珍珠地划花等优秀品种的发现，加深了我们对磁州窑的认识。磁州窑不仅善于吸取其他窑的优点，而且具有创造性，同时影响其他各窑。因而可以说它代表了我国北方民间瓷器的烧造水平与艺术风格。

我们这次在磁县北部的隋代青瓷窑址贾壁村的复查中，没有发现晚于隋代的遗物。在南部各窑也未发现早于北宋的遗物。这是否表明在磁州的范围内没有唐代的遗存呢？唐代是我国陶瓷大发展的时期，而河南、河北又是当时北方烧瓷的集中地，近年来唐代窑址不断被发现就说明了这一点，然而磁州既然在隋代就已开始烧制青瓷了，而且到了北宋烧瓷水平又达到了这样的高度，很难想象磁州在唐代停烧而到北宋又突然兴起，这个问题有待将来调查发现。

磁州窑遗址广泛地分布在漳河两岸，此次因时间关系，我们只就上述几处遗址进行了调查，据当地农民反映，从观台镇到东、西艾口村一带，沿漳河两岸还有很多窑址。这次发现的烧“张家造”枕遗址只是其中的一处，如果能对这一地带再进行一次深入的调查和发掘，对研究北方民间瓷器的发展会有更大的帮助。

（原载《文物》1964 年第 8 期）

注释：

1《文物参考资料》1954 年第 4 期。

2《文物参考资料》1952 年第 1 期。

3《巨鹿宋器丛录》第一编瓷器题字。

Abstract of an Investigation into the Ruins of Cizhou Kiln

Li Huibing

The investigation into the ruins of Cizhou kiln in Guantai Town, Dongaikou, Handan City and at Yezi Village, southern Cixian County was made in April, 1964. Of the three sites investigated, Guantai Town site is the largest in term of area and the richest in varieties of porcelains fired. A dozen of porcelain varieties were fired in the three places, including white glaze, black glaze, dark brown glaze, white or green glaze with design of black patterns, white glaze with design of dark brown patterns, white glaze with cut design, white glaze with incised design, wares with incised design over pearl-pattern ground, wares with brown splashes, green glaze, wares with decoration in three colors, etc. Of the porcelain varieties found, six were newly documented. The majority of porcelain parts from the ruins are bowls and plates of similar type. The decoration style of Cizhou ware varied greatly. The dozen of porcelain varieties mentioned above say it all. Each decoration style has its artistic effects. Decorative themes, the characteristics of civil kilns, are leaf or branch scrolls, interlocking peony or lotus, lotus-petal, water ripples, butterfly, egret, phoenix, duck, fish, etc. The investigation shows Cizhou kiln operated from Northern Song dynasty to Yuan dynasty. Cizhou ware has a certain relevance to that of nearby kilns. For instance, white glaze with design of black patterns from Cizhou kiln is very much similar to that of Bacun kiln of Yuxian County, Henan Province. So are white glaze with incised design of Cizhou kiln and Dangyangyu kiln and wares with incised design over pearl-pattern ground from Cizhou kiln and Dengfeng kiln.

邢越二窑及定窑

陈万里

一 邢越二窑

李唐一代的工艺美术，是有它伟大的成就，以陶瓷来说，由陶而进展到瓷，唐代不仅是一个过渡时期，也可以说是完成时期。邢、越二窑，就是这个时期里的产物。邢是白，越是青，北方之白与南方之青，就平分秋色似的代表着南北的两个系统的作品。

（一）邢窑

邢窑之见于记载的，《新唐书·地理志》里载："河南府土贡埏埴盎缶，邢州巨鹿郡土贡磁器，越州会稽郡土贡磁器。"而李肇《国史补》里，亦有："凡货贿之物，侈于用者，不可胜记，丝布为衣，麻布为囊，毡帽为盖，革皮为带，内丘白瓷瓯，端溪紫石砚，天下无贵贱通用之。"是《新唐书》里所说的邢、越二窑，当时并贡于朝的；《国史补》则证明了邢窑是在内丘的。

李肇的《国史补》是写唐开元、贞元间（713～804年）的见闻，来补国史之缺，这就说明邢瓷在开元、贞元间，已为天下无贵贱所通用的器物。自然，它的创作时代，定在开元之前，也可以说就是在初唐，而盛行的时期则中唐可以肯定了的。《俑庐日记》里，提到清光绪三十三年定州发现李基墓，墓中明器瓷坯坚固如石，釉色如玻璃，色白而不滞，略如定器，而墓志年月，是咸亨二年（671年）四月，那是初唐时期，其为邢瓷无疑。因为有唐一代文献里提到白瓷的，就是邢窑，而那时候还没有定瓷，又是可以肯定了的。

嗣后大中初（847～859年，已在中唐之后），有一个郭道源的，擅击瓯。文献里这样说："用越瓯邢瓯十二，旋加减水，以筋击之，其音妙于方响。"云云；到了唐肃宗上元（760～761年）的时候，陆羽在他所著的《茶经》里，把邢、越二窑所出的瓷碗批评了一下，就是说："磁碗，越州上，鼎州次，婺州次，寿州次，岳州、洪州次。或者以邢州处越州上，殊为不然。邢磁类银，越磁类玉，邢不如越一也。邢磁类雪，越磁类冰，邢不如越二也。邢磁白而茶色丹，越磁青而茶色绿，邢不如越三也……越州磁、岳州磁皆青，青则益茶，茶作白红之色。邢州磁白，茶色红；寿州磁黄，茶色紫；洪州磁褐，茶色黑，悉不宜茶。"可见当时邢、越二窑已经并重，绝不是天下无贵贱通用之内丘白瓷独步的时代。而且陆羽还抑邢扬越，对于人们所称赞的邢瓷，抱着不以为然的态度。懿宗咸通（860～873年）的时候，皮日休的诗里，也有"邢客与越人，皆能造磁器……"之句，是邢与越，在晚唐的时候，依然是并重一时的两种瓷器，可是自此以去，就不再有人提及邢瓷，越瓷则徐寅、陆龟蒙辈，都有诗赞美它。而越瓷到了五代，更是独步一时。北方之邢，恐怕就在此时，黯淡下去。因此就会使人揣想到那时的邢窑工人，会在曲阳，另烧白瓷，开创了定瓷，或许有相当理由。不过邢瓷早为社会所通用，又何致一蹶不振到此地步。我个人认为内丘窑的白瓷，既为民间所好，自会延续下去。只是自晚唐以至五代及北宋初期，几成越瓷独霸的局面，所以邢瓷就没有什么记载；愈不能说，就会黯淡到一点没有前途。近 30 年来，巨鹿出土物品中，很多光素的白瓷，有的说是定瓷，有的说是北方影青。其实定瓷是有的，不成问题，因为大观（巨鹿城在大观二年为大水所淹没）的时候，正是定瓷出品最优美的时期，而其他白瓷之并非定窑的制作，或是不近定瓷的作风，概以所谓北方影青目之，这是一种曲解，毫无根据的。此种物品的器型，并非一般的盘、碗常品，颇多奇特的制作，如鸭座灯台等。我以为或者就是五代以至北宋的邢瓷，这是很可能的。否则为什么有这种优秀的作品，不能明确指出它的烧窑所在呢？此后如能找到邢窑地点，或者可以能解答此问题。

20 余年前在印度勃拉名纳巴特废址里，发现中国瓷片 4 片。其中两片是邢瓷，一片是越瓷，一片是宋以后作品。该城在公元 7 世纪时，最为繁荣，废灭于 1020 年（宋真宗时）。在印度这样一个僻远的地方，而有邢瓷碎片的发现，实一极可注意的事情。

此外，在唐的时代，平定、平阳、霍州均烧白器，平定窑又俗称“西窑”，是否对于邢窑之在河北为东而言，亦是一个问题。

关于邢瓷的本质，可以一谈的，就是它的胎土色白细洁，而极坚硬。釉白颇润泽，有时微微闪黄，带一点乳白色。胎与釉之间，有一层下釉，就是俗称的护胎釉。它的制品，就现在所认为是邢瓷的，平底折边（就是边的外缘凸起一条边沿，是别的瓷器上所不曾见到的）。胎厚重，平底处有没釉的。短嘴的把壶，纯然的唐的作风。白釉很厚，有到底的，亦有不到底的。烧成火度，已达千度以上。观察器型全面，令人有一种浑厚凝重的感觉，这与后来的定瓷，大不相同。并且邢瓷的器物上，没有一点花纹，质朴素净，正是唐代邢瓷的优点所在。它的烧造地点，说在内丘，可是在内丘县境内，未能找到烧窑的遗址。又说在临城，最近在内丘临城的邻接地带，有一处地名磁窑沟，发现烧窑遗址。可是在一块有明弘治七年及隆庆三年的窑神庙碑记里，未曾提到唐代。所得碎片，亦非白瓷，不能证明为邢窑所在的地方。因此邢窑遗址，究在何处，尚需等待以后的发现。

（二）越窑

越器的发现，是在抗日战争的前二三年间，当时杭州及绍兴方面所发现的，多为晋的时期的作品，最后发现了三国孙吴时期的越器，为数亦属不少。下面谈谈关于唐代的越器。

唐代越器，见于唐代文人记载的甚多，为方便起见，列表如次：

唐代文人记载越器表

姓　名	提到越器的词句	大概时期
顾　况	“越泥似玉之瓯……”（《茶赋》）	肃宗至德进士，约 757 年前后
陆　羽	《茶经》提到越器已见前文	肃宗上元间，约 761 年前后
孟　郊	“越瓯荷叶空……”	德宗贞元进士，约 785 年前后
施肩吾	“越碗初盛蜀茗新……”	宪宗元和进士，约 806 年前后
许　浑	“越瓯秋水澄……”	文宗太和进士，约 827 年前后
皮日休	“邢客与越人，皆能造瓷器……”	懿宗咸通间，约 861 年前后
郑　谷	“茶新换越瓯……”	僖宗光启进士，约 886 年前后
徐　寅	《贡余秘色茶盏》诗	昭宗乾宁进士，约 894 年前后
韩　偓	“越瓯犀液发茶香……”	昭宗龙纪进士，约 889 年前后
陆龟蒙	“九秋风露越窑开，夺得千峰翠色来……”	昭宗光化间，约 899 年前后

从这许多记载文字里，我们知道差不多自中唐以后的越器，更为人们所重视。王仁裕的《开元天宝遗事》里说：“内库有青瓷酒杯，纹如乱丝，其薄如纸，以酒注之，温温然有气相次如沸汤，名自暖杯。”徐寅的《贡余秘色茶盏》诗中有：“陶成先得贡吾君……”之句，又明确地知道青瓷之在宫中应用的，已在唐玄宗的开元天宝时候（713～755 年）；而到了徐寅那时候，已是晚唐的最后期。此种青瓷以及秘色茶盏，除了越窑以外，还有哪一种窑烧青色的物品呢？所以我说在这一段时期，宫上用此越器，民间又这样地重视，那么越窑之在当时，岂是所谓“天下无贵贱通用之”的邢瓷所能与之抗衡？不过在千载以下，要知道越器是怎样一种制作，真是有“李唐越器人间无”之叹！而自宋至清代的著作中，都找不到有什么人收藏着越器，或是看到过越器的记载。及至最近 20 年来，发现了余姚的上林湖窑以后，于是对于五代钱氏所烧造贡宋的瓷器，能够知道了它的真面目。只是李唐一代的越器，是怎样的一种制作，还不能肯定下来。最后经过几次的出土物品，才证实了唐代的越窑。

第一个发现，是有唐长庆三年（823 年）年号的一块墓志铭，那是 1934 年在浙江慈谷县鹤鸣场出土的。当时出土的情形不明了，所以墓中有无其他物品，那就不得而知了。这块墓志铭，先到了杭州，随后到了上海，卖给毛姓的，后来又听说转到一个广东商人的手里。原件全面作淡橄榄色青釉，略带灰色而有气泡，系半瓷胎性质。铭文在釉下，刻阴文，首行是：“唐故彭城钱府君姚夫人墓志并序”，文中的姚夫人，长庆二年死的，三年八月葬于上林东皋山之冈，这是一件有年代的青瓷墓志，亦可以说是证实唐代越窑的第一个发现。不过这块瓷版很粗劣，决不能代表唐代越窑的制作。

随之而来的第二个发现，是在1936年绍兴古城发现了一个唐户部侍郎北海王府君夫人的墓。有一块墓志砖，砖上有唐元和五年（810年）年号。自墓中出土的瓷器有好几件。青釉极光亮润泽，壶及小水池的制作都是很精美的，这才是唐代越瓷的标准物品，我在当时曾经写过一篇文章，中间有这么几句话："……就此仅有的实物来研究当时造瓷的进展，就技巧上说，确乎已经到了成熟的时期。"[1] 因此这个发现，对于究竟唐代的越器是怎样的，有了一个明确的答案。

王墓中所见越器，并无花纹，后又在市场上见到碎片一块，有"会昌七年（847年）改为大中元年三月十四日清明故记之耳"三行文字，是在釉里的，有划花，后来这块碎片，到了上海估客手里，竟复原了。同时我在杭州得到了一个小碗，碗心划花，跟碎片的划花完全是一个作风，可以确定是同一时期的制作。所划花纹，虽极简单，可是开辟了以后五代越器上繁复花纹的途径。这就是为什么我有"吾们看到了永康太康圹里的实物，同时看看五代时候精美的作品，就晓得在这时期中形成了一架桥梁的过渡产物，那就是现在元和圹里所见到的物品"[2] 这样的说法了。

由于以上的发现，可以确实知道唐代越器的究竟。而此种瓷器之在国外发现它的碎片，就现在所知道的，有以下几处：

埃及京城开罗南郊福司脱特，是一个荒废了的都城，在公元9世纪的时候，非常繁盛，到13世纪初叶，成为废墟。30年前有好些人在这废墟上发掘，得到碎瓷片很多，并且写了好些报告，其中就有越器的碎片，为数也不少。此种越器之到埃及，正是该城繁盛的时期，也就是公元9世纪，正当晚唐的时候。当时越器是经由阿拉伯人、波斯人的关系，到达埃及的。

波斯沙麻拉遗迹于1910年及1913年间，经过了两次发掘，发现了越窑的碎片。该地于838年（唐文宗开成三年）建筑成一都市，仅仅50年，就于883年（唐僖宗中和二年）成为废墟。越器就在那个时候，到了波斯各地方，因为那时候波斯湾是我国与波斯贸易上重要的港口，尤其是在公元9世纪中叶，阿拉伯商人跟我国贸易上的关系极为密切，东西交通，盛极一时，越器就大量地经由我国南部出口，到了波斯。由于以上两处发现了越器的碎片，说明了唐代已与埃及、波斯往来，是一个极重要的资料。

印度勃拉名纳巴特遗址，发现青瓷碎片，亦经证明是越器。

以上所谈的邢、越二窑，在完成中国瓷器的制作方面，有它重要的地位；何况由于邢、越二窑的发展，才开辟了宋代瓷器一个灿烂的局面，这一点，更是值得我们注意。此外，在唐代的鼎州、婺州、岳州、寿州、洪州各地，所烧造的物品，是怎样的器型与色釉，除了往年在长沙所出土的似可确定为岳州窑外，其他地方所烧造的，此刻还不能确切地指明，这又需要等待以后窑址的发现了。

至于唐以前的越器，上面已经说过，从三国的孙吴以至西晋，出土的实物极多，尤其是冢墓中的明器，如：粮食坛，上面附有凸雕的亭台人物禽兽；五壶尊，是在尊的肩部上面附着四个小壶，连着尊的口是5个，所以名为五壶尊；洗的种类颇多；此外天鸡壶、多孔双耳罐、耳杯、兽盘、猪栏、蛤蟆水丞等，种类真是繁多极了。窑址今人发现的，在萧山有九严窑，而我在萧山方面发现的有王家窑，在绍兴的有庙前窑、古窑庵前窑多处，因在越州区域以内，是以普通均称越窑。

唐以后的越窑，一般是专指余姚的上林湖窑。自五代以至北宋初期，由于钱氏的割据东南，大量烧造进贡的物品[3]，因之越器的制作，比之唐代的，有着显著的进步。同时开始了极繁复的图案花纹，这是唐代所没有的。

因此，在那时候的越器，是有着极高度的艺术。这就是为什么越器之在今日有它极崇高地位的缘故。及至吴越钱氏于太平兴国三年举地降宋以后，在文献方面还能知道兴国七年，尚有所谓殿前承旨监越州瓷窑赵仁济的记事[4]；而《宋会要·食货》第六“诸郡进贡”条下也有“熙宁元年十二月，尚书户部上诸道贡物……越州……秘色瓷器五十事”的一段记载。不过在这近百年间，太平兴国元年（976 年）至熙宁元年（1068 年）的越器是怎样的一种制作，并无实物可以证明。大约此后的上林湖窑，渐次走上了下坡路。所以《六研斋笔记》里，说到南宋时余姚秘色瓷，粗朴而耐久，这是很值得注意的。另外，《余姚县志》里说：“上林湖烧秘色磁器颇佳，宋时置官监窑焉，寻废。今各邑亦俱有民窑，然所烧大率砂罐瓦尊之类，不出境，亦粗拙，不焉佳器。”是上林湖窑最后的结果仅能烧些粗拙的东西，而十余年前我去调查时，并此粗器亦已不再烧造，只见砖瓦窑几处而已。

二 定窑

定窑向来说在定州，但是究在定州何处，没人能回答，只是近人叶麟趾有以下一段记载：

“定州窑在今河北曲阳县。定州窑地址，考诸文献所载，皆指为今之河北省定县。然经实地调查，则绝无窑址可寻。当地之大白村，虽属近似，亦无确实之证明。或谓自唐以来，所谓定州，非只限于今之保定与正定之间者，其地域较为广大，即保定、正定、平定等处，亦皆包括在内，总名曰定州，故凡由此等地方所出窑器，均称为定窑云。是说未免过于广义者，因平定之窑，俗称西窑，其器与所谓定器比较，显有不同之点。且保定、正定，亦皆无相当之窑址也。曩者闻说曲阳产磁，偶于当地之剪子村发现古窑遗迹，并拾得白瓷破片，绝类定器，据土人云，昔之定窑，即在此处。又附近之仰泉村，亦为定器出产地，然已无窑迹矣，此说诚有相信之价值。且旁考地理上之关系，则曲阳距定县四十里，唐名恒阳，原属定州，盖所称定州，乃指其大地名而言，非专指今之定县。即如唐之邢州窑，在距今邢台县约五十里之内邱县，饶州窑在距今鄱阳县即昔之饶州府约一百八十里之浮梁县，是其最明显之比例也。现今曲阳县尚有制陶者，器虽粗糙，然确属定窑之本派。或谓定窑废灭于元末，盖因当时已无优良之品，因无关于此后曲阳之制作也。”这是一个极重要的发现。同时检查《曲阳县志》，亦有以下的记载：

卷一下“舆地”条：“……涧磁村：县北四十五里，东至北镇二里，西至韩家村五里，南至灰岭村十里，北至树沟村十里……”

卷六《山川石迹考》:“……涧磁岭，采访册在县北六十里。按岭在龙泉镇之北，西北灵山镇十里，上多煤井，下为涧磁村，宋以上有磁窑，今废。”

“……龙泉镇，今俗称南北镇，镇旧有镇使副瓷窑税使等官。”

卷一〇、卷一一《土宜物产考》第六条:“……土性:山岭——县境三面皆山，土石相间多不能种禾麦，尚宜树木。露山一带，惟出煤矿，龙泉镇则宜瓷器，亦有出滑石者。”

“……土产：黄瓷盆瓮之属，出恒水左右。白瓷龙泉镇出，昔人所谓定瓷是也。亦有设色诸式，宋以前瓷窑尚多，后以兵燹废。宜请求旧法，参以新式，以复其利。”

《曲阳县志》里明明说有瓷窑，而且说及定瓷，并旧有瓷窑税使等官，这是极重要的记载。抗战期间，曲阳沦于敌区，当时日人小山富士夫曾经去过，并采取碎片极多。我于1951年间去该县调查，目的是要采集些碎片，并确定它是否定窑遗址。

由定县先到曲阳，再由曲阳去北乡灵山镇，往东是涧磁村，往西是东西燕山村。现在分别就调查所得述之如次：

涧磁村即叶麟趾记载的剪子村，也就是县志所称的“涧子里”、“涧子村”。从灵山镇往东，经过王家村、岗北村，计7里。该村西南有一小溪流，南面是大溪（即恒水），旱季时，都干枯无水。大溪南是灰岭，北是马头山。东去北镇二里，过大溪后，就是南镇，南北镇合起来就是志书上的龙泉镇。

村直北，跨过几处高地，是一个很大的土丘，高约八九米，径约30米，完全是碎片同工具所堆成的。土丘之东，又一土丘，较小一点。由此往东，有一东西方向的地沟，两边尽是碎片。在此地区，假定它是第一区窑址。碎片中划花的特多，素地的较少。胎骨洁白细腻，色釉润泽、匀净，是定窑标准的作品。碎片中得到一块瓷枕的侧面，这是很重要的，因为由此可以知道定窑的瓷枕是怎样的一回事了。

村东约一里半路，快到北镇了，田间有巨碑二，及白石狮子一对，即是法兴寺的故址。寺毁于当时日敌的三光政策之下，已无一间房间留存。附近有云龙的碎片极多，去年还出过整器10件，都是划龙的，其中有一件，盘底有“尚食局”三字。

村西约半里地，在山溪北面的高原上，碎片又是成丘地堆积着。此处除划花外，印花的也不少，是为第二区窑址，不过较之第一区范围略小。

东西燕山村两村相连，离灵山镇西8里，叶麟趾所未曾提及的，或即叶所称仰泉村之误。村西有一条溪河。村北凤凰山，西北高峰是鸡冠岩山。远望东西燕山村，是在山坡上。碎片散在两燕山村之北，两燕山之间，及西燕山村之西，发现有印花、划花及素地的三种，纯系习见之定窑风格。在当地人家，见有印花云龙盘残片。村西地区，白釉不到底的粗瓷碎片不少，可见此处所烧造的，有粗细两种不同的作品。另有玻璃块随处都可拾得，有黑色的，有暗蓝色、暗绿色的，想亦系当年烧造过的东西。

西村之南，有近代式民窑一处，成立在“七七事变”以前，抗战期间，机器被敌寇搬走了，窑场房屋全毁。胜利后恢复，烧造坩埚，极耐用，惜以技师他去，因而停顿。瓷土用本地北山所产，釉石在30里外的山里，用煤亦取之本地，烧瓷的一切条件俱极优越，如能开发，颇有前途。

就涧磁及东西燕山两处比较来说，当然窑场区域，以涧磁为广，在西燕山就差得远了。作品方面，东西燕山优秀的也有，可是比较粗一点的都在东西燕山。工具中，独多圆圈式的，大小不一，这是定窑覆烧用的工具，到处都是，可见当年生产能力之高。

此外在灵山镇之东，约三里左右岗北村，现有窑20余座，大都烧缸，也有几处烧黑釉粗瓷的。《大明会典》第一一册卷一九四《工部》一四里关于陶器部分，宣德年间题准光禄寺每年所需酒缸瓶坛，分派河南布政司方面，除钧磁二州外，"真定府曲阳县酒缸一一七只，十瓶坛四二七四个，七瓶坛六一〇〇个，五瓶坛六二四〇个，酒瓶一〇三四一个，每年烧造解寺应用"。又嘉靖三十二年题准："曲阳县缸瓶共一七七六五件，该银一九九两八钱八分，外增脚价银一八五两九钱九分三，总该银一一四〇两六银五分八，通行解部。召商代买，如遇缺乏，止行磁州真定烧造，免派钧州。"此为曲阳在明代宣德年间，只烧缸窑之证。而明代曲阳的缸窑是在灵山附近，大致也不会错的。

就瓷窑所发现的遗品说，可以确定此处为定窑遗址，毫无疑问，因为定器有它的特征，如刻划花纹的图案，如釉上的泪痕，以及细腻洁白瓷胎等，都是很容易与其他仿定的瓷器区别的。

至于定窑的创始，是否在李唐时期，实在是一个不易解决的问题。可是在《曲阳县志》卷一一记载着，五（王）子山院和尚舍利塔记碑，说碑石在五（王）子山法兴院之西数十步[5]，额篆题"大周五（王）子山禅院长老和尚舍利塔"。而在立碑人的姓名中，有"□□使押衙银青光禄大夫检校太子宾客兼殿中侍御史充龙泉镇使钤辖瓷窑商税务使冯翱"的题名，而碑石建立于大周显德四年二月。那么，在五代后周的时候，曲阳龙泉镇已确有瓷窑，而且规模已是相当的大，出品又是相当的多了，所以有瓷窑商税务使，在龙泉镇以监收税银，这就可以证明龙泉镇在五代的时期中，已经烧造所谓定窑的瓷器，同时还可以证实一点，就是五代时期中的定器，已经大量地生产了，那么定器的技术，在那时候必定发展到了相当成熟的阶段。因此曲阳龙泉镇瓷器，在唐时已经烧造，又是可以确信的事实。而唐代所烧造的遗片，假定能够发掘遗址，必能充分证实这一点。

定瓷到了北宋，已为宫廷中所应用，《宋会要》里是这样记载的："磁器库在建隆坊，掌受明越饶州、定州、青州白瓷器及漆器以给用。……宋太宗淳化六年七月，诏拣出纳磁器库诸州磁器缺璺。"同时一方面供宫中应用，另一方面亦供应着社会上需要。《曲阳县志》有一段记载，说明这个事实。就是在天成元年（后唐明宗时，926年）乡贡进士马夔重修五（王）子山院碑，碑面的右侧，有一段"贩磁器客赵仙重修马夔碑记"碑文行书，文云："愚尝谓此山乃境中绝胜之所也。然有记事之碑，经其雨雪，字体亏残，愚虽不达，恻然悯之，于是请匠以重镌之，庶后观者得以（缺），时宋宣和二年（宋徽宗时，1121年）庚子八月十五日中山府贩磁器客赵仙修记。"下题"院主僧智弁岳阳杨刊"。就这个史实可以知道当时的定瓷是有着广大市场的。而《格古要论》里，也提到"宋宣和政和间窑最好"。可见当时出品，最为优秀。同时在这样大量生产之下，定会发生粗制滥造的弊病，因此，这就是可以说明东西燕山村所发现的遗片，为什么会远逊于涧磁村遗片的理由了。

同时并因定器有芒（疑是覆烧的毛边），宫中改用汝瓷。不久有靖康之变，北方瓷场受到极大波动，烧定瓷的优秀工人，南边到景德镇，遂烧所谓影青的青白瓷，这是有一脉相承的事实可以证明的。其次，景德镇居民的祖先，颇多是曲阳籍贯，也是一个很可以注意的事情。而北方的定瓷，就在这样的情况之下衰落下来。不过定瓷的存续时间有多么长，此时还未易肯定下来。

就定瓷的制作说，所谓划花、刻花是模仿着越器的。因为唐至五代的越器，在国内有着极大的声誉，定瓷之受到它的影响，可以想象而知。不过印花的方法，却是定窑的独创，即在越器中亦未曾见到此种制作。而定器的来源，或者是由制作邢瓷的工人，转而在曲阳方面，开一新局面，亦有此种揣测，这是值得注意的事。至于定窑所制作的器具，以盘、碗为最多，瓶、壶为最少。瓷胎洁白，色釉微带黄而润泽异常。印花的图案，编排配置，极为整齐。大盘的盘心用莲花鲤鱼为图案的较多，四围多以牡丹、萱草、飞凤为图案。划花的花纹，自由放纵，跟印花的大不相同。刻花的刚劲有力，要以刻莲花瓣的算是典型。瓷枕极少见，故宫藏有一件，以孩儿侧卧的姿态作为枕面的长方枕，雕刻最精，是定瓷中极为少见的。定瓷中还有如苏东坡诗中所赞美的“定州花瓷琢红玉”的红定。周辉的《清波杂志》、蒋祈的《陶记略》都有记载。究竟是怎样的一种作品，至今还是疑问。墨定在项子京《历代名瓷图谱》中，曾经说到，仅见一种，就是一件墨定凫尊，在明代已成为稀有的珍品了。唯近来出土的黑釉碎片，真如漆黑，胎质、器型，都是定的作风，是否就是墨定，亦属疑问。紫定，项谱中有 5 件，说明釉色是“烂紫晶澈，如熟葡萄，璀璨可爱”，又说：“色紫若茄苞，晶莹润澈”云云。是紫定色釉的紫，如葡萄，又如紫茄，绝不是普通一般人所指的紫定了。《格古要论》中说到定器，亦以紫定色紫，黑定黑如漆，价高于白定云云。此外，定瓷中还有画金花的。南宋末周密的《志雅堂杂抄》中说：“金花定碗，用大蒜汁调金描画，然后再入窑烧，永不复脱。”徐兢《宣和奉使高丽图经》中亦有“金花乌盏，翡色小瓯，银炉汤彝，皆窃效中国制度”的说法，是墨定上有金花之证。而东坡诗上所谓“定州花瓷琢红玉”，又是说明红定上是有金花的。抗战前，据闻出土过几件金花的定碗，可惜都流落到海外去了。

南渡后，各处仿烧定窑的不少，见之记载的，如昌南（景德镇）仿定，亦名粉定。元时彭窑仿定器，土脉细白，与定相似，称为新定。象山窑（浙江象山县）所烧的似定器，磁州白釉器，无泪痕，亦有划花、印花及素瓷诸种，价高于定。萧窑（江苏徐州萧县白土镇）烧白釉器，胎质颇薄。宿州专仿定器，釉色酷似北定。临川窑（江西临川）胎薄，白釉微带黄色。南丰窑（江西南丰县）胎虽厚，白瓷跟临川相近。德化窑（福建德化）称为白建。耀窑（陕西耀县）白似牛乳，似粉汁，似熟米，薄胎，有暗花，白釉极厚。有开片，胎比定厚，色白比之定瓷稍黄，因有暗花及开片，所以跟定瓷有区别。饶州窑体薄，釉润，色白，但是不及定器。此外，吉州、泗州、宣州各窑，均是仿造定器的。究竟怎样可以区别各处所烧造的仿定瓷器，必须在各地找得窑址后，才能解决这些问题。

（原载《文物参考资料》1953 年第 9 期）

注释：

1 见《瓷器与浙江》书中《唐代越器专集》引言。

2 见《唐代越器专集》引言。

3 详见《十国春秋》、《宋会要》、《宋史》、《吴越备史补遗》、《宋两朝供奉录》、《枫窗小牍》诸书，以及我著的《瓷器与浙江》。

4 周密：《志雅堂杂抄》。

5 县志里说，五（王）子山在涧磁岭西北，下有五（王）子山院。

Abstract of Xing Kiln, Yue Kiln and Ding Kiln

Chen Wanli

Xing kiln represented the northern white glaze, whereas the Yue kiln represented celadon of the South. Xing kiln was recorded in literatures. Intellectuals had made comments on then famous Xing and Yue kiln. According to literature record, Xing kiln was reportedly located in Neiqiu County, Hebei Province. The body of white glaze ware of Xing kiln is pure white and hard and the glaze is fine and glossy. It was fired at a temperature of over 1,000 °C. The shaping of Xing kiln ware is simple but vigorous. It has a flat bottom and everted flange. It is generally without ornamentation, reflecting the decorative style of Tang dynasty, i.e. simple and elegant. The discovery of white glaze porcelain of Xing kiln in India indicates that the porcelain was widely used domestically and abroad, matching the records in books of Tang dynasty. Yue kiln was located in Yuyao and Cixi City, Zhejiang Province. Based on the descriptions and praises of many literati, Yue kiln was prominent at the time. Before the discovery of Yue kiln site at Shanglinhu, knowledge on Yue kiln was gathered from its earlier products and the Qian's tribute porcelains in Five Dynasties were not known. Knowledge on Yue kiln in Tang dynasty was gathered from unearthed artifacts with date. The discovery of Yue kiln wares in Egypt, Persia, India, etc. suggests their widespread use at the time. Ding kiln was documented, too. Information on the kiln is controversial, though. In 1951, the author conducted an investigation into the kiln sites at Hejian and Dongxiyanshan Village. The investigation confirmed those kiln sites were the ruins of Ding kiln. It started to fire in Tang dynasty and did not stop until Jin dynasty or even later. Ding kiln wares are with incised design and glaze drops. The making of the Ding wares and the imitation by other kilns were discussed.

邢窑刍议

叶喆民

邢窑是我国陶瓷史上驰名古今、蜚声中外的一处窑场，也是悬而未决的一个疑团。尽管早在唐人李肇、陆羽、皮日休等的诗文里都曾提到过它的烧造地点和器物特征[1]，多年来人们根据文献到河北内丘去寻访，始终未能找见其窑址。5年前河北邯郸陶瓷公司曾派人去它的邻县临城南程村一带调查，找到过大批白瓷残片及窑具，送来故宫博物院鉴定其年代。鉴定结果虽属宋代之物，但我们认为很有可能发现更早的唐代白瓷。我们于1977年春去该地，在南程村与射兽村一带找见不少白釉、黑釉、青釉和附有印花、划花、绘花装饰的宋金元时期的瓷片，但未发现唐代瓷片。

1980年夏，河北临城二轻局陈二印、张书太等同志会同县局领导及文化馆、河北师大等有关同志沿北渠两岸调查了7处窑址。找到了具有唐代特征的粗白瓷片，取得了令人可喜的成果。同年秋，笔者与傅振伦先生及王舒冰、杨文山二同志应邀去临城、内丘古窑址进行复查，在同志们的通力合作下，又获得了新的线索及大批资料。除在河北岸的岗头、澄底一带发现具有唐代"玉璧底"特征的白瓷残片之外，还见到个别平底足的白釉残器，以及具有金代鸡腿瓶特点的黑釉残器。邢瓷研制小组的林玉山、陈二印、陈月恩等同志，终于在更北方的祁村、双井一带发现了质地精白、具有初唐特征的一件白瓷壶残器，此壶短流，圆肩，丰腹，平底，胎釉细白莹润，正与陆羽"邢磁类雪"的誉词相合。这些都为探讨邢窑创造了十分有利的条件。现就两次见闻略抒管见，以供邢瓷研究的参考。

邢窑白瓷，前人多与越窑青瓷并论。除陆羽《茶经》外，皮日休《茶瓯》诗有"邢客与越人，皆能造瓷器。圆似月魂堕，轻如云魄起"的赞语。国外文献中提到埃及福斯塔特(Fostat)和伊拉克萨麻拉(Samarra)等地发现的唐代白瓷残片也多认为是邢窑制品。所以一般很少考虑它的上限究竟早到何时。而今在临城祁村、双井一带发现的平底白瓷壶和短流青瓷壶残片，说明其上限至少是唐初，烧造历史有可能上溯到隋代。这不仅符合多年来我们调查唐宋古窑所见的一般规律，而且有传世的遗物可以参照。例如故宫博物院陈列的隋代白瓷碗、罐，以及历史博物馆陈列的隋李静训墓出土的大量白瓷器，其中著名的白釉天鸡壶，胎釉的精细洁白与祁村出土的白瓷壶近似。而隋代白瓷迄今犹未找见窑址，是否可与今天的初步发现联系一起来考虑？就是说至少有一部分隋代白瓷将可能因此而找到归宿，这是值得深入调查研究的一个问题。

过去由于邢窑窑址未曾发现，人们对于传世或出自邢台地区唐墓中比较精致的白瓷，多根据《茶经》

所谓“类银”,“类雪”的说法而假定为“邢窑”瓷器,其中有的同临城窑址出土的唐代白瓷残片的特征相似。而祁村出土的瓷片，其胎釉坚细白润的程度比之近代白瓷略无逊色。特别是平底或玉璧形底的作品均未见有白土化妆的迹象，并且在玉璧形圈足心内施加白釉。这一做法与唐代曲阳窑(定窑前身)完全一致，说明当时瓷土的淘练和釉料的调配，以及制作技术都已相当精工。而在岗头附近所出玉璧形底的白瓷，胎质灰粗，釉光混浊，有的显然施加了化妆土，圈足周围露胎无釉，制作远较祁村白瓷粗陋。至于澄底村所出晚唐五代白瓷，有的只在器里施加一层白土化妆，釉色洁白，器外则薄施亮釉，露出胎体本色有如银灰。三者对比可以看出邢窑并非一概使用化妆土，而是因其时代早晚、烧制地点乃至瓷土质量、工艺精粗之不同而异。从而进一步体会到“雪”白与“银”灰的形容非常真切。

但是，以前一般中外文献在谈到瓷器上最初使用化妆土的方法时往往即指为邢窑白瓷。今日看来这一说法至少不够全面。尤其近年在一些隋代青瓷中也曾见有使用化妆土的现象，也说明这一问题值得商榷。前几年有关科研单位曾对隋代白瓷与山西浑源出土的唐代白瓷作过鉴定，前者白度为 60.5 度，后者为 61.8 度。今日所得临城祁村白瓷，如能再作测试，将不仅有助于了解邢窑白瓷的质量，而且有利于区别窑口和全面认识唐代制瓷工艺水平。此外，该地还出土有唐代青瓷残片，也是说明邢窑烧制品种与白瓷发展历史的重要物证。

唐代白瓷除邢窑外，尚有不少名窑。仅就个人足迹所至和从文献所知，有河北曲阳，河南密县、巩县，山西浑源，江西婺源和四川大邑以及广州的瓷窑等。例如唐代大诗人杜甫《又于韦处乞大邑瓷碗》诗中写道:“大邑烧瓷轻且坚，叩如哀玉锦城传。君家白碗胜霜雪，急送茅斋也可怜。”唐人李奉敕修撰的《本草》有“白瓷屑，平无毒，广州良，余皆不如”的说法。结合杜甫、皮日休、陆羽等人的形容、比喻，对照今日祁村出土的白瓷壶、碗，不难看出当时的白瓷质量是相当高的。又如清人蓝浦的《景德镇陶录》中说，唐初武德年间 (618～626 年)，镇民陶玉、霍仲初已能烧制“土惟白壤”、“体稍薄”、“色素润”、“佳者莹缜如玉”、“称为假玉器”的白瓷。祁村出土的白瓷，无论在胎釉的白度和坯体的薄度乃至瓷化程度方面都可与之比拟。此外，唐人段安节《乐府杂录》说:唐大中年间 (847～859 年)，乐师郭道源“用越瓯、邢瓯十二，旋加减水，以筋击之，其声妙于方响”(“方响”是一种铜铁制打击乐器，其声清浊随质之厚薄而不同)。这一记载说明邢瓷胎体如不能充分烧结就不可能发出像金属那样清脆动听的声音。我国文物界至今仍保留着一种用指叩敲以鉴别陶瓷的传统方法，一般认为声音清脆嘹亮的就已瓷化。而在西方则习惯于使用迎光透视的鉴别方法。这些都是合乎科学道理的，因为它们表明坯胎中未能融熔的部分之间，充满玻璃相与否，纯净度和均匀程度如何，我国古瓷的主要特征就是玻璃相较多。可惜祁村出土的白瓷尚无完整器物可供试验，但从其胎体的坚致与细薄程度来看，这段记载似非无稽之谈。古代阿拉伯商人苏林曼 (Suleinman) 在 851 年 (唐大中五年，与郭道源击瓯的故事同时) 所写的笔记中说："中国人持有白色黏土制作的碗，它像玻璃一样美丽，可以看见里面所盛的液体。"由祁村出土的白瓷看来，还不具备这样的透影性能。

关于临城、内丘的地理沿革，据《新唐书》卷三九《地理》三，临城隶属"赵州赵郡"。注："本房子，天宝元年更名，天祐二年更曰房子。"内丘则隶"邢州巨鹿郡"。注："武德四年隶赵州，五年来属。"如此，则内丘、临城二地过去在同一大行政区内时合时分。若从当前实际情况观察，则传为邢窑遗址的磁窑沟而今已半部划入临城境内。类似这种区划的变迁在历史地理上亦不乏其例。以河北名窑而论，如举世闻名的磁州窑产地磁县，在最近几十年间，就曾时而划入河南，时而划归河北；号称"五大名窑"的定窑，却不在定县而在曲阳。既然"河北三大古窑"中的两处如此饱经沧桑，而其余的一个邢窑又何独不然呢？根据上述一些文献、事例和目前掌握的实物资料看来，我认为临城的几处唐代窑址就是所谓"邢窑"的一部分，至少也是邢窑的正统或亲支近派，这一点是可以肯定的了。

值得注意的是，通过两次实地调查，初步发现一些有趣的现象和线索，即出土瓷片从时代风格看愈往北愈早。例如前面所举初唐平底白瓷壶和短流青瓷壶等残片只在祁村、双井一带有所发现。而岗头出土者多是玉璧形底的中、晚唐作品，澄底所见最早的白瓷不过是晚唐、五代之物。至于射兽、南程二村以及东、西磁窑沟所出瓷片则是宋元以后之物。最近又在山下村发现了宋代的印花白瓷，而未见有唐代产品。另一迹象是，在岗头与南程发现有金代常见的鸡腿瓶残片。这类黑釉器物在以前两度去定窑调查时也发现不少，联系《金史》关于"真定府土产有瓷器"的记载，说明它们到金代并未断绝烧造。

据南程村老年人说，南程村原名"大碗窑"，相传本地制瓷工人曾迁移去观台 [2]。而 1977 年去该村调查时还听说县城西北约 20 公里的官都曾发现过窑址，但因时间仓促，未能进行实地考查。另外，在西磁窑沟北坡一带堆积瓷片及窑具甚多。附近有俗称"尧舜庙"的遗址，庙已无存，据说有一石碑已断作桥基，过去烧窑时在此祭神。按北方不少唐宋古瓷窑曾有窑神庙之设，如陕西耀州窑，河南当阳峪窑、鹤壁集窑、禹县扒村窑、宜阳二里庙窑以及山西榆次窑等，皆有窑神庙。神名"柏林"、"百灵"或"伯灵"，碑亦名"德应侯碑"。估计"尧舜"或是"窑神"之讹称。惜已无碑记可考。又于农民家中曾见白地黑花题诗瓷枕残片，似北宋磁州窑而不加化妆土，胎质缜密，釉色白中泛青，黑中发褐，别具一格。据说出自地下约 7 米的土层内。联系前面所闻，对当地有可能发现较早的窑址提供了一点线索。是否内丘邢窑的古窑址由于地貌的变迁已被埋没也未可知。

在两次调查临城古窑址过程中，所见到的瓷器残片多是碗、盘、壶、罐、盆、钵、枕之类的日用器皿，而最近在祁村所获残片中尚有小瓷马及骑马俑（儿童玩具）各一件。这些现象同其他唐宋民窑产品之粗细兼备是一致的。而且它自唐以来一直未断烧造，一方面固然由于本身具有得天独厚的资源与优良传统的技术，另一方面也是和它那面对人民生活的生产方向分不开。因此它能在划时代的白瓷中名列前茅，流芳千古。只是比起当时与之齐名的越窑来，除了二者在釉色上各有千秋外，邢窑无论在造型的多样或纹饰的变化方面均显得美中不足。尤其到晚唐五代时期竟被越窑"秘色"瓷[3]所专美，形成所谓"陶成先得贡吾君"[4]的局面。同时在部分越窑青瓷中还有釉下彩镂孔和所谓"金釦越器"的贴金、镶金装饰技法。相对而言，邢窑却不似从前那样为人重视了。至于后来居上的宋代定窑、磁州窑，更以其精湛的印花、刻花、剔花、绘花等多种技法取胜，尤其是剔划花的方法使化妆土的利用在磁州窑型的装饰上出现一个崭新的阶段，在造型方面更加丰富多样，实用美观。虽然这些都与当时的社会风尚、时代背景有关，然而目前所见传世唐代邢窑作品多是光素无纹，式样单调，个别窑址出土的五代残片偶有划花之作，宋以后愈加粗率。尽管如此，并不等于否定它在唐代陶瓷史上的地位。我认为邢窑到后来显然有些故步自封，甚至一蹶不振，例如在东西磁窑沟窑址所出元代以后残片，极少精细的白瓷而多是黑釉粗制的缸、盆之类。这一点或许也是它之所以昙花一现而终于默默无闻的一个原因。

在总结历史经验的同时，却见南至磁窑沟以北 20 公里范围内，至今蕴藏有大量的瓷土、石英、长石和煤矿。面对如此取之不尽、用之不竭的制瓷大好资源，倘能就地取料，充分利用这些优越条件，在传统的基础上取长补短，推陈出新，深信古树新花，必将重放异彩，为我国陶瓷史谱写出更加光辉的篇章。

（原载《文物》1981 年第 9 期）

注释：

1（唐）李肇《国史补》："凡货贿之物，侈于用者，不可胜记。丝布为衣，麻布为囊，毡帽为盖，革皮为带，内丘白瓷瓯，端溪紫石砚，天下无贵贱通用之。"

（唐）陆羽《茶经》："邢磁类银"、"邢磁类雪"。

（唐）皮日休《茶瓯》诗："邢客与越人，皆能造磁器。圆似月魂堕，轻如云魄起。枣花势旋眼，苹沫香沾齿。松下时一看，支公亦如此。"

2 河北邯郸所属，观台为宋磁州窑主要产地。

3（宋）叶寘《垣斋笔衡》："秘色唐世已有，非始于钱氏，大抵至钱氏始以专供进耳。"

（清）蓝浦《景德镇陶录》及朱琰《陶说》中也说："越州烧进，为供奉之物，臣庶不得用，故云秘色。"

4（唐）徐寅《贡余秘色茶盏》诗："捩色融青瑞色新，陶成先得贡吾君。巧剜明月染春水，轻旋薄冰盛绿云。古镜破苔当席上，嫩荷涵露别江濆。中山竹叶醅初发，多病那堪中十分？"

Abstract of a Discussion on Xing Kiln

Ye Zemin

Xing kiln is a well-known kiln. Following the clues in literatures, the author paid several inspection visits to Neiqiu County, Hebei Province, but no ancient kiln sites were found. In 1977, the author paid another visit to Lincheng County, no relics of Tang dynasty was found either. During the 1980s, local relic experts conducted seven investigations into ancient kiln sites, leading to the finding of coarse white glaze porcelains. The same year, the author re-visited the site where coarse white glaze porcelains were found, and new clues and information were gathered. Later on in Qicun, Shuangjing, fine white glaze porcelains were found, matching literature records of as white as silver or snow. The firing history of Xing kiln may be traced back to Sui dynasty. Some of the Palace Museum, the History Museum of China collections of white glaze porcelains and unearthed tomb artifacts may be from Xing kiln. Specimens of white glaze collected from Xing kiln sites show some of its products are fine and some applied with engobe. The idea that all Xing kiln white glaze porcelains applied with makeup soil is inaccurate. Apart from Xing kiln, there were many other kilns fired white glaze porcelains in Tang dynasty. Historically, Lincheng and Neiqiu belong to the same administrative region. The finding of porcelains of Song and Jin dynasties in Lincheng suggests Xing kiln did not stop firing during this time period. The existence of Yao and Shun Temple and the discovery of porcelain toys, such as pony, in the kiln sites, indicate that just as other kilns, Xing kiln produced both fine and coarse wares. It started to fire in Tang dynasty.

唐代邢窑窑址考察与初步探讨

李辉柄

邢窑是唐代著名的瓷窑之一，在中国陶瓷发展史上占有十分重要的地位。过去，由于它的窑址未被发现而长期得不到解决，对于它的庐山真面目也一直没能搞清楚。

1980 年 8 月，邢窑窑址被发现，获得了邢窑的实物标本。1981 年 4 月 25 日，笔者应邀赴邢窑窑址考察并参加了有关邢窑的学术讨论会。会上学者们一致认为邢窑窑址的发现，解决了中国陶瓷史上的一个重大问题。

一 邢窑在中国陶瓷发展史上的地位

我国陶瓷远在唐代就已销往海外，对世界一些国家产生了影响。

唐代，出现了以浙江越窑为代表的青瓷和以河北邢窑为代表的白瓷两大系统。因之瓷器研究者就以"南青"、"北白"而概之。1949 年以来的考古资料证明，青瓷、白瓷南北皆有，所谓"南青"、"北白"指的是代表当时青瓷发展成就的是南方的越窑青瓷，代表白瓷发展成就的是北方邢窑白瓷。从陶瓷发展上看，青瓷为早，白瓷是在青瓷的基础上发展起来的。邢窑白瓷质地坚硬，制作精致，洁白如雪，是其他白瓷无法比拟的，时代也较其他瓷窑为早。唐代陆羽《茶经》有："邢磁类银，越磁类玉"，"邢磁类雪，越磁类冰"。邢瓷类银、类雪与越瓷类玉、类冰，应当是陆羽对邢、越二窑的高度评价。

隋代白瓷，突破了传统青瓷的格调，为白瓷的发展打下了良好的基础。邢窑白瓷较之隋代又前进了一大步，改变了以青瓷为主导的发展方向，迅速地发展起来。在邢窑白瓷的影响下，北方又出现了另一个烧白瓷的定窑。以邢窑为代表的白瓷与越窑青瓷从此并驾齐驱。唐代瓷器生产的成就，与邢窑的出现有着直接的关系。

二 邢窑窑址未发现前的情况

邢窑在文献中虽有较详细的记载，但长期以来由于邢窑窑址未被发现，就在一部分学者中或多或少地产生了一些疑问。坚信邢窑窑址存在的学者，尽管把一些白瓷定为邢窑，但因证据不足而缺乏说服力。

在邢窑窑址未发现以前，学术界对邢窑的看法主要有以下三种：

第一，对邢窑持怀疑态度。1949 年以来，考古事业迅速发展，新发现的古代瓷窑数以百计，大大充实了我国陶瓷史的内容。唐代瓷窑如陆羽《茶经》所提及的越州窑、鼎州窑、婺州窑、岳州窑、寿州窑和洪州窑六大青瓷窑，除鼎州窑外，皆有发现。邢州窑遗址长期未被发现，引起了人们对邢窑的存在、文献记载的可靠性，产生了疑问。

第二，以为邢窑的存在无可置疑，窑址迟早将会发现。其理由：一为文献有征；二为唐代的白瓷窑如河南的巩县窑、密县西关窑、登封曲河窑，山西的浑源窑以及河北的定窑等都已发现，有的还进行了发掘。它们烧制的白瓷，大都白中闪黄，真正够得上“邢窑”白瓷的器物则未发现。而 1949 年以来，陕西、河南、河北等省的唐墓里出土了大量的白瓷，其中有一部分精致优质的白瓷，不同于上述地区所出的白瓷，很可能就是邢窑的制品。

第三，对邢窑持慎重态度。在邢窑窑址未发现以前，既不肯定邢窑，也不否定邢窑。

三 对邢窑窑址考察后的意见

根据李肇《国史补》中“内丘白瓷瓯，端溪紫石砚，天下无贵贱通用之”的记载，一般认为邢窑窑址在内丘。但多年以来内丘境内并未发现任何窑址遗迹。而近年在临城、内丘交界的瓷窑沟和临城县境内的程村、解村、澄底、岗头等地则发现窑址多处。在岗头窑址群中还发现唐代的遗物。岗头以北的祁村和双井村一带又发现了中唐和初唐时期的窑址，尤以祁村窑烧制的白瓷具有典型邢窑白瓷的特征。这样看来，邢窑窑址既不在邢台，又不在内丘，而是在与内丘交界的临城县。现通过考察作以下探讨。

第一，陆羽《茶经》于邢瓷有“类银”、“类雪”的评语。《茶经》成书于唐肃宗年间 (756～761 年)，祁村窑址的时代上限经调查为唐代初期，与文献记载相符，说明祁村窑至少在 756 年以前就已建窑烧造白瓷了。

第二，祁村窑烧制精致的白瓷的同时，还大量烧制粗瓷。白瓷造型规整，胎质坚硬，釉色洁白，与《茶经》“邢磁类雪”相吻合。过去窑址未发现，一般将制作精致、釉色洁白的器物暂定为“邢窑”。常见的多为玉璧形底的碗和小短流的壶以及丰肩平底罐等。这在研究者中间似已视为“邢窑”的基本特征，因之往往把一些早期定窑的制品也误定为邢窑。祁村窑烧制器物主要有碗、盘、壶、罐、盏托等，工艺上一丝不苟。如玉璧形底碗，多为浅式，敞口，口沿往往凸起一道边沿，底足短浅，底足外沿略高于内沿，底内心微凸。碗壁内外一般不见有旋纹。除底足部外施满釉，玉璧中心施釉，釉稳定不下垂，没有定窑那种“泪痕”的流釉现象，这些都为其他白瓷窑所不及。唐代定窑白瓷虽也比较精细，然而与邢窑制品相比，还是有区别的。定窑玉璧形底碗，底足外沿与内沿平坦，玉璧中心不施釉，这是由于唐代定窑在做法上与邢窑不同；邢窑拉坯成型时，先挖足，后施釉，再将足部釉磨掉，留下底足中心的釉。定窑则先施釉，然后在磨平底足的同时挖足，因而底中心无釉。定窑质坚而不甚白，釉色微黄，制作也不如邢窑精致。河南其他瓷窑的玉璧形底碗，胎质不如邢、定二窑，制作粗糙，胎体厚重，以唇口者居多。釉色闪黄，往往有细小开片，底足无釉。祁村窑器物如此精致是与烧窑技术之高分不开的。尽管未发现窑炉，不了解它的结构，但它的窑具比较先进而多样，除了一般所见到的漏斗状匣钵、桶式匣钵以外，还有一种盒式匣钵。这种匣钵有盖有底，坯体置其中，然后放在漏斗状匣钵之上，它是烧造高档白瓷专用的一种匣钵。这种匣钵不见于其他唐代的白瓷窑中。使用漏斗状匣钵在祁村窑也是比较早的。祁村窑在烧窑技术上要求严格，废品较少。出土的高档白瓷残片尤为少见。

第三，窑以地名。陆羽《茶经》里提到的越州窑、鼎州窑、婺州窑、岳州窑、寿州窑和洪州窑都是如此，邢州窑亦然。祁村窑的窑址所在地在唐代不属于邢州的内丘，而是属于赵州的临城。由于李肇《国史补》有“内丘白瓷瓯”的记载，所以一般认为邢窑窑址应在内丘。然而内丘到目前为止并没有发现任何窑迹。内丘在唐武德四年属赵州，次年改隶邢州；临城在唐则一直属赵州管辖。内丘与临城的交界处的地理区划，时分时合，窑址正处于这一地带。从内丘、临城交界的瓷窑沟往北，中经解村、南程村、河北岸、澄底、岗头直到祁村、双井村，长达 12 公里，发现了古窑遗址 12 处，其中岗头、祁村、双井为唐代瓷窑区。鉴于此种地理情况，这应当是唐代邢窑窑址所在地无疑。另外，唐代以州名窑当是泛指，正如邢窑不在邢台而在内丘（内丘、临城交界地带），定窑不在定县而在曲阳。将来如果在内丘发现了窑址，也不能否定祁村窑之为邢窑，就像定县如果发现窑址，也不能否定曲阳窑是定窑一样。

第四，1949 年以来，在大量唐墓里出土了不少白瓷，尤其是陕西、河南、河北出土的白瓷更多。这些白瓷的窑址在哪里，一直是大家特别关心的问题。其中有些白瓷可能属于邻近瓷窑的产品。一部分精致的白瓷，如邢台唐墓出土的白瓷碗、河南安阳薛家庄唐墓出土的白瓷碗和盏托等[1]，与祁村窑烧制的器物在造型、釉色以及玉璧形底中心施釉等方面具有共同特征。特别是盏托制作精工，在其他唐代白瓷窑中还未发现，可见它们是邢窑制品无疑。过去一般把它们定为“邢窑”是有一定道理的。

第五，唐代的邢窑白瓷与越窑青瓷，在当时就已远销海外。在埃及著名的福斯塔特、印度勃拉名纳巴特等古代遗址中，都有邢窑白瓷的发现。日本的平城京和平安京及其周围地区出土的唐代白瓷中也有邢窑的制品[2]。如京都市下京区七条唐桥西寺遗址出土的白瓷碗就与祁村邢窑窑址出土物相同。可见邢窑白瓷真如李肇《国史补》所说“天下无贵贱通用之”了。

根据实地考察以及上述分析，可以证明祁村窑就是文献所记载的邢窑。

四 对邢窑烧瓷历史的分析

在邢窑窑址未发现以前，对唐墓中出土的白瓷，研究者根据文献记载来鉴定它们的窑口。现在邢窑窑址已经发现，对于邢窑的历史，结合文献加以印证也是非常必要的。陆羽《茶经》除了邢窑白瓷以外，还记载了当时著名的越州窑、鼎州窑、婺州窑、寿州窑和洪州窑六大青瓷窑。除鼎州窑尚未发现外，其余五窑都已发现，有的还进行了发掘。从考古资料上看，这些青瓷窑历史悠久，延续的时间也长。越州窑、婺州窑、洪州窑从晋、南朝时期开始，延续到唐代。寿州窑与岳州窑至少也滥觞于隋代以前。这些瓷窑的产品到唐代已享盛名，普遍被用作茶具，因而陆羽才把它们写入《茶经》。

邢窑在《茶经》里出现是值得注意的一个问题，这是否意味着邢窑在时代上能与这些青瓷窑相比，或者也如上述那些青瓷窑，至少在隋代以前就开始烧制白瓷？1949 年以来，在北方发掘的隋墓，如西安西郊隋大业四年李静训墓[3]、西安郭家滩隋墓[4]，都出土有白瓷。这些隋代白瓷与邢窑有没有关系？这是值得探讨的重要问题。从现在已发现的唐代烧白瓷的窑如河南巩县窑、密县窑、登封窑以及河北曲阳窑看，都没有发现隋代白瓷，相反地在巩县窑址中却发现了隋代的青瓷[5]。邢窑白瓷质量优于其他瓷窑，在时代上也较其他瓷窑为早，因此才被收入《茶经》。至于隋代墓中出土的白瓷是哪个窑的产品，是否即唐代邢窑白瓷的前身，也就是说邢窑在隋代是否已经开始烧制白瓷，这一问题还有待今后的发掘工作来证实。

经过调查证明，在邢窑分布的内丘、临城交界的磁窑沟和临城境内的其他地区，除了岗头、祁村、双井村发现了唐代的窑址外，其余均为金代以后或元代的窑址，烧制的器物与唐代邢窑并无渊源关系。这似乎说明祁村邢窑白瓷在唐代以后就衰落了，继之而起的曲阳定窑在唐代晚期受邢窑的影响开始烧制白瓷并很快发展起来。北宋时期定窑大量烧制带有印花装饰的白瓷，成为当时北方最有名的瓷窑。祁村邢窑停烧以后，中间相隔了一段时间，又受到定窑的影响，烧制印花瓷器。这就形成了内丘、临城交界地区瓷窑发展的基本状况。祁村邢窑遗址的发现是中国陶瓷史上一项重大收获。至于内丘境内是否如文献记载的有窑址的存在，邢窑白瓷的创烧年代，以及它衰落原因等问题，还有待于进一步探讨。

（原载《文物》1981 年第 9 期）

注释：

1 河南文化局文物工作队：《河南安阳薛家庄殷代遗址、墓葬和唐墓发掘简报》，《考古通讯》1958 年第 8 期。

2 [日]长谷部乐尔：《日本出土的中国古陶瓷特别展览》，东京国立博物馆，1975 年。

3 唐金裕：《西安西郊隋李静训墓发掘简报》，《考古》1959 年第 9 期。

4 陕西省文管会：《西安郭家滩隋墓清理简报》，《文物参考资料》1957 年第 8 期。

5 冯先铭：《河南巩县古窑址调查记要》，《文物》1959 年第 3 期。

Abstract of the Investigation into Xing Kiln Sites of Tang Dynasty and Discussions

Li Huibing

The paper discusses the status of Xing kiln in the history of the development of Chinese ceramics, knowledge about Xing kiln before and after the discovery of its kiln sites and the firing history. After typical white glaze porcelains of Xing kiln being found in Qicun Village in the 1980s, a conclusion was draw that Xing kiln is neither in Xingtai, nor in Neiqiu, but in Lincheng. The reasons behind are as follows. First, in the book, Tea, there was a comment on white glaze porcelain of Xing kiln which says it is as white as silver or snow. The book was written during the Suzong Period (761-762) of Tang dynasty by Lu Yu. According to investigation, Xing kiln at Qicun Village started to fire in early Tang dynasty, matching the record in the book; Second, Xing kiln at Qicun Village fired both fine and coarse white glaze porcelains; Third, kilns were generally named after places. Qicun Village in Tang dynasty belonged to Zhaozhou and latter on was under the administration of Xingzhou where the name of the kiln came from; Fourth, a large number of white glaze porcelains were unearthed from tombs of Tang dynasty. Some of which are products of Xing kiln; Last, Xing kiln wares had been sold overseas in Tang dynasty. The discovery of Xing kiln wares abroad well matches the records in literatures. Xing kiln was located in Lincheng and at Ciyaogou, the border of Neiqiu and Lincheng. Tang dynasty kiln sites were only found at Gangtou, Qicun and Shuangjing. The rest of kiln sites are from Jin and Yuan dynasties. Xing kiln at Qicun Village once stopped firing for some time. As affected by Ding kiln, it re-opened and fired white glaze porcelains with stamped design during Jin and Yuan dynasties.

内丘邢窑的重大发现

李知宴

1986 年我到河北内丘对邢窑窑址做过一次考古调查，在调查中搜集了一些瓷片资料，也思考了一些问题，现在就这些问题报告如下：

一 内丘瓷窑的发现为邢窑研究打开新局面

邢窑在我国封建社会陶瓷发展中占有重要地位，不但开始生产的时间早，而且以其精湛的技艺推动着整个北方瓷器工艺的发展。在唐代有所谓“南青北白”的局面，这是以越窑为代表的南方青瓷和以邢窑为代表的北方白瓷并驾齐驱。越窑在 1949 年前就发现窑址，许多问题讨论相当深入，而邢窑由于窑址没有发现，研究工作遇到许多困难，不能深入进行。

1980 年河北临城发现隋唐时期的白瓷窑址，还有时代更早的青瓷窑址。其中有的精细白瓷水平很高，符合唐人歌颂、评价的邢瓷标准，引起广泛的讨论[1]。比较一致的认识是，这就是唐代盛名的邢窑窑址所在地，有人甚至提出邢窑就在临城，不在内丘，文献记载有误。但是在讨论中也有一些问题尚未解决。例如，临城瓷窑分散，大多数窑址工艺水平不高。就从水平最早的祁村窑址采集的瓷片标本初步统计，精细白瓷只占 20%，大多数是青瓷、粗白瓷和其他品种，为唐人歌颂的精细白瓷数量太少，不可能产生很大的社会影响。临城在内丘的北边，根据地质勘察和考古调查，这一带只有内丘产优质瓷土，唐代以来都在内丘取土，直到今天都是这样。临城没有内丘条件优越，那么唐代为什么不在内丘建窑而在临城建窑？再有，既然邢窑不在内丘而在临城，李肇在《国史补》上为什么不说“临城白瓷瓯”而说内丘呢？临城在隋唐一直属于赵州，内丘只在唐高祖武德初年属赵州，以后一直属邢州，整个唐朝二百多年的时间里赵州、邢州所辖范围一直没有多大变化，内丘和临城地界清楚稳定，唐朝文人不至于弄错。临城和内丘都与隆尧为邻，隆尧就是隆平和尧山，隆平是唐高祖李渊的祖宗坟地（开元八代宣简公并七代祖懿王陵）所在地，坟地就在县南的王尹村北。邢、赵二州官员要在每年春秋二季率领百官前往祭谒，在地理上，政治意义如此重要，在唐代的邢、赵二州是不许混淆不清的[2]。李肇在《国史补》中明确指出邢窑在内丘，他的《国史补》十分严肃，他在《自序》中说：“予自开元在长庆，撰《国史补》，虑史氏或阙则补之。”他是在很认真地记录社会现实，以补国史，他不敢也不可能把邢、赵二州搞错。其他文献也明确指出在内丘。既然文献不可能写错，那么窑址就不可能不在内丘，既然窑址不可能不在内丘，那么临城所发现的窑址就可能不是邢窑的中心窑场。因为唐代以州命名的瓷窑，一般都包括一个相当大的地理范围，相同的产品可能超过州界。临城瓷窑可能属于邢窑的一个组成部分。大家一直在等待内丘能发现唐代白瓷窑址。

1984年内丘县开展文物大普查，在京广铁路两侧，小马河、李阳河两岸，即县城周围，冯村、永安、五部等乡120平方公里的范围内发现了28处古窑址。特别在内丘县周围发现密集的窑群，其中包括过去在唐大明宫遗址发现的刻有“盈”字款和用笔书写“翰林”、西安唐墓出土底部刻写“翰林”那样的精细白瓷，而且细白瓷生产的比例，比临城任何一个窑址都大，这里出土的白瓷质地细密，与陆羽在《茶经》里描写的“如银似雪”、“邢磁白”完全相符。产品品种之丰富，数量之大，也与李肇在《国史补》中评价的“天下无贵贱通用之”相符。1985年我们到内丘调查之后，将临城和内丘窑址标在地图上，发现内丘窑址和临城窑址连成一片，是一个巨大的瓷窑生产区，作坊相邻而建。内丘的窑址范围大，密集，细白瓷的比例高，还生产粗白瓷、三彩釉陶、青瓷、黑瓷、黄釉瓷和芝麻酱釉瓷。很明显内丘是这个陶瓷生产区的中心，原料也在内丘，得天独厚，且交通发达，商业繁盛。根据临城陈刘庄千佛寺碑记载的内容，内丘是临城与内丘一带商品集散中心。所以文献记载邢窑在内丘是完全正确的，而临城的瓷窑群则是邢窑的有机组成部分。

这次发现对邢瓷的研究意义十分重大，为邢瓷的研究打开了一个新局面，从考古学上寻找邢窑的任务算是实现了。

二 自然条件和窑址布局的特点

根据窑址调查了解到内丘有发展瓷器生产优越的自然条件。内丘县在河北省南部偏西。窑址在滏阳河上游的小马河、寺阳河、泜河、泜北渠一带。地处太行山麓，是丘陵和平原交汇之地。南起内丘县城，北至临城的竹壁水库，南北25公里，东西宽约5公里的范围，蕴藏着丰富的瓷土。许多煤层把瓷土层分割成若干小条小块。有优质瓷土，也有质量一般的瓷土。在内丘县城附近优质瓷土埋藏较浅，易于开采[3]。临城和内丘自古以来就在这里取土，滏阳河及其支流水源丰富，保证了制瓷用水。内丘地处丘陵，林木茂盛，柴草砍之不尽。就地取材是我国陶瓷作坊建立的一个原则，上述条件形成陶瓷发展的良好基础。

唐代的内丘，李肇在《国史补》中说："凡货贿之物，侈于用者，不可胜纪。"交通四通八达，这里的货物贩运到很远的地方。可以想见，内丘、临城的瓷器汇集于市，地方官挑选优秀之作上贡，皇室也派人来征购，商人贩运到各地销售。从活跃的商业交通线来看，陆路往北联通曲阳、保定、通县、涿县、北京等地，往南联通邢台、邯郸、安阳、洛阳、西安，联通丝绸之路。邢瓷可以运往西域。水陆交通也很方便，小船将邢瓷运往滏阳河，经子牙河进入天津，再由北运河进入长江，直接运到扬州、镇江，或经南方水系、陆路交通可运往广州、明州等海港城市输出海外。生产和销售的畅通，推动着生产的发展。

邢窑生产有一个发生、发展、兴盛和衰落的过程。窑址的分布，从临城来说早期青瓷、白瓷窑址主要分布在城南的陈刘庄、贾村。兴盛时期的青瓷、白瓷、黑瓷窑址有陈刘庄、贾村、澄底、岗头、祁村、西双井、东双井等。晚期窑址在北程村、南程村、解村、山下、西瓷窑沟等。窑址布局表明，当时作坊的建立离城较远，也比较分散，没有发现集中的窑群，就是最兴盛的盛唐时期，细白瓷的比例也极小。

内丘的窑址群有三大部分。第一部分在城的西边、北边和东边，生产早期的青瓷和白瓷。第二部分在城的周围，尤其西关、南关地区瓷窑集中，在范围不大的地区就发现窑址 14 处之多。生产粗白瓷、细白瓷、黑瓷、黄釉瓷和乳浊窑变釉瓷、酱釉瓷、三彩釉陶等。第三部分，比较边远部和与临城交界的东瓷窑沟等。瓷窑的布局和临城相似，早期比较分散，离城比较远。盛唐时期，也就是邢窑最兴盛的时期，瓷窑集中在城周附近，密集，规模也比较大，带"盈"字款的白瓷主要在这一带几处窑址里有发现。离城（即市场）近，离优质瓷土近。作坊的建立，经过精心选址，原料、市场、运输等因素都考虑到了。时代偏晚的窑址，多在内丘和临城交界的瓷窑沟，品种单调，就地销售。

三 对时代的判断看清了邢瓷发展的过程

邢瓷生产时间很长，品种也很丰富，有青瓷、青黄釉瓷、黄釉瓷、黑瓷、酱釉瓷、乳光窑变釉瓷、白瓷、三彩釉陶等。

青瓷、青黄釉瓷和黄釉瓷。产量大，都是青灰胎，坚硬厚重。施青釉，器物里壁满施，外壁只在上腹或口沿部分施釉。釉质凝厚，玻璃质强。有的青黄釉瓷在胎体上施一层白色化妆土，釉层青绿深沉而泛黄，同一件器物上，不施化妆土的釉色深青或灰青色。黄釉瓷器，釉色一致，成黄色或淡黄色，釉质较细。这三类制品工艺接近，呈色物质主要是铁的氧化物。深青色或灰青色是还原焰烧成，不衬化妆土的青黄釉和黄釉是由氧化焰烧成。北方的馒头窑容易烧成氧化焰，所以一般青釉都有点泛黄。器物主要有碗、盘、罐、壶、钵等生活用具。这些制品的胎釉特征和厚重、坚硬的质感方面，与河北景县封氏墓群、河南濮阳李云墓出土的青瓷接近，从河北邺城相当于北齐时期遗址采集到的青瓷碗片，与它完全一样。碗类的造型与河间邢氏墓、安阳范粹墓、太原娄睿墓出土的青瓷相类似。窑址中的青瓷钵，特点是敛口、圆唇，底部很小，接近环底，与娄睿墓出土的釉陶钵相近。青瓷盘，口沿较尖，胎体略外斜，平底，与洛阳王湾北朝地层中出土的陶盘一样。这些窑址一般埋藏都比较深，种类少。从河北临城及内丘露出的窑炉残体观察，体积小，有的直径只有 2 米，结构简单，窑具也没有发现匣钵。用土坯砖砌窑的墙壁，器物底部只用泥条卷成一个圈来垫烧。这些都是早的特征。邢窑初创时期定在北朝后期比较合适。河北、河南、山东等地一些北朝晚期的瓷窑，产品没有邢窑质量好。

还有青瓷注壶、直筒腹碗、四耳罐、盘口细颈瓶等属于隋代，而胎体厚重的执壶，则是初唐的产品。邢窑里发现有口呈梯形的扁壶，双系，腹周为联珠纹，中间二人着胡服，在莲蓬形台上跳舞，这是初唐之作。故宫博物院珍藏的青釉龙柄凤头壶很可能是邢窑初唐时期的产品[5]。

黄釉瓷器。胎体厚重，用宽肥的三叉支钉支烧，与寿州窑的黄釉瓷风格一样，应该是初唐的产品，到盛唐时期变化不大，胎做得薄一些，只是器物品种减少。

黑瓷。多数产品较粗，形体大而厚重。部分黑瓷釉层凝厚，莹润光亮。在内丘西关窑群中发现的黑瓷三足鍑，是盛唐时期的产品。在临城的射兽、南程村一带发现的黑瓷鸡腿坛是金元时代的产品。

酱釉瓷。包括质量相当好的，釉色呈芝麻酱颜色的唐代作品。

乳浊窑变釉瓷。在内丘的河村遗址有发现，底釉是黑釉或褐黄釉。与河南鲁山、郏县、禹县的花瓷一样，在底釉上出现花斑，这是一种二液分相釉，与宋代的钧瓷釉工艺密切，河南考古工作者称为“唐钧”。

白瓷。产量大，在社会上流传很广，技艺水平高。有粗白瓷、细白瓷，覆烧白瓷、划花白瓷和白釉黑花瓷。

粗白瓷有杯、碗、壶、罐、钵等。有一种碗，口沿略外撇，圆唇，腹体宽而浅，胎色白中发灰，有的不施化妆土，有的里壁全施化妆土，外壁只在口沿部分施化妆土。施白釉，有的制品白色一致，有的白釉不均匀，下腹壁及底足不上釉。这些特点和河南安阳武平六年范粹墓出土的白瓷一样，还有双耳罐都应该是北朝的产品。根据魏晋南北朝瓷器发展的情况来看，北朝完全具备了生产白瓷的条件，古代文献记载的白瓷还会更早一些。《笙赋》注引吕忱《字林》:“瓷，白瓶长颖”，“颍”就是“躲’字，《玉篇》“躲”，“身也”。吕忱是西晋时人[6]，如果文献记载确实的话，西晋时已经有了白瓷长颈瓶了，所以北朝发现白瓷毫不奇怪。

内丘的北双流和临城贾村等窑址出土一批白瓷，有深腹杯和深腹碗，深腹杯的口微侈，口沿尖薄，中腹至底器壁逐渐加厚，底部很小，圆饼状足，足的边棱略为外侈，有的底部稍宽一些。白胎，施化妆土，白釉玻璃质强，下腹近底处露胎，具有隋代白瓷的特征。河南安阳张盛墓，西安李静训墓、姬威墓的白瓷基本上与它一致。邢台隋大业四年墓出土的白瓷双龙柄盘口尊、天津市文管会收藏的双龙柄双身尊都是隋代邢窑的产品。在内丘窑址里发现的白瓷双耳扁瓶，耳是忍冬叶形，腹部粗大的联珠纹有北朝的特征，范粹墓出土的黄釉扁瓶就是这样，联珠围成杏仁形装饰圈，则像隋李静训墓出土的白瓷扁壶一样，腹部的缠枝花卉则是唐代的式样。这件作品定在唐朝初期比较合适。

在内丘窑址出土一件白瓷素坯的佛龛，名为善事泥，根据佛的形象、发型、佛、弟子、力士和狮子、童子等组合，这件作品定在初唐比较合适。在粗白瓷中，碗类的形体比较大，器壁弧度不大，圆饼足又宽又矮，足径超过口的1/2，胎厚，施化妆土，釉色银灰，积釉处泛青或泛黄。敛口钵一类厚胎作品，与西安地区初唐墓出土的白瓷一样。还有白瓷砚台与总章元年（668年）李爽墓出土的瓷砚一样。直口平底白瓷盘，也与李爽墓出土的白瓷盘一样。

在粗白瓷中，那种形体较矮，侈口，腹体较斜，弧度不大，玉璧形足的碗、盏、盒子以及腹体饱满圆鼓的罐都是盛唐时期的产品，在各地盛唐墓中出土较多，陕西西安唐大明宫遗址、西市遗址均有出土。在内丘窑址中发现的白瓷折腰碗与陕西乾县神龙二年永泰公主墓出土的三彩折腰碗一样。

细白瓷有碗、盏、瓶、罐、盆、盒、凤头壶等。

1978年河北临城东镇公社农民取土时挖出一批白瓷。有白瓷凤首，可能是凤头壶的盖，两件三足盘，两件玉璧底碗，一件白瓷三足鍑，一件罐盖，一件翻沿圆唇深腹碗，动物形象有狮、大象。大象身披毛毯，前面有一个驯象的人物。这批作品是邢窑的细白瓷。同时出土的还有一件海兽葡萄镜，镜体小，直径9.5厘米，厚1厘米。边厚，唇尖，花纹严谨，中圈是一组联珠纹。海兽葡萄镜在我国流行于唐高宗、武则天至唐玄宗的天宝时期。临城发现的海兽葡萄镜是较早的一种，应是初唐至盛唐之间的产物。河南陕县刘家渠唐墓出土的邢窑白瓷长颈瓶是盛唐之物。

邢窑中的刻“盈”字款、“翰林”款，或书写“翰林”字样的作品是邢窑的精细产品，主要用于向宫廷上贡。西安地区唐开元二十四年墓里出土一件白瓷罐，底部刻“翰林”字样，说明它们是盛唐之物。临城窑址出土的细白瓷皮囊壶，在西安地区盛唐墓里有出土，英国维多利亚和阿尔伯特博物馆收藏一件白瓷褐彩皮囊壶，也是盛唐之物。西安何家村出土一件银质鎏金舞马衔杯皮囊壶，造型与邢窑的皮囊壶一样，是盛唐时期之物。白瓷中仿金杯的高足杯、环耳杯，其时代也应是盛唐之作。荷叶口、菱花口、葵口的碗、盏类作品是晚唐时期的产品。

细白瓷中，有一类碗、盏、盏托、盒、瓶、执壶等作品，胎体较薄，腹体加深，颈部加长，圈足加高，以及一些精巧的小动物形象，根据西安和河南三门峡地区唐墓出土的瓷器相比较，应该是晚唐至五代时期的作品。

内丘窑址中的三彩釉陶都是盛唐时期的产品。

在内丘和临城交界的瓷窑沟，临城的南程村，东、西双井村生产的粗白瓷、覆烧瓷器、白釉黑花瓷器都是宋金元时代之作。

四 邢瓷的分期研究有了可靠的依据

内丘邢窑资料极其丰富，可以看出邢瓷的发展有明显的阶段性，能够按照考古学的方法进行分期。北朝至初唐是第一期，盛唐是第二期，晚唐五代是第三期，宋金元是第四期。

第一期，北朝、隋、初唐是邢窑的创立时期，也是我国北方瓷系形成和初步发展的时期，窑址作坊分散，建作坊主要注重瓷土原料和水源，以生产方便为主。生产的瓷器有青瓷、青黄釉瓷、黄釉瓷。北朝发明白瓷，工艺不够成熟，但比青瓷质量高，产量小。到隋朝白瓷发展较快。但整个来看，第一期瓷器的特点是质地粗厚坚致，原料没有良好加工，气孔率大。辘轳成型，轮旋纹理不匀，稳定性不佳，胎色为灰色，深浅不一，有的青瓷也加化妆土，火焰气氛控制不稳定，有的瓷器露胎部分成褐红色，没有任何装饰，靠化妆土来增加釉色的美观。釉面流釉、滚釉现象常见。白瓷也粗，白度不高，釉色白中泛黄或泛灰，玻璃质强，工艺上比青瓷考究一些。生活用具种类不多，但烧出了佛龛（即善事泥）及佛的形象。

流通情况，邢瓷的发现主要在河北、河南、陕西一些达官显贵的大墓中。其他地区、沿海港口城市没有发现。

第二期，即盛唐时期，邢瓷迅速发展，在内丘城周形成中心窑场，作坊密集，生产兴旺，上述各类瓷器和三彩釉陶品种均能生产。工艺精细，社会影响广泛，向宫廷进贡，也输出到海外许多国家和地区。这个时期的白瓷分为粗白瓷和细白瓷。所谓粗白瓷是与该窑精细白瓷相比而言的。但与全国各地唐代白瓷相比，水平还是高得多。细白瓷原料经过仔细加工，成型稳定性能良好，规格精巧，一件作品从中心轴线向四周测量，没有任何厚薄不匀和歪扭变形的现象。这个时期的邢瓷可以和越窑比肩抗衡。唐朝著名诗人皮日休在《茶中杂咏·茶瓯》诗中把它与越窑器一起来歌颂，称颂它们“圆似月魂堕，轻如云魄起”[7]。用辘轳成型，修坯精细，胎面看不到任何轮旋纹理，白釉直接施在胎体上，不施化妆土，全凭工匠的精工细作，获得洁白的效果。釉质细腻，釉光莹润，色白如雪。陆羽在《茶经》中评价“邢瓷类雪”。根据化学分析，与景德镇、德化白釉相比，釉中 MgO 含量较高，CaO 较低，属 $MgO—CaO—Al_2O_3$ 一 SiO_2 系统，称“镁一灰”釉，用还原火焰烧成[8]。这种瓷器原料特性是，火候要求高，但细白瓷没有烧到家，所以吸水率较高，各类生活用具如碗、盘、盏、杯、碟、瓶、壶、罐、烛台等产品数量很大，种类多，凤头壶、皮囊壶等白瓷作品别具一格。

邢瓷到这个时候成熟了，技艺精湛，做工细腻。邢瓷不讲究色彩和花纹装饰，但在器物的造型结构、线条处理上很富匠心，把庄重典雅的造型美，陶瓷胎釉的质感美发挥到最高水平，表现出大唐盛世宏伟气魄的时代精神，在我们中华民族的工艺史上放射出一片光彩。一些精巧的葵口碗、菱花口碗也是在这个时期出现的，碗类器物较矮，碗壁弧度不大，胎略厚，足径一般是口径的 1/2，高度一般只有口径的 1/4，底足外墙壁略高于内墙或相当，足心挖得很浅，足高只有通高的 1/10。许多作品足心刻“盈”字款、“翰林”款，或墨书“翰林”字样。

施釉也改为里外壁、足心满施，只在足沿露胎。

瓷器的品种也齐全，能满足各个阶层的需要，正如李肇在《国史补》中所说：“内丘白瓷瓯，端溪紫石砚，天下无贵贱通用之。”正是反映这种实际情况。《新唐书·地理志》：“邢州巨鹿郡……土贡……磁器。”确实也向宫廷进贡。带“盈”、“翰林”款，或书写“翰林”字样的瓷器在大明宫遗址里出现就是证明。这个时期邢窑白瓷还作为重要商品向国内、国际市场销售。除长安、洛阳等政治经济城市大量发现以外，通往河西走廊的甘肃，丝路重要地段的新疆地区均有发现。其他山西、河北、北京等地经常发现。南方的重要港口城市如宁波、扬州、广州等地也有发现。故宫博物院收藏一件花口瓶，釉下刻“丁大刚作瓶大好”一行字，该瓶的窑口尚需考虑，但可以说明唐代白瓷生产商品性增强，既能满足统治者上层的需要，也能满足市民有钱之家选用，或销售到海外。

第三期，晚唐至五代，白瓷继续得到发展，包括生活用具、陈设艺术品和人物、动物等艺术形象。细白瓷数量相对增加，工艺也提高，胎体变薄，作品更精巧，葵口、荷口、菱花口作品主要在这个时期流行，器物底部宽平，圈足高而窄，称为“玉环底”。烧窑工艺更加提高，过去生烧的现象消失，敲击起来有清越的金属声，晚唐人段安节撰写的《乐府杂录》“方响”条中记载：“武宗朝，郭道源为凤翔府大兴县丞，充太常夺调音律官，善击瓯。率以越瓯、邢瓯共十二只，旋加减水于其中，以箸击之，其音妙于方响。”河北一些小型唐墓中也发现邢瓷殉葬，而且是质量很高的细白瓷[9]。说明民间人家也能买到以前只有宫廷才能使用的东西。

与整个唐朝社会艺术与工艺发展趋势相比，邢瓷只追求质感美和质量的提高，新品种增加不多，也不追求色彩和装饰花纹。

第四期，宋金元时期，细白瓷已经不生产，粗白瓷的质量也明显下降，工艺落后，模仿定窑、磁州窑生产一些民间用瓷，但工艺水平远远落后于定窑和磁州窑。作坊零落，成为一般民间生产粗瓷的场所，失去了唐代邢窑白瓷的艺术光辉。

关于邢窑细白瓷中带“盈”字款的作品，近来发现越来越多。过去作过种种推测，都不够准确。在唐代，各地官吏常将一些地方名产或精细高级工艺品向皇帝进贡，中央或地方官吏均有，这些都是按规定进贡的额外进献。这些贡品都被纳入皇宫中的“琼林”或“大盈”二库，专门供皇帝私人使用，任何人不得使用，邢瓷中精细白瓷自然也是进献而受到皇帝欣赏之物，故此，在社会上享有盛名，精巧玲珑的瑰宝自然也就是能讨得皇帝喜欢的献纳物了，窑址发现的带“盈”字款的细白瓷可能就是专门纳入“大盈”库中的贡品。邢窑白瓷在各地大官僚墓葬中出土很多，但带“盈”字款的作品没有见到，唯独在大明宫有发现，恐怕就是这个原因。

（原载《河北陶瓷》1986年第4期）

注释：

1 河北临城邢瓷研制小组：《唐代邢窑遗址调查报告》，李辉柄：《唐代邢窑址考察与初步探讨》，叶喆民：《邢窑刍议》，《文物》1981 年 9 期。

2 程在廉：《何处是邢窑》，《河北陶瓷》1984 年 1 期。

3《笔记小说大观》第 30 册第 1 页，江苏广陵古籍刻印社。

4《笔记小说大观》第 30 册第 1 页，江苏广陵古籍刻印社。

5 见《故宫博物院瓷选集》。

6 转引自唐兰《长沙马王堆汉侯妻辛追墓出土随葬遣策考释》，《文史》第十辑。

7《全唐诗》卷二三《皮日休》五。

8 盛厚兴：《唐代邢窑白瓷的研究》，《中国古代陶瓷科学技术第二届国际讨论会论文提要》第 15 页。

9 石家庄地区文物研究所：《河北晋县唐墓》，《考古》1985 年 2 期。

Abstract of an Important Discovery of Xing Kiln in Neiqiu

Li Zhiyan

The author conducted an investigation into Xing kiln in Neiqiu in 1986. The discovery of Tang dynasty white glaze porcelain kiln sites at Qicun Village, Lincheng County in 1980 had drawn lots of attentions. A popular point of view was that Lincheng is the place where locates Xing kiln. Some even suggested that Xing kiln was actually located in Lincheng, not in Neiqiu for there might have been an error in literatures that mistook Lincheng for Neiqiu. However, some issues still remain unresolved. The 1984 survey in Neiqiu found 28 ancient kiln sites from where a large number of white glaze porcelains were unearthed. No kiln sites in Lincheng had ever unearthed so large number of white glaze porcelains. With fine texture, white glaze porcelain of Neiqiu confirmed the reliability of the description appeared in the book, Tea, which says that the porcelain is as white as silver or snow. Relying on its high-quality raw materials and convenient waterway transportation, Neiqiu must have witnessed a smooth development of the porcelain industry. Grouped kiln sites have never been found in Lincheng. Even during its heyday, the proportion of fine white glaze porcelains fired was still low in Lincheng. Whereas in Neiqiu, three groups of kiln sites have been found in the west, north and east part of the county. Early celadon and white glaze porcelains were fired there. Around the county town, 14 kiln sites were found. At those sites, coarse and fine white glaze, black glaze, yellow glaze, flambé glaze, dark brown glaze porcelain and three-color glazed pottery were fired. Xing kiln had a long firing history, from the Northern dynasties, Sui dynasty to Jin and Yuan dynasties. It can be roughly divided into four stages: the Northern dynasties, Sui dynasty and early Tang dynasty; the golden ages of Tang dynasty; late Tang and Five Dynasties; Song, Jin and Yuan dynasties. Apart from white glaze, it fired a variety of colored porcelains and earthwares as well.

从隆化窑的调查看河北陶瓷的发展

李知宴

隆化窑陶瓷在过去一些著作中提到过，但内容都不详细。我在承德工作期间，与国家文物局在承德举办的文物博物馆培训班的同志们一起，在1982年6月23日对隆化窑进行了调查，采集了一些研究标本。在承德博物馆、隆化县文化馆看到收藏的隆化窑作品，《河北陶瓷》编辑部的同志希望将调查公布出来，供研究者参考，现在就调查所得谈一点粗浅的认识。

一 地理位置和窑址情况

隆化在河北省北部，承德以北滦河的东边，伊逊河和伊玛图河交汇处。窑址在隆化县城东北方向一公里的地方，地势起伏，但窑场地区地势比较平坦。北边与内蒙古自治区、辽宁、吉林相通，南边与承德、唐山、北京相通，交通方便。隆化出瓷土，山丘林木茂盛，水源丰富，周围产煤，具备古代发展陶瓷手工业的理想条件。

隆化窑遭到极大的破坏。窑址范围已经完全开辟为菜地。看不到古窑场的完整轮廓，只看到农民开菜地时拣出来扔在一边一堆堆的窑具、瓷片。农民说烧瓷的窑炉早就挖烂、填平，有的挖成了粪池，找不到任何窑迹了。在农田周围察看，在田坎上尚能看到一些灰渣、窑具和瓷片堆积的断面，有这样堆积的范围大约有几万平方米，说明当时这里是作坊群。

二 瓷器的种类

根据调查所采集的标本进行整理，隆化窑瓷器的器物种类有碗、盏、钵、水盂、高足杯、罐、鸡腿坛、缸、器盖等。

（1）碗

是该窑生产最多的品种，各类碗可能要占该窑产品的70%以上，根据器物排比，可分为11式：

Ⅰ式。碗体比较坦平，胎体比较薄，最厚的地方也只有1厘米，接近腹中部的地方厚为0.5厘米，口沿等最薄的地方大约只有0.3厘米，平底，圈足，圈足比较宽，旋削整齐，足心平坦。

Ⅱ式。碗形坦平，胎体比较薄，最厚的地方只有0.5厘米，平底，圈足，足沿切削整齐，中心有一个极小的钮。

Ⅲ式。碗形较深，腹壁微曲，底心略凹，圈足，足沿比较浅，底心下凸，腹上沿至碗底厚薄相差较大。

Ⅳ式。标本残破太甚，看不清整体结构，能看出的部分是圈足很浅，足沿比较窄，足心一个乳状突起，碗心出现一圈因叠烧黏结而出现的砂泥。

Ⅴ式。侈口，曲腹，平底，圈足，足心有一个乳突，口沿和底厚薄相差约三倍，圈足很小。

Ⅵ式。形体较大，胎体厚实，侈口，曲腹，底心微凹，圈足，外底中心微凸，胎体较粗厚，碗心有因叠烧而留下的黏结疤痕。

Ⅶ式。侈口，腹壁微曲，平底，腹壁和底成二层阶状，圈足很浅，足心微突。

Ⅷ式。侈口，曲腹，腹壁较深，底心下凹，圈足，足沿较窄，足的根部较宽。

Ⅸ式。侈口，圆唇，曲腹，腹体较深，胎体较薄，底部略下凹，圈足，足沿很浅，足心外突部分只比圈足略为矮一点。

Ⅹ式。侈口，翻沿，圆唇，器型比较大，腹壁较坦，圈足很小，足壁较深。

Ⅺ式。敛口，圆唇，曲腹，腹体较深，器物外壁口沿之下有两道棱线，施钧釉。

（2）钵

只有一种形体较小的直口钵，唇沿略为外突。

（3）水盂

敛口，唇沿尖薄，腹壁浅而微凹。

（4）罐

在窑址中的残片很多，但未能找到能复原的，根据采集到的标本看，其口沿结构有两式：

Ⅰ式。敛口，圆唇，颈部较粗，上腹鼓出，下腹较瘦，胎体较薄。

Ⅱ式。直口，圆唇，颈部很短，肩部高耸。

此外，在隆化县文化馆收藏一件直口、平唇的双耳罐，肩和上腹鼓出，腹体扁圆，平底。

（5）盆

可分为二式：

Ⅰ式。是一种卷沿曲腹盆。

Ⅱ式。形体很大，侈口，口沿很粗，腹壁很直，成圆筒形。

（6）瓶

小口瓶数量很多，侈口，尖唇，细颈，肩部特别丰满而高耸。

（7）高足杯

侈口尖唇，腹壁深而微曲，足呈喇叭形，足沿尖而外侈。

（8）器盖

盖沿成子母口，唇沿尖薄，盖面隆起，上面有宝顶。

（9）鸡腿坛

主要特点是小口，半肩，腹体较高，圈足的足沿略外侈。这类坛有两种式样，一种从颈至腹部都比较丰满，另一种则比较瘦长。

（10）窑具主要有三种

匣钵。呈直筒形，比较粗大厚重。

支圈。学习定窑覆烧工艺，这类窑具使用量很大，碗类制品基本上都采用这种方法。

支柱。剖面呈工字形，一般是三个支柱支撑一件产品。支柱的规格大小不同。

三 胎质和胎色

隆化陶瓷作坊，生产时使用的是当地生产的矸子土，即北方瓷土。没有精细加工，质地比较粗，含有细砂，从烧成的成品看好像坚硬的细砂岩。根据胎质胎色，可以分为5类：

1. 白胎

略为泛黄，能看见白色石英砂粒和细小的黑砂点，但量少而细微。在放大镜下可以看到很小的孔隙，胎体比较薄，造型稳定，一般没有变形，也不施化妆土，釉面光平。这是隆化窑瓷器中的上乘之作。

2. 灰胎

灰胎略为发褐，质地也较细，致密，没有看到气孔和断裂的现象，但在放大镜下能看到坚硬的细砂颗粒，也是灰胎中较好的作品。钧瓷的胎体多属这一类。还有一种深灰胎，颜色成青灰色，像砂岩，很坚硬，但是比较粗糙，有石英和细颗粒。

3. 褐色粗胎

类似耐火砖的结构，但很坚硬，在放大镜下可以看到蜂窝状的孔隙。釉层覆盖在上面虽然比较亮，但釉面出现许多大小不均匀的棕眼。这类制品在隆化窑中数量很大。

4．缸胎

胎体粗厚，颗粒很粗，成浅褐色，胎体中有白色小点，坚硬厚重。

5．陶胎

属釉陶作品，胎体没有烧结。所用原料和瓷器原料一样，只是器物表面施铅釉，以低温烧成，胎体比较粗松，颜色白中泛黄，胎体也比较厚实。

四 釉质釉色

根据调查得到的资料，隆化窑瓷器有白釉、黑釉、青釉、酱釉、钧釉、茶叶末釉、绿釉（即铅釉）等。如果按釉色来划分，隆化窑生产了7个品种。釉色的质感方面，白釉玻璃质相当强，开细碎冰片，黑釉、酱釉、绿釉都没有开片现象，但比较光润。

1．白釉

由于白瓷是该窑生产的主要品种，白釉对配方要求很严，对胎色、窑中焙烧的气氛反应很敏感，所以白色变化很大。隆化窑的白釉有以下几种：

（1）银白色釉

釉光莹润，取得这种效果是在胎体上施了洁白的化妆土，加之釉质的细腻，所以白釉的质量就很高，从其洁白度看不次于河北曲阳定瓷水平。

（2）象牙白釉

白色略为泛黄，釉层和胎体之间施白色化妆土，类似定窑的象牙白釉，只是釉质比较粗。

（3）白釉

黄色的成分很重，釉层中有泪痕状流釉现象，釉层较厚，在碗类制品的中心有较厚的积釉现象。这类制品也属于质量相当高的一类品种。

（4）灰白釉

釉层较薄，虽然比较明亮，但釉面不平整，施釉也不均匀，这类制品胎体上没有上化妆土。由于粗糙色深的胎体衬托的缘故，釉色成灰白色，数量相当多，属于质量不高的低档产品。有的制品可能由于烧窑时氧化焰控制不严格，产生还原气氛，导致釉色发青。

2．青釉

青瓷数量很少，青釉有三种。

第一种，由于胎色发白，青釉颜色比较淡，只在口沿或积釉的地方颜色较深，釉层比较厚，相当光润，釉面不平。

第二种，釉色发灰，属灰青釉，实际上是白釉，由于施在深灰色的胎体上，釉色发青。因为透明白釉很容易受到胎质胎色的影响。这种釉质相当细腻，釉层和胎体结合得很好。

第三种，质量不高，釉层和釉色都不均匀，有深浅不钧匀的许多斑点。

隆化窑的青瓷，釉色均不典型，没有一般青瓷那种美丽的青绿颜色，说明当时工匠配制青釉的技术不够成熟。

3. 黑釉

隆化窑黑瓷生产数量与白瓷差不多，属于大窑产品。在一般的陶瓷作坊里，黑瓷是用比较粗的原料来制作，而隆化窑的黑瓷和其他瓷种在胎体上没有特别的不同。有的胎料粗，有的胎料较细，这种情况与定窑一样。仔细分析隆化窑的黑瓷有 4 种类型：

第一种，黑釉相当细腻，釉色均匀，光泽度不高，但相当润泽，施釉均匀，没有流釉和积釉的现象，胎体薄而细匀，这种黑釉的水平与曲阳燕山村的黑瓷水平一致。

第二种，黑中发褐，釉层较薄，在高温中釉层被胎面的孔隙吸收，釉面出现许多橘皮状棕眼，釉层麻麻达达的。

第三种，凝厚光亮，在器物的口沿出现天蓝色乳絮现象，施在褐色粗胎上。

第四种，颜色很黑，釉面出现银灰色光泽，很亮，很像铅板上出现的银光。这种釉多施在粗厚的胎体上，例如粗大的鸡腿坛的表面常有这种现象。

4. 钧釉

在隆化窑调查中不少同志采集到钧釉标本，有的同志采集到相当大的瓷片。我在调查中采集到两个标本。钧釉数量虽然不多，但确实说明该窑生产过钧釉。第一个标本是浅灰胎，釉色为黑褐色，釉层里满是天蓝、白、淡黄色组成的乳絮状斑块。这是高温中铁、铜、磷酸钙等物质在釉层中熔融、浸漫形成的窑变现象；第二个标本，胎体颜色比较浅，釉层比较凝厚，釉色成天蓝色，山西浑源界庄窑就有与此相似的作品。隆化窑钧瓷釉色的突出的特点是釉层凝厚，釉层和胎体结合的一条洁白的中间层看得很清楚，釉面相当光亮。钧釉作品只发现碗类的个体。这一点也与河南、山西一般民间窑场生产钧釉瓷器的情况一致。

5. 茶叶末釉

颜色就像茶叶的碎末聚集在一起一样，釉面不光亮，但比较典雅。根据观察分析，这种釉本来是为了烧黑釉瓷而配制的，由于烧成温度和火焰气氛的关系而烧成了茶叶末的颜色，有的也像鳝鱼的青皮，数量很少。

6. 酱色釉

釉面像芝麻酱的酱褐色，有的器物胎体很薄，颜色较淡，像定窑中的紫定。有一种在粗厚胎体上施酱色釉的器物，就像现代民间烧制的铁褐釉大缸一样。还有一种小口瓶，施一种略为发黑的深酱色釉，釉面不光亮。

7. 绿釉

深绿色铅釉，釉面有一层浮光。

施釉的方法一般为蘸釉法，多数作品釉面不平。器物里壁有积釉现象，外壁釉层不均匀，有流釉现象。施釉很注意实用的效果。在器物的内壁、外壁的口沿及上腹部分上釉，因为这些部位或者盛物，或者使用时嘴唇接触，上了釉光滑干净，而外腹壁的下部至底足均不施釉。这种做法在中原地区早期瓷器中普遍采用。有的器物内外壁均满施釉，釉层将底足裹住。

8. 釉色搭配

隆化窑既有器物内外壁均施一色釉者，也有施两色釉者。有的器物外壁施褐绿色釉，内壁施白釉；外壁施茶叶末釉，内壁施白釉；外壁施酱褐色釉，内壁施白釉。钧釉瓷器是内外壁施相同的釉，内壁满施，外壁口沿至上腹施釉，下腹露胎。

隆化窑瓷器胎体虽然比较粗糙，直接影响到釉的艺术效果，但该窑配的各种釉大多数明亮光润，使民用的普通粗瓷获得较好的美感。同时，该窑虽然器物种类不够丰富，釉色品种也不多，但同一器物釉色的搭配很有变化，这样做没有单调之感，正是资金不太雄厚的民间瓷窑的可贵之处。

五 隆化窑瓷器的装饰

隆化窑瓷器没有华贵的装饰，属于民用粗瓷的范围，有胎上装饰和白釉黑彩装饰两种。

1. 胎上装饰

是指成型时在辘轳车上转动，刻划出旋纹，或用光滑的工具压印胎壁出现又浅又宽的瓦沟纹，在一些鸡腿坛或小口瓶瘦长的下腹部分出现这种纹路。隆化窑瓷器上这类纹饰不清晰，图案性不强，为了增强釉面的艺术效果，部分制品在胎体表面施一层洁白细腻的化妆土，上了化妆土的制品，釉层明亮而光润，提高了瓷器的质量。在隆化县文化馆珍藏一件搅胎高足杯，用事先配好的灰褐色胎泥和白色胎泥做出树木年轮的纹理，上施淡青色透明釉。

2. 白釉黑彩

主要是花卉和题诗。这是隆化窑较好瓷器的主要装饰。根据调查所见，白釉黑花的主要纹饰有弦纹、圆圈纹、光芒纹，在罐、瓶一类制品最圆鼓的部分画出牡丹花和其他一些朵花。在调查中，有的同志采集到用黑彩画竹子的瓷片。在隆化县文化馆展出一件白瓷罐，腹部画枝叶茂盛的竹子，挺拔有力，相当别致，这在北方磁州窑白釉黑花的作品上是很少见的，在大盆一类的器物腹部，用黑彩十分醒目地写出“君子爱财，取之有道” 8 个大字。竹子产自南方，别的地方的白釉黑彩瓷器中从来没有见到过。

六 隆化窑的装烧方法

根据调查所见，隆化窑采用以下几种方法把坯件装进窑里焙烧：

1. 垫圈支烧

将碗类器物一个个堆叠起来，装入匣钵，放在窑里焙烧。在采集的标本中，有的碗一圈刮釉，作用是支撑坯体而不黏结，也有垫圈因周围釉层流动而粘在碗心的。

2. 托柱支烧

钵、盆类制品用托柱支撑，托柱有大小不同的规格。

3. 套烧

小口瓶类制品，肩部有一周涩圈，有的瓷瓶还残留有别的瓶体粘在肩上的残片。这说明它们采用的是一个瓶足套在另一个瓶的肩部，一个套一个放在窑里焙烧。

4. 支圈覆烧

学习定窑覆烧工艺，将碗类制品扣在支圈上，支圈层层相叠，窑里占有的空间范围比用单个匣钵要小得多。在隆化窑址里，这类工具数量最多，大多数碗类制品都是芒口，说明隆化窑各个作坊相当广泛地采用这种装窑的方法。

七 时代的判断

隆化窑出土的一种碗，腹体较宽而平坦，碗足比较宽，碗底中心部位刮去一圈釉，露出一个涩圈，装窑时用垫圈支垫，一个接一个地装上去，这种造型和装窑方法是北方辽金时代用得最多的方法。白釉黑花瓷器中画竹子、牡丹花、卷枝花的从质地和艺术风格上看属金代风格。窑址中采集到的钧瓷片，釉质釉色和山西大同浑源金元时期的钧瓷相同。隆化窑址中有许多鸡腿坛的遗物，在调查中了解到形体结构有两种：第一种比较粗大，尤其上腹比较圆鼓，下腹又比较短；第二种比较瘦长，中腹以下是一圈圈瓦沟纹，圈足特别高。根据墓葬出土资料判断，第一种属金代，第二种属元代。大量的碗类制品，圈足很小，足心一个乳状突起，这是元代瓷器的典型风格。

隆化窑大量采用覆烧工艺，覆烧工艺是北宋定窑创造的先进工艺，由于它对提高产量有突出的作用，金代的北方，南宋的南方广泛采用，而像福建的德化窑，在元朝还在采用此法。北方元朝都不再用覆烧法，而隆化窑比较突出的是元朝大量使用，这是隆化窑的特殊之点。

从这些资料判断，隆化窑的生产时代是金代至元代。

八 从隆化窑看河北地区陶瓷的发展

河北是我国古代经济、文化、手工业很发达的地区，也是我国古代陶瓷发展的重要地区。早在7000多年前的磁山文化就有了陶器生产，到仰韶文化、龙山文化，以至奴隶社会、封建社会，这里的制陶业都很发达。在北朝时期建立了我国最早的瓷器生产体系。河北临城的陈刘庄发现北朝晚期的青瓷窑址，在贾村发现了质量相当高的隋代白瓷窑址。在唐代，河北的邢窑把我国白瓷的生产水平提高到一个崭新的阶段，如银似雪的白瓷制品在社会上产生广泛的影响，达到“天下无贵贱通用之”的地步。在邢窑的推动下，曲阳窑在唐代中晚期开始生产具有邢窑艺术风格的白瓷。在宋代，曲阳定窑成为我国艺术瓷器的杰出代表，成为宋代五大名窑之首。在中国和亚洲地区陶瓷发展中影响深远。在磁县有专门生产青瓷的贾壁窑，宋代兴起了代表我国北方民间瓷器生产的磁州窑，艺术上有许多创新，有浓郁的地区特色和民间艺术的情趣，深受人民的喜爱。磁州窑的工艺不但在河北，而且在山西、河南、甘肃、陕西都得到发展，生产时间延续到今天，一千多年赓续不衰，这种艺术扎根于民间，有雄厚的基础。河北地区陶瓷在我国陶瓷生产中一直处于举足轻重的地位。

在北京门头沟的龙泉务，发现了辽金时期的重要窑址，生产白瓷、黑瓷和辽三彩。隆化在河北省的最北边，根据发现的资料看，河北古代陶瓷生产，南部地区发现较早，规模最大，影响也最深远。到辽金元时期，也就是北方在少数民族政权控制的时期，我国北方广大地区形成了陶瓷生产的区域，时间在12世纪至14世纪。这个时期瓷器在人民生活中比较广泛使用，民间瓷窑大量兴起。就河北地区来说瓷器手工业生产的布局更加均衡了。

从工艺风格来看，隆化窑属于磁州窑系统，但工艺上又广泛接受定窑的先进技艺。在金元时期它与北京门头沟的龙泉务窑，内蒙古自治区的赤峰窑，山西的大同窑、浑源窑形成一个风格更为接近的生产区域。在金元时期成为我国的一个重要产瓷区。在唐山陶瓷兴起之前，隆化窑担负着供应河北北部地区民间生活用瓷的需要，从这个意义上来说，隆化窑的地位就比较重要了。

隆化窑发现了钧瓷，扩大了钧瓷生产的地域范围。与之相似的钧瓷产品在山西的临汾、长治、浑源等都有生产。根据在内蒙古自治区工作多年的李作智同志告之，在内蒙古自治区有的瓷窑也产钧瓷，这些情况增进了我们对钧瓷生产的认识。蜚声中外的钧瓷在元代北方广大地区都生产，范围远远超过宋朝的版图。这进一步说明隆化窑的发现有相当重要的科学价值。

（原载《河北陶瓷》1985年第4期）

Abstract of Interpretation of the Development of Ceramics in Hebei Province through the Investigation of Longhua Kiln

Li Zhiyan

Longhua kiln was investigated in 1982. Since the kiln was not documented, little was known before. The article introduced the kiln in 8 dimensions: location, porcelain varieties, texture and color of the body, glaze, porcelain decoration, firing method, dating of its products, position of Longhua kiln in the development of ceramics in Hebei Province. The kiln is located in the northern part of the Province. It mainly fired bowls, saucers, alms bowls, containers, stemmed cups, jars, drumstick-shaped altars, vats and covers. The bodies of Longhua kiln wares are white, gray, brown and with coarse texture, vat alike or pottery. Glazes applied are white, green, black, Jun, tea dust, dark brown or green. The common way of decoration is white glaze with design of black color. Four firing techniques were applied by the kiln. Judging by the shaping of the wares and firing methods, Longhua was a civilian kiln of Jin and Yuan dynasties. From Sui, Tang and Song to Jin and Yuan dynasty, a fast development of porcelain-making was witnessed in Hebei Province. There are some links in decorative style between Longhua and Cizhou kiln. Although the decorative style of Cizhou wares was seen on Longhua wares, the shaping and coloring are different. The discovery of Jun glaze wares in Longhua kiln adds new information about the distribution of Jun kilns.

窑址调查纪要

窑址	调查时间	调查人
贾壁窑	1959.6	冯先铭　叶广成
磁州窑	1951.4	陈万里　杨忠礼
	1964	李辉柄　姚万青
	1977.5	冯先铭　叶喆民
	1984.5	冯先铭　李毅华
	2005.5	冯小琦　蔡　毅　赵　山 王　琎　孙志远　王桂林
邢窑内丘窑	1962	冯先铭
	2005.5	冯小琦　蔡　毅　赵　山 王　琎　孙志远　王桂林
邢窑临城窑	1977.5	冯先铭　叶喆民
	2005.5	冯小琦　蔡　毅　赵　山 王　琎　孙志远　王桂林
定窑	1951.4	陈万里　杨忠礼
	1957.3	冯先铭　李辉柄　王莉英 郭　仁　葛季芳
	1977.5	冯先铭　叶喆民
	1982.9	李辉柄　王莉英　杨静荣
	1991	冯先铭　冯小琦
	2000	王莉英　冯小琦
	2005.5	冯小琦　蔡　毅　赵　山 王　琎　孙志远　王桂林
井陉窑	2005.5	冯小琦　蔡　毅　赵　山 王　琎　孙志远　王桂林
隆化窑	1982	李知宴
	1984	冯先铭　李毅华

注：以上统计以故宫博物院现存瓷片为准，无标本的调查不计在内。

后记

《故宫博物院藏中国古代窑址标本》一套书经过近20年的酝酿，今天终于要逐卷面世了。本书是由故宫博物院几代陶瓷研究者——陈万里、冯先铭、李辉柄、叶喆民、王莉英、叶佩兰、李知宴、何俊义、欧志培、刘兰华、李毅华、邵长波、杨静荣、冯小琦、蔡毅、吕成龙、徐巍、王健华、刘伟、纪伟、董健丽、赵聪月、郑宏、高晓然、郭玉昆、韩倩、黄卫文、赵晓春等深入考古第一线采集的众多标本汇集而成。这些标本的收集历经了半个多世纪，经过三次大的整理。第一次是在1988年，由冯先铭先生负责，参加者有刘兰华、冯小琦、纪伟，主要整理存放在故宫文华殿与研究室的标本；第二次是在2004年，由冯小琦负责，主要参加者有杨静荣、蔡毅、刘伟，是在第一次的基础上，把数十年散放在承乾宫、永寿宫等数处的标本集中整理。整理工作从搬运开始，逐个开箱、清洗，并分省按窑口进行编目；第三次从2008年至今，由冯小琦负责，董建丽、韩倩参加。在前两次的基础上，对所有标本进行重新排柜位，核对数字，特别是对2005年以后调查的标本进行整理、拍照，对前两次整理的遗留问题进行解决。窑址标本文字介绍以冯先铭先生关于古窑址的论述为基础，由冯小琦进行整理与补充。附图说明由蔡毅、徐巍、董健丽、韩倩、黄卫文、郑宏、赵聪月、高晓然完成。此书得以出版，特别要感谢各级领导的大力支持与协调，感谢陶瓷组全体同人的合作，感谢资料信息中心的全力支持与配合。感谢各地博物馆、考古部门以及各地文保单位对故宫窑址调查工作的大力支持。

编辑出版委员会

主任

单霁翔

副主任

李　季　王亚民

委员

纪天斌　陈丽华　宋纪蓉　冯乃恩

娄　玮　胡建中　闫宏斌　任万平　杨长青

宋玲平　赵国英　赵　杨　傅红展　苗建民

石志敏　余　辉　张　荣　章宏伟　尚国华

主编

冯小琦

副主编

蔡　毅

编委

吕成龙　杨静荣　刘　伟

徐　巍　黄卫文　韩　倩

赵聪月　高晓然　郑　宏

英文翻译

郑弘毅　于全文　方　妍

薛　云　薛秀康　陈　希

摄影

马小旋　赵山

图片资料

故宫博物院资料信息中心

责任编辑

万　钧

装帧设计

北京颂雅风文化传媒有限公司

郑子杰　陈晓晓

图书在版编目（CIP）数据

故宫博物院藏中国古代窑址标本．河北 / 故宫博物院编．
-- 北京 ：故宫出版社，2013.11
ISBN 978-7-5134-0511-9

Ⅰ．①故… Ⅱ．①故… Ⅲ．①古代陶瓷－标本－中国－图录 ②古代陶瓷－标本－河北省－图录 Ⅳ．① K876.32
中国版本图书馆 CIP 数据核字（2013）第 267821 号

故宫博物院藏中国古代窑址标本

河北

编　　者：故宫博物院
出版发行：故宫出版社
地址：北京东城区景山前街4号　邮编：100009
电话：010-85007808　010-85007816　传真：010-65129479
网址：www.culturefc.cn
邮箱：ggcb@culturefc.cn
制版印刷：北京雅昌彩色印刷有限公司
开　　本：878×1092毫米　1/16
印　　张：25.5
版　　次：2013年11月第1版
2013年11月第1次印刷
印　　数：1～2300册
书　　号：ISBN 978-7-5134-0511-9
定　　价：190.00元